Research Methodology in Library and Information Science

Research Methodology in Library and Information Science

Utpal Sharma

RANDOM PUBLICATIONS
NEW DELHI (INDIA)

Research Methodology in Library and Information Science

ISBN 978-93-5111-567-0
© Reserved

All Rights Reserved. No Part of this book may be reproduced in any manner without written permission.

Published in 2015 in India by

RANDOM PUBLICATIONS

4376-A/4B, Gali Murari Lal, Ansari Road
New Delhi-110 002
Phone : +9111-43580356, 011-23289044, 011-43142548
e-mail: sales@randompublications.com,
info@randompublications.com, randomexports@gmail.com

Reprinted 2026

Type Setting by : Friends Media, Delhi-110089

Preface

Research in library and information science is necessary for maintenance pace with all of the recent trends in the developing field of library study.

Library and information science (LIS) (sometimes given as the plural library and information sciences) is a merging of the two fields library science and information science. The phrase "library and information science" is associated with schools of library and information science (abbreviated to "SLIS"), which generally developed from professional training programs (not academic disciplines) to university institutions during the second half of the 20th century.

Researchers have recently reviewed the status of some digital libraries from around the globe. These reviews reveal that while the digital libraries have very good information access and retrieval mechanisms in place, there is almost no provision for quality reference and information services.

However, these studies show that there is a trend towards the personalisation of digital library service, as in case of HEADLINE and GEMS (presently called iGEMS, a digital library developed at Nanyang Technological University in Singapore). Some recent research efforts have been directed at building personalised digital library environments. These studies can be grouped into three categories: user needs assessment, personalised user interface and personalised digital library, researchers reviewed literature on user interfaces, particularly in a digital library environment, and suggested the need for a task-based digital library.

Researcher discussed the personal digital library (PDL) that acts as a front-end to other electronic library systems and manages the user's information needs. Barry and Barbara discussed the creation of personal digital libraries. The North Carolina University Library developed MyLibrary @NCState as a portal application to the NCSU Library's information resources. This portal allows user profiling to build a dynamic, customised gateway to both general and discipline specific resources. MyLibrary is a Cornell University Library initiative to provide personalised library services to their students, faculty and staff on the basis of a focus group study to gauge library users.

This book is useful for students, teachers and researchers engaged in library and information science research.I would like to thank my team for standing beside me throughout my career and writing this book. My special thanks go to "Random Publications" who have published the book.

– Utpal Sharma

Contents

1

Information Science

What is information science? The question, while seemin-gly simple, begs another, more complex one: *How is information science, or for that matter any field, to be defined?* This is a complex problem dealt with at length in philosophy and in other fields. Lexical definitions are necessary for providing a broad description and boundaries of the subjects covered by a field, but they cannot provide for a deeper understanding. Webster does not a field define. This is not to reject clear lexical definitions—not at all—just to establish their limitations. In approaching the discussion of information science, I am taking the problem point of view as elaborated by Popper who argued that:

- Subject matter or kind of things do not, I hold, constitute a basis for distinguishing disciplines....*We are not students of some subject matter, but students of problems*. Any problem may cut right across the border of any subject matter or discipline.

Our emphasis is on problems addressed by information science. Although we provide definitions of information science and other fields in interdisciplinary relations with information science later in the chapter, we are doing this solely to advance the understanding of problems addressed by different fields and their relation to information science problems. Debates over the "proper" definition of information science, as of any field, are fruitless, and in expectations naive. Information science, as a science and as a profession, is defined by the problems it has addressed and the methods it has used for their solutions over time.

Any advances in information science depend on whether the field is indeed progressing in relation to problems addressed and methods used. Any "fixing," if in order, will have to be approached by redefining or refocusing either the problems addressed, or the methods for their solutions, or both. Information science has three general characteristics that are the leitmotif of its evolution and existence. These are shared with many modern fields. They can also be viewed as problem areas with which infor-mation science has to deal on a general level:

- First, information science is interdisciplinary in nature; however, the relations with various disciplines are changing. The interdisciplinary evolution is far from over.

- Second, information science is inexorably connected to information technology. A technological imperative is compelling and constraining the evolution of information science, as is the evolution of a number of other fields, and moreover, of the information society as a whole.
- Third, information science is, with many other fields, an active participant in the evolution of the infor-mation society. Information science has a strong social and human dimension, above and beyond technology. A number of works that I freely consulted dealt with various historical aspects of information science.

Among those works are:

- Shera and Cleveland,
- Bourne,
- Herner,
- Salton,
- Cleverdon,
- Swanson,
- Lilley and Trice,
- Farkas-Conn,
- Buckland and Liu, and
- Rayward.

Still, a comprehensive history of information science is a project for a future historian of science. As yet only historical pieces and different perspectives of pieces exist. A history of any field is a history of a few powerful ideas. I suggest that information science has three such powerful ideas, so far. These ideas deal with processing of information in a radically different way than was done previously or elsewhere. The first and the original idea, emerging in 1950s, is *information retrieval*, providing for processing of information based on formal logic. The second, emerging shortly thereafter, is *relevance*, directly orienting and associating the process with human information needs and assessments.

The third, derived from elsewhere some two decades later, is *interaction*, enabling direct exchanges and feedback between systems and people engaged in IR processes. So far, no powerful ideas have emerged about *information*, as the underlying phenomenon, or *"literature"*, as the object of processing.

However, one can argue that the idea of mapping of "literature," that started with exploitation of citation indexes in 1960s, may also qualify as a powerful idea. In a non-historical sense this stage deals with these powerful ideas and with leitmotifs. They form a framework for understanding the past, present, and future of information science.

WHAT IS "INFORMATION" IN INFORMATION SCIENCE

In a scientific sense, the answer to the question is "We don't know." Yes, we can and do provide various lexical definitions of information, and we have an intuitive understanding of its meaning that we apply daily and widely. Thus, we do understand the message-sense in which we deal with information in information science. But that does not provide for a deeper and more formal understanding and explanation. Information is a basic phenomenon. For all basic phenomena—energy or gravity in physics, life in biology, justice in jurisprudence—the same "we-don'tknow" answer applies.

However, the investigation of the basic phenomena is proceeding—that is the basic point of all these fields. It is proceeding by investigating the *manifestations, behaviour,* and *effects* of phenomena under question. While we do not know what information is, or what some of its derivative notions, such as relevance, may be, over the years we have learned a lot about their various manifestations, behaviours, and effects. And we are continuing to learn about them through scientific investigations. "Information" has a variety of connotations in different fields. For instance, from the standpoint of physics and biology, a number of highly ambitious attempts have undertaken to explore information as a basic property of the universe.

In psychology, information is used, at times, as a variable dealing with sensory perception, comprehension, or other psychological processes. These senses of information are very different than the one in information science. In some fields, information science included, the notion of information is broadly associated with messages. For this sense, a number of interpretations exist, which are assumed in different theoretical and pragmatic treatments of information. We can present them as related, but differing manifestations of information in an ordered sequence or a continuum of increasing complexity.

Narrow Sense

Information is considered in terms of *signals or messages for decisions* involving little or no cognitive processing, or such processing that can be expressed in algorithms and probabilities. Information is treated as the property of a message, which can be estimated by some probability. Examples are information in terms of uncertainty in information theory, "perfect infor-mation" in game theory, or information as related to decision-making and market equilibrium in the theory of uncertainty and information in economics of information.

The latter has been surveyed by Hirshleifer and Riley, who provide this illustrative explanation: In the economics of uncertainty, an individual is assumed to act on the basis of current *fixed beliefs, e.g.*, deciding whether to carry an umbrella based on one's present estimate of the chance of rain, while in the economics of information a person typically is trying to arrive at *improved beliefs, e.g.*, by studying a weather report before deciding to take an umbrella.

Information may be considered as causing a difference between fixed and improved beliefs. The value of information is calculated as the difference between the decision maker's expected utility of the decision made without the information, and the expected utility of the best possible choice in decision made after receiving and analysing the information. The huge, and sometimes insurmountable, problem, of course, is estimating appropriate probabilities. A number of pragmatic applications follow this interpretation, such as computerized trading.

Broader Sense

Information is treated as directly involving *cognitive processing and understanding.* It results from interaction of two cognitive structures, a "mind" and a "text." Information is that which affects or changes the state of a mind. In cases of information services, information is most often conveyed through the medium of a text, document, or record, *e.g.*, what a reader may understands from a text or document. The interpretation by Tague-Sutcliff fits:

- Information is an intangible that depends on the conceptualization and the understanding of a human being. Records contain words or pictures absolutely, but they contain information relative only to a user... Information is associated with a transaction between text and reader, between a record and user.

Broadest Sense

Information is treated in a context. That is, information involves not only messages that are cognitively processed but also *a context*—situation, task, problem-at-hand, and the like. Using information that has been cognitively processed for a given task is an example. In addition to other senses, it involves motivation or intentionality, and therefore it is connected to the expansive social context or horizon, such as culture, work, or problemat-hand.

In information science, we must consider the third and broadest sense of information, because information is used in a context and in relation to some reasons.

The point was implicitly understood from the beginning of information science, particularly as reflected in the practice of information retrieval. This interpretation of "information" in information science is not new. Such a broad interpretation of information that explicitly incorporates cognition and context was, among others, elaborated by Wersig and Neveling and Belkin and Robertson. It is also implicit in the social role of information science.

DEFINITIONS OF INFORMATION SCIENCE

An early definition of Information science is:

- "Information science is that discipline that investigates the properties and behaviour of information, the forces governing the flow of information, and the means of processing information for optimum accessibility and usability.

- It is concerned with that body of knowledge relating to the origination, collection, organization, storage, retrieval, interpretation, transmission, transformation, and utilization of information. This includes the investigation of information representations in both natural and artificial systems, the use of codes for efficient message transmission, and the study of information processing devices and techniques such as computers and their programming systems. It is an interdisciplinary science derived from and related to such fields as mathematics, logic, linguistics, psychology, computer technology, operations research, the graphic arts, communications, library science, management, and other similar fields. It has both a pure science component, which enquires into the subject without regard to its application, and an applied science component, which develops

Some authors treat informatics as a synonym for *information science*, especially related to the concept developed by A.I. Mikhailov and other Soviet authors in the mid sixties, which suggested that informatics is a discipline related to the study of Scientific Information. Because of the rapidly evolving, interdisciplinary nature of informatics, a precise meaning of the term "informatics" is presently difficult to pin down.

Regional differences and international terminology complicate the problem. Some people note that much of what is called "Informatics" today was once called "Information Science" at least in fields such as Medical Informatics.

For example, when library scientists began also to use the phrase "Information Science" to refer to their work, the term informatics emerged:

- In the United States as a response by computer scientists to distinguish their work from that of library science, and
- In Britain as a term for a science of information that studies natural, as well as artificial or engineered, information-processing systems.

There is considerably differences between what is considered a subfield of information science and what is not (or what belongs to one information science and what belongs to another. If we take *information systems* as an example, Vickery is a book written by a leading information scientist and that book places information systems within IS. Ellis, Allen, and Wilson is, on the other hand a bibliometric investigation describing the relation between two different fields: "Information science" and "information systems".

A Multitude of Information Sciences

Michael Buckland wrote an article *What Kind of Science Can Information Science Be?* from the perspective of Library and information science: "other important fields have also used the name "information science." One is computer science, concerned with the theory and application of algorithms. Another, concerned with entropy, probability, Shannon-Weaver information theory, physical patterns, and related topics, is sometimes referred to as the "physics of information." Also, the word information is, of course, used in information technology, but largely restricted in practice to the use of electronics for communication and computation. These other areas are not considered here. Instead, we are concerned with those areas generally understood as being within the scope of *library and information science* (LIS) and the interests of the American Society for Information Science and Technology."

PHILOSOPHY OF INFORMATION

Philosophy of information (PI) studies conceptual issues arising at the intersection of computer science, information technology, and philosophy. It includes the investigation of the conceptual nature and basic principles of information, including its dynamics, utilisation and sciences, as well as the elaboration and application of information-theoretic and computational methodologies to its philosophical problems.

ONTOLOGY

In computer science and information science, an ontology formally represents knowledge as a set of concepts within a domain, and the relationships between those concepts. It can be used to reason about the entities within that domain and may be used to describe the domain.

More specifically, an ontology is a model for describing the world that consists of a set of types, properties, and relationship types. Exactly what is provided around these varies, but they are the essentials of an ontology. There is also generally an expectation that there be a close resemblance between the real world and the features of the model in an ontology.

In theory, an ontology is a "formal, explicit specification of a shared conceptualisation". An ontology renders shared vocabulary and taxonomy which models a domain with the definition of objects and/or concepts and their properties and relations.

Ontologies are the structural frameworks for organizing information and are used in artificial intelligence, the Semantic Web, systems engineering, software engineering, biomedical informatics, library science, enterprise bookmarking, and information architecture as a form of knowledge representation about the world or some part of it. The creation of domain ontologies is also fundamental to the definition and use of an enterprise architecture framework.

HISTORY OF INFORMATION SCIENCE

Early Beginnings

Information science, in studying the collection, classification, manipulation, storage, retrieval and dissemination of infor-mation has origins in the common stock of human knowledge. Information analysis has been carried out by scholars at least as early as the time of the Abyssinian Empire with the emergence of cultural depositories, what is today known as libraries and archives.

Institutionally, information science emerged in the 19th century along with many other social science disciplines.

As a science, however, it finds its institutional roots in the history of science, beginning with publication of the first issues of *Philosophical Transactions,* generally considered the first scientific journal, in 1665 by the Royal Society.

The institutionalization of science occurred throughout the 18th Century. In 1731, Benjamin Franklin established the Library Company of Philadelphia, the first library owned by a group of public citizens, which quickly expanded beyond the realm of books and became a center of scientific experiment, and which hosted public exhibitions of scientific experiments.

Benjamin Franklin did invest a town in Massachusetts with a collection of books that the town voted to make available to all free of charge, which formed the first Public Library. Academie de Chirurgia (Paris) published *Memoires pour les Chirurgiens*, generally considered to be the first medical journal, in 1736.

The American Philosophical Society, patterned on the Royal Society (London), was founded in Philadelphia in 1743.

As numerous other scientific journals and societies are founded, Alois Senefelder develops the concept of lithography for use in mass printing work in Germany in 1796.

19th Century

By the 19th Century the first signs of information science emerged as separate and distinct from other sciences and social sciences but in conjunction with communication and computation. In 1801, Joseph Marie Jacquard invented a punched card system to control operations of the cloth weaving loom in France. It was the first use of "memory storage of patterns" system.

As chemistry journals emerged throughout the 1820s and 1830s, Charles Babbage developed his "difference engine," the first step towards the modern computer, in 1822 and his "analytical engine" by 1834. By 1843 Richard Hoe developed the rotary press, and in 1844 Samuel Morse sent the first public telegraph message. By 1848 William F. Poole begins the *Index to Periodical Literature,* the first general periodical literature index in the US.

In 1854 George Boole published *An Investigation into Laws of Thought...*, which lays the foundations for Boolean algebra, which is later used in information retrieval. In 1860 a congress was held at Karlsruhe Technische Hochschule to discuss the feasibility of establishing a systematic and rational nomenclature for chemistry. The congress did not reach any conclusive results, but several key participants returned home with Stanislao Cannizzaro's outline (1858), which ultimately convinces them of the validity of his scheme for calculating atomic weights.

By 1865, the Smithsonian Institution began a catalog of current scientific papers, which became the *International Catalogue of Scientific Papers* in 1902. The following year the Royal Society began publication of its *Catalogue of Papers* in London. In 1868, Christopher Sholes, Carlos Glidden, and S. W. Soule produced the first practical typewriter.

By 1872 Lord Kelvin devised an analogue computer to predict the tides, and by 1875 Frank Stephen Baldwin was granted the first US patent for a practical calculating machine that performs four arithmetic functions.

Alexander Graham Bell and Thomas Edison invented the telephone and phonograph in 1876 and 1877 respectively, and the American Library Association was founded in Philadelphia. In 1879 *Index Medicus* was first issued by the Library of the Surgeon General, U.S. Army, with John Shaw Billings as librarian, and later the library issues *Index Catalogue,* which achieved an international reputation as the most complete catalog of medical literature.

European Documentation

The discipline of *documentation science*, which marks the earliest theoretical foundations of modern information science, emerged in the late part of the 19th Century in Europe together with several more scientific indexes whose purpose was to organize scholarly literature. Many information science historians cite Paul Otlet and Henri La Fontaine as the fathers of information science with the founding of the *International Institute of Bibliography* (IIB) in 1895.

A second generation of European Documentalists emerged after the Second World War, most notably Suzanne Briet. However, "information science" as a term is not popularly used in academia until sometime in the latter part of the 20th Century.

Documentalists emphasized the utilitarian integration of technology and technique towards specific social goals. Ronald Day, "As an organized system of techniques and technologies, documentation was understood as a player in the historical development of global organization in modernity–indeed, a major player inasmuch as that organization was dependent on the organization and transmission of information."

Otlet and Lafontaine (who won the Nobel Prize in 1913) not only envisioned later technical innovations but also projected a global vision for information and information technologies that speaks directly to postwar visions of a global "information society."

Otlet and Lafontaine established numerous organizations dedicated to standardization, bibliography, international associations, and consequently, international cooperation. These organizations were fundamental for ensuring international production in commerce, information, communication and modern economic development, and they later found their global form in such institutions as the League of Nations and the United Nations.

Otlet designed the Universal Decimal Classification, based on Melville Dewey's decimal classification system. Although he lived decades before computers and networks emerged, what he discussed prefigured what ultimately became the World Wide Web. His vision of a great network of knowledge focused on documents and included the notions of hyperlinks, search engines, remote access, and social networks.

Otlet not only imagined that all the world's knowledge should be interlinked and made available remotely to anyone, but he also proceeded to build a structured document collection. This collection involved standardized paper sheets and cards filed in custom-designed cabinets according to a hierarchical index (which culled information worldwide from diverse sources) and a commercial information retrieval service (which answered written requests by copying relevant information from index cards).

Users of this service were even warned if their query was likely to produce more than 50 results per search. By 1937 documentation had formally been institutionalized, as evidenced by the founding of the American Documentation Institute (ADI), later called the American Society for Information Science and Technology.

Transition to Modern Information Science

With the 1950s came increasing awareness of the potential of automatic devices for literature searching and information storage and retrieval. As these concepts grew in magnitude and potential, so did the variety of information science interests. By the 1960s and 70s, there was a move from batch processing to online modes, from mainframe to mini and microcomputers.

Additionally, traditional boundaries among disciplines began to fade and many information science scholars joined with library programmes. They further made themselves multi-disciplinary by incorporating disciplines in the sciences, huma-nities and social sciences, as well as other professional programmes, such as law and medicine in their curriculum. By the 1980s, large databases, such as Grateful Med at the National Library of Medicine, and user-oriented services such as Dialog and Compuserve, were for the first time accessible by individuals from their personal computers.

The 1980s also saw the emergence of numerous special interest groups to respond to the changes. By the end of the decade, special interest groups were available involving non-print media, social sciences, energy and the environment, and community information systems. Today, information science largely examines technical bases, social consequences, and theoretical understanding of online databases, widespread use of databases in government, industry, and education, and the development of the Internet and World Wide Web.

STRUCTURE OF INFORMATION SCIENCE

Any field is structured along some distinct, larger areas or subdisciplines of enquiry or practice. Think of a number of areas of medicine, computer science, librarianship, and so forth. Information science is not an exception. It has a distinct, two-partite structure. A number of authors observed that the work in information science falls in two large areas or subdisciplines, each, of course, with further subareas or specialties.

White and McCain conducted a monumental bibliometric study of the domain of information science by providing extensive analysis of co-citation patterns for 120 authors over a period of 23 years. Borrowing from White and McCain, visualize a map of information science as an ellipse with authors inside, distributed or clustered according to their connections. There are two large clusters at each end of the ellipse, with only a few authors spanning both. In other words, there are two major areas or subdisciplines. I liked their metaphor:

As Things Turn Out, Information Science Looks Rather like Australia:

Heavily coastal in its development, with a sparsely settled interior.

In one of the coastal sections, fall authors that worked on analytical study of literatures; their structures; studies of texts as content-bearing objects; communication in various populations, particularly scientific communication; social context of information; information uses; information seeking and behaviour; various theories of information and related topics.

As yet, there is no good label for that cluster. Some call it "information analysis." For simplicity, lets call this the *domain cluster,* as did White and McCain, although "basic" may be a good label. In the other coastal section are authors who concentrated on IR theory and retrieval algorithms; practical IR processes and systems; human-computer interaction; user studies; library systems; OPACs; and related topics.

Let's call this cluster the *retrieval cluster,* although "applied" may also be a good label. Basically, most of the areas in the domain cluster are about study of fundamental manifes-tations and behaviour of phenomena and objects that information science is all about. They are centered on the phenomenon of information and its manifestations in literature. The retrieval cluster deals, by and large, with a variety of implementations, on both practical and theoretical levels.

It is about implementation, behaviour, and effects of the interface between literatures and people, including, of course, all kinds of retrieval aspects. Unfortunately, these two main clusters are largely unconnected.

Only a very small number of authors spanned the two clusters. In other words, there are very few integrating works. The last text that undertook an integrative approach encom-passing both clusters. A rare example of such an effort in research is the last work by Tague-Sutcliffe, where she related the notion of informative-ness with evaluation of IR systems.

Several modern texts are specifically aimed at IR but none on information science as a whole. I dare to venture a prediction: fame awaits the researcher who devise a formal theoretical work, bolstered by experimental evidence, that connects the two largely separated clusters, *i.e.*, connecting basic phenomena with their realization in the retrieval world. And a bestseller is awaiting an author that produces an integrative text in information science. Information science will become a full-fledged discipline when the two ends are connected successfully. The two clusters are not equally popu-lated. The retrieval cluster has significantly more authors, not to mention total number of works. As in many other fields, more effort is expanded on the applied side than on the basic side.

In part, this is due to availability of funds for given topics—not surprisingly, research goes after moneyed topics. By and large, over the last decade or so, major granting agencies funded only applied research in information science. For instance, I have been unable to identify a single grant addressing any of the topics in the domain or basic cluster from NSF Division of Information and Intelligent Systems since its preceding Division of Information Science and Technology was reorganized and included in the Directorate for *Computer and Information Science and Engineering* (CISE) in 1985. In de Solla Price's concepts and words, the domain cluster is "little science", while the retrieval cluster is "big science," and the connection between the two has presently no science.

PROBLEMS ADDRESSED

General

Webster routinely defines information science as "the science dealing with the efficient collection, storage, and retrieval of information." It is a general definition of problems addressed by information science. The definition follows pretty much an early and popular one given by Borko as a part of a wide discussion and controversy about the nature of the field in the 1960s. More specifically, information science is a field of professional practice and scientific enquiry addressing the problem of effective communication of knowledge records—"literature"—among humans in the context of social, organizational, and individual need for and use of information. The key orientation here is the problem of need for and use of information, as involving knowledge records.

To provide for that need, information science deals with specifically, oriented information techniques, procedures, and systems.

To elaborate, the specific concentration of information science is on human knowledge records as *content-bearing objects*, in all forms, shapes, and media. The primary emphasis is on content of these objects, in terms of their potential for conveying information. "Literature" may be used as a generic term for these knowledge records, but "literature" has many other connotations, thus requiring a careful restriction in its use in information science. Because of these connotations, "literature" will not become popular in information science. Realizing this, I am using the term here only as a shorthand, as did White and McCain, when they elegantly stated:

> "The proper study of information science is the interface between people and literature... modeling the world of publications with a practical goal of being able to deliver their content to enquirers on demand... While many scientists seek to understand communication between persons, information scientists seek to understand communication between persons and certain valued surrogates for persons that literature comprises.

In all of this there is a technological imperative, reflected in efforts to take advantage of modern information technology. While information science is not about technology, the problem of providing effective computer applications pervades the field. Following is a word on the extent and borders of infor-mation science.

Focusing information science on the content-bearing properties of literature, and on associated techniques and systems dealing with providing effective access to and use of literature, provides a restriction for information science.

Thus, the field does *not* deal with great many other information systems, such as payroll, inventory, decision support systems, data processing, airline schedules, and a zillion others, nor does it deal with direct communication among and between persons. Information science is about a specific manifestation or type of information that defines its scope and its systems. Information science, as many other fields, also involves a professional component. Starting in 1950s, the profession of information science grew from research and applications in IR, to become a powerful component of the field, and in many ways a leading one in respect to innovation.

As in many other fields, there is an uneasy relation between the scientific or research-oriented component and the professi-onal or practice-oriented one. The profession is responding in its own way to needs of its users and organizations, and chartering its own technological applications, many times independently of research advances, and even in different directions. At present, the connection and feedback between profession and research in information science is not as well established as it is in older fields, such as engineering or medicine. This is a serious inhibitor for progress of both.

More Specific

A number of authors suggested a breakdown of specific areas of information science, beyond the structural analysis offered above. The breakdown among different authors is in significant agreement, although the labels differ somewhat. I will take the breakdown and labels provided by White and McCain. They provided a factor analysis of co-cited authors and extracted 12 factors as specialties. In descending order of how authors loaded, they labelled the specialties as:

- Experimental *information retrieval* (IR);
- Citation analysis;
- Practical retrieval;
- Bibliometrics;
- General library systems theory;
- Science communication;
- User studies and theory;
- OPACs;
- General imported ideas—other disciplines;
- Indexing theory;
- Citation theory; and
- Communication theory.

While one may quibble with some of the classes and labels, these specialties provide a fairly accurate picture of problem areas in which information scientists worked over the past quarter of a century.

Over time, there were shifts in emphasis and there were movements between specialties. Nothing is permanent. But these are the specialties of information science. New areas are clearly on the horizon. For the 1990s, I would suggest that the major new areas include interaction studies; searching of the Internet; multimedia IR; multilanguage IR; and digital libraries.

SOCIAL CONTEXT OF INFORMATION SCIENCE

Information science is a field that emerged in the after-math of the Second World War (WW II), along with a number of new fields, with computer science being but one example. The rapid pace of scientific and technical advances that were accumu-lating since the start of the 20th century, produced by mid-century a scientific and technical revolution. A most visible manifestation of this revolution was the phenomenon of "information explosion," referring to the exponential and unabated growth of scientific and technical publications and information records of all kinds, so masterfully synthesized and illuminated by de Solla Price.

In a remarkable turn of events, the impetus for the development of information science, and even for its very origin and agenda, a respected MIT scientist and, even more importantly, the head of the U.S. scientific effort during WW II. Bush did two things:

- He succinctly defined a critical and strategic problem that was on the minds of many, and
- Proposed a solution that was a "technological fix", and thus in tune with the spirit of the times.

Both had wide appeal and Bush was listened to because of his stature. He defined the problem in almost poetic terms as "the massive task of making more accessible a bewildering store of knowledge". In other words, Bush addressed the problem of information explosion. The problem is still with us. His solution was to use the emerging computing and other information technology to combat the problem. But he went even further. He proposed a machine named Memex, incorporating a capability for "association of ideas," and duplication of "mental processes artificially." A prescient anticipation of information science and artificial intelligence is evident.

Memex, needless to say, was never built, but to this day is an ideal, a wish list, an agenda, and, some think, a utopia. We are still challenged by the ever-worsening problem of the information explosion, now universal and in a variety of digital formats. We are still trying to fix things techno-logically. We are still aspiring to incorporate Memex's basic ideas in our solutions. A number of scientists and professi-onals in many fields around the globe listened and took up Bush's challenge.

Governments listened as well and provided funding. The reasoning went something like this: Because science and technology are strategically important for society, efforts that help them, information activities in particular, are also important and need support. In the U.S., the *National Science Foundation* (NSF) Act of 1950 established NSF and provided a number of mandates, among them "to foster the interchange of scientific information among scientists in the U.S. and foreign countries" and "to further the full dissemination of information of scientific value consistent with the national interest". The 1958 National Defence Education Act enlarged the mandate:

> "The National Science Foundation shall..undertake programme to develop new or improved methods, including mechanized systems, for making scientific information available".

By those mandates, an NSF division, which after a number of name and direction changes is now called the Division of *Information and Intelligent Systems* (IIS), has supported research in these areas since the 1950s. Importantly, the field-defining studies that NSF supported included, among others, Cranfield IR evaluation studies in the 1950s and 1960s, large chunks of SMART studies from the 1960s to 1990s, and now the Digital Libraries Initiatives. In the U.S., information science developed and began flourishing on its own in a large part due to government support by a host of agencies, as did many other fields. Historically, the support was a success—it was instrumental in creation of the whole enterprise of information science and even of the information online industry based on IR. But to the credit of information science it kept growing on its own even after government support slackened substantially. This cannot be said of a number of other fields or areas that floundered after government stopped being their main source and resource.

Social Context

It is a truism to state that information was always important for any society in any historical period. But the role of information and its degree of importance differed. With the evolution of the social order to a "post-industrial" society, or "post-capitalist" society or what we now commonly also call "information society," knowledge and information is assuming an increasing central role in every aspect of life. The classic study by Machlup, followed by a number of similar studies, documented the startling structural changes in the economy and society as driven by the growth of information and knowledge production and processing. Popularly, they were summarized by Drucker:

> The change in the meaning of knowledge that began two hundred fifty years ago has transformed society and economy. Formal knowledge is seen as both the key personal and the key economic resource... [K]nowledge proves itself in action. What we now mean by knowledge is information effective in action, information focused on results.... The actual products of the pharmaceutical industry is knowledge; pill and prescription ointment are no more than packaging for knowledge.

Addressing the problem of information explosion, information science found a niche within the broader context in the evolution of the information society. In its various manifestations and attempted solutions, the niche is getting broader and bigger. But by no means does information science hold a monopoly in that niche. As the importance of infor-mation is increasing in society, more and more resources and expenditures are channeled into various information-related activities.

More and more research funds, projects, and initia-tives are devoted to information in various disguises. It is not surprising then that more and more fields, researchers, professionals, and businesses are turning to information, and even "discovering" information. There is gold in information. Information science has many competitors—it may be even swamped by them.

INFORMATION RETRIEVAL IN LIBRARY

In the early and mid-1950s, a critical mass of scientists, engineers, librarians, and entrepreneurs started working enthusiastically on the problem and solution defined by Bush. By 1960s this became a large and relatively well-funded effort and organized activity. Often, there were heated arguments and controversies about the "best" solution, technique, or system.

These arguments brought on the tradition of evaluation, a major staple of IR research and development. What is now TREC started with Cranfield evaluations in the late 1950s and early 1960s. Remarkably, the basic evaluation principles developed then are still the underpinning of TREC today. Calvin Mooers, an active and highly visible pioneer of information science, coined the term *information retrieval* in 1951. The term took hold, and today is a part of the English language. At that time, Mooers not only coined the term, but also defined the problems to be addressed:

> "Information retrieval embraces the intellectual aspects of the description of information and its specification for search, and also whatever systems, techniques or machines that are employed to carry out the operation.

Today, we would add that IR also and particularly involves interaction in all of these, with all the contextual-cognitive, affective, situational—aspects that interaction embraces. An expanded Mooers' conception is still valid. As it advanced, IR produced a number of theoretical, empirical, and pragmatic concepts and constructs. Numerous IR systems were developed and successfully deployed.

A great many historical examples can be given to illustrate the remarkable evolution of IR systems and techniques, adapting the ever-evolving information technology, from punch cards in the midcentury to the Internet at its close. Based on IR, an online information industry emerged in the 1970s, and grew through its own version of information explosion, as chronicled by Hahn. IR is one of the most widely spread applications of any information system worldwide. It has a proud history. Surely, information science is more than IR, but many of the problems raised by IR or derived from objects and phenomena involved in IR, are at its core.

Approaches and Paradigm Split

The approach taken by Mooers was to concentrate on the building of systems. This systems emphasis which was formulated early in the 1950s, was the sole approach to IR for some decades. It still predominates in a good part of IR research to this day.

Consequently, most of the IR research and practice concentrated on retrieval systems and processes. However, starting in the late 1970s and gaining steam in the 1980s, a different line of reasoning and research evolved-one that concentrates on the cognitive, interactive, and contextual end of the process. It addressed users, use, situations, context, and interaction with systems, rather than IR systems alone as a primary focus.

The retrieval cluster started splitting into subclusters, as noted by White and McCain, and before by others such as Saracevic and Harter. We now have two distinct communities and approaches to research in the retrieval cluster. They became commonly known as *systems-centred* and *user-centred.* Both address retrieval, but from very different ends and perspectives. The split is not only conceptual, looking very differently at the same process, but also organizational. The systemscentered side is now mostly concentrated in the *Special Interest Group on Information Retrieval* (SIGIR) of the *Association for Computing Machinery*

(ACM), while the user-centered cluster congregates around the *American Society for Information Science* (ASIS).

Each has its own communication outlets-journals, proceedings, and conferences. There is less and less overlap of authors and works between the two outlets. We have two camps, two islands, with, unfortunately, relatively little traffic in-between. The systems-centered approach is exemplified by work on algorithms and evaluation based on the traditional IR model, a model that does not consider the users or interaction. The massive research that evaluates a variety of IR algorithms and approaches within TREC is a culmination of this approach.

In contrast, cognitive, situational, and interactive studies and models, involving the use of retrieval systems exemplify the human-centered approach. Following that approach, interactive models, differing significantly from the traditional IR model, started to emerge. Even in TREC, a group of researchers started an interaction track, but so far have a hard time conceptually and methodologically, thus demonstrating the difficulty in merging the traditional and interactive models and approaches. Let me characterize, in a simplified way, the relationship between the two approaches or subclusters addressing different sides of retrieval.

On the one hand, the human-centred side was often highly critical of the systems side for ignoring users and use, and tried valiantly to establish humans as the proper center of IR work. The mantra of human-centred research is that the results have implications for systems design and practice. Unfortunately, in most human-centred research, beyond suggestions, concrete design solutions were not delivered. On the other hand, the systems side, by and large, ignores the human side and user studies, and is even often completely ignorant of them. As to design, the stance is "tell us what to do and as suggested, do it." But nobody is really telling, or if telling, nobody is listening.

As a rule, in systems-oriented projects, people and users are absent. Thus, there are not many interactions between the two camps. Let me provide some examples. A rough analysis of the 1997 SIGIR proceedings found only 3 papers of some 34 that dealt in some way with people and users; in the ACM's Digital Libraries 1997 conference proceedings, of 25 papers only 3 mentioned people and users. If one reads authors such as Dervin and Nilan, and many of their successors, who champion the human centered approach, one gets the impression that there is a real conflict between the two sides and approaches, and that there is an alternative way to the "dreadful" systems approach.

In a way, this stance is a backlash caused by the excesses, failures, and blind spots of systems-centered approaches not only in IR, but also in great many other technological applica-tions. Unfortunately, sometimes the backlash is justified. All of us who work on the humancentered side are not that dismissive of the systems side. But the issue is not whether we should have systems-*or* humancentered approaches. The issue is even less of human*versus* systems-centered. *The issue is how to make human*and *systems-centered approaches work together.* In this sense, a number of works have addressed integrating usercentered and systems-centered approaches in IR, but this has been discussed mostly by researchers from the usercentered side. Examples are works by:

- Bates,
- Belkin,
- Cool,
- Stein,
- Thiel,
- Fidel
- Efthimidiadis,
- Robertson and
- Beaulieu.

To reiterate, it is not one camp against the other but how can we incorporate the best features of both approaches and make them work jointly. The issue is how to deliver and incorporate the desired design features that will improve systems orientations towards users, integrate them with systems features, and use advantages provided by both, humans and technology.

In other words, the issue is *putting the human in the loop* to build better algorithms and to exploit computational advantages. Real progress in information science, and by extension in IR, will come when we achieve this. Lately, the NSF has championed human-centered design involving an interdisciplinary approach to information systems. Hopefully, this will go beyond rhetoric. It is not easy to do. But, that is what research is for—to address difficult, not only easy problems.

Proprietary IR

By the 1980s, the commercial information industry based on IR became successful and profitable. Out of academe, grants, and government, IR became a money-making propo-sition. This, of course, is another and important sign of success. Not surprisingly, a number of former IR researchers, practitioners, and graduates of IR programmes ventured out to become IR entrepreneurs.

Sure enough, throughout information science history there were many entrepreneurs, and they were highly significant in development of the field. But this generation of entrepre-neurs was different. They ventured to develop and market a variety of IR procedures based on algorithms, applicable and scalable to large files, multiple applications, and/or various advanced technologies. It was knowledge industry at its purest. But, as in all commercial knowledge industries, the product was proprietary. While it was not that hard to guess the base of these various proprietary algorithms and how they worked—after all they were derived from publicly available knowledge and experiences, such as those that came from SMART experi-ments—they remain unpublished and "secret."

A new kind of IR evolved, separate from the rest, not communicating as to intellectual advances with the rest. None of these ventures became a high commercial success, as measured by Silicon Valley standards. But the World Wide Web, emerging in the first half of the 1990s, changed all this. The acceleration of the growth of the Web is an information explosion of the like never before seen in history. Not surprisingly then, the Web is a mess. No wonder that everybody is interested in some form of IR as a solution to fix it.

A number of academic-based efforts were initiated to develop mechanisms, search engines, "intelligent" agents, crawlers, and so forth, to help control the Web. Some of these were IR scaled, and adapted to the problem; others were a variety of extensions of IR. Many had few, if any original, developments, besides new packaging or labeling; and a good number were just the usual hype. The wheel was reinvented a number of times. But out of this, and fast, came commercial ventures, such as the pioneering Yahoo!, whose basic objective is to provide search mechanisms for finding something of relevance for users on demand.

And to make a lot of money. These enterprises pride themselves on having proprietary methods by which they are accomplishing the retrieval tasks. The connection to the information science community is tenuous, and almost non-existent. The flow of knowledge, if any, is onesided, from IR research results into proprietary engines. The reverse contribution to public knowledge is zero. A number of evaluations of these search engines have been undertaken simply by comparing some results between them or comparing of their retrieval against some benchmarks.

Some evaluations were done within, others outside of information science. Results were not complimentary. The Web-based proprietary IR is expanding and flourishing outside of the field. It is addressing a vexing problem, the like we have not seen before. But as yet, the success is elusive and questionable.

RELEVANCE

As information science pioneers developed IR processes and systems in the 1950s, they defined as the main objective retrieval of *relevant* information. Effectiveness was expressed in terms of relevance. From then to now, IR is explicitly geared not towards any old kind of information, but towards *relevant information*. Various IR approaches, algorithms, and practices were, and still are, evaluated in relation to relevance.

Thus, relevance became a key notion in information science. It is also a complex phenomenon with a long and turbulent history in information science transcending IR, going back to early 1950s. Of course, there was a choice. Relevance did not have to emerge as the key notion. Uncertainty was one choice suggested by a number of theorists to be the base of IR, and thus to reflect effectiveness. But it did not take. In contrast, uncertainty is the basic notion underlying expert systems. If the pioneers had not embraced relevance, but instead, let's say, uncertainty, as the base for IR, we would have today a very different IR, and probably not that successful. In general, relevance, according to *Webster*, means having significant bearing on matter at hand. As with many other concepts, relevance assumes related but more specific meaning in more specific contexts and applications.

In the context of information science, relevance is the attribute or criterion reflecting the effectiveness of exchange of information between people and IR systems in communi-cation contacts based on valuation by people. With relevance as the criterion, and human judgements of relevance of retrieved objects as the measuring instrument, the measures of precision and recall are widely used in evaluation of IR systems. The strength of these measures is that they involve people—users—as judges of effectiveness of performance. The weakness is the same: it involves judgement by people, with all the perils of subjectivity and variability. Relevance indicates a relation. For relevance, many relations have been investigated. An consensus has emerged in information science that we can distinguish between several differing relations that account for different manifestations or types of relevance:

- *System or Algorithmic Relevance:* Relation between a query and information objects in the file of a system as retrieved, or as failed to be retrieved, by a given procedure or algorithm. Comparative effectiveness in inferring relevance is the criterion for system relevance.
- *Topical or Subject Relevance:* Relation between the subject or topic expressed in a query and topic or subject covered by retrieved texts, or, more broadly, by texts in the system file, or even in existence. Aboutness is the criterion by which topicality is inferred.
- *Cognitive Relevance or Pertinence:* Relation between the state of knowledge and cognitive information need of a user and texts retrieved, or in the file of a system, or even in existence. Cognitive correspondence, infor-mativeness, novelty, information quality, and the like are criteria by which cognitive relevance is inferred.
- *Situational Relevance or Utility:* Relation between the situation, task or problem at hand and texts retrieved by a system, or in the file of a system, or even in existence. Usefulness in decision making, appropriateness of information in resolution of a problem, reduction of uncertainty, and the like are criteria by which situational relevance is inferred.
- *Motivational or Affective Relevance:* Relation between the intents, goals, and motivations of a user and texts retrieved by a system, or in the

file of a system, or even in existence. Satisfaction, success, accomplish-ment, and the like are the criteria for inferring motivational relevance.

Practically, IR systems assess systems relevance only-that is, they respond to queries-hoping that the objects retrieved may also be of cognitive relevance, and even more so of utility. However, a user may judge an object by any or all types of relevance-for a user they may interact dynamically. Difficulties arise when an object is of system relevance but not of cognitive relevance or utility, or conversely.

If items are of cognitive relevance or utility, but were not reflected in the query, they are not and cannot be retrieved. At the bottom of IR research is a quest to align systems with other types of relevance. People all over have a strong intuitive understanding of relevance, thus, they intuitively understand, without manuals, what IR is all about. This makes IR systems generally understandable and acceptable-a critical attribute in their widespread application.

DISCIPLINARY RELATIONS

Two things introduced interdisciplinarity in information science. First and foremost, the problems addressed cannot be resolved with approaches and constructs from any single discipline-thus, intedisciplinarity is predetermined, as it is in many modern fields. Second, interdisciplinarity in information science was introduced and is being perpetuated to the present by the very differences in backgrounds of people addressing the described problems. Differences in background are many; they make for richness of the field and difficulties in communication and education. Clearly not every discipline in the background of people working on the problem made an equally relevant contri-bution, but the assortment was responsible for sustaining a strong interdisciplinary characteristic of information science. I will concentrate on interdisciplinary relations with two fields: librarianship and computer science. Obviously, other fields, most notably cognitive science and communication, have also interdisciplinary relations, but these are the most significant and developed ones.

Librarianship

Librarianship has a long and proud history devoted to organization, preservation, and use of graphic records and records in other media. This is done through libraries not only as a particular organization or type of information system, but even more so as an indispensable social, cultural, and educational institution whose value has been proven manifold throughout human history, and across all geographic and cultural boundaries. Researcher defines the library as:

- ...Contributing to the total communication system in society... Though the library is an instrumentality created to maximize the utility of graphic records for the benefits of society, it achieves that goal by working with the individual and through the individual it reaches society.

The common ground between library science and information science, which is a strong one, is in sharing of their social role and in their general concern with effective utilization of graphic and other records, particularly by individuals. But there are also very significant differences in several critical respects, among them:

- *Selection of Problems Addressed and the Way they were Defined*: A majority of the problems were not and are not addressed in library science;
- *Theoretical Questions Asked and Frameworks Established*: The theories and conceptual frameworks in librarian-ship have no counterpart in information science, and *vice versa*;
- *The Nature and Degree of Experimentation and Empirical Development and the Resulting Practical Knowledge and Competencies Dderived*: There is very little overlap in experimentation and development between the two, and professional requirements differ as well to a significant degree;
- *Tools and Approaches Used:* A most telling example is the very different approach undertaken in relation to utilization of technology in IR and in library automation; and
- *The Nature and Strength of Interdisciplinary Relations Established and the Dependence of Progress on Inter-disciplinary Approaches*: Librarianship is much more selfcontained.

All of these differences warrant a conclusion that librarian-ship and information science are two different fields in strong interdisciplinary relations, rather than one and the same field, or one being a special case of the other. This is not a matter of turf battles, or of one being better or worse than the other. Such arguments, while common between many fields, matter little to progress of either field. But differences in selection and/or definition of problems addressed, agenda, paradigms, theoretical base, and practical solutions *do* matter. Thus the conclusion that librarianship and information science, while related, are different fields. The differences are most pronounced in the research agenda and directions. Interestingly, research on OPACs, now that they are incorporating more and more IR features, is bringing the two fields in closer relation. Probably, so will the research in digital libraries, but at this time, it is too early to tell. The conclusion is not without heated controversy. Among other authors, Vakkari contends on information science and librarianship being one and the same field, with the now commonly used name of "library and information science." Does it matter? Administratively yes, very much so, particularly in universities and professional societies. Otherwise, no. The issue is, and always will be, in the problems addressed and solutions undertaken. I contend that they differ significantly.

Computer Science

The basis of relation between information science and computer science lies in the application of computers and computing in IR, and the associated products, services, and networks. In the last few years, this relation also involves research on the evolving digital libraries, with their strong technological base. To illustrate the connection, we use a definition by Denning:

> "The discipline of computing is the systematic study of algorithmic processes that describe and transfer information: their theory, analysis, design, efficiency, implementation, and application. The fundamental question underlying all of the computing is: "What can be automated?"

Computer science is about algorithms related to infor-mation interpreted in the first, whereas information science is about the very nature of information and its use by humans, interpreted in the third or broadest sense. Computer science is about symbol manipulation, whereas information science is about content manipulation, where symbol manipulation is the indispensable infrastructure. The two concerns are not in competition, they are complementary—they lead to different basic and applied agendas. Computer science is also many times larger than information science.

A number of computer scientists have been involved in research and development on information and its many spin-offs, to the point of being recognized leaders in information science. Gerard Salton is a prime example. In addition, there are several streams of research and development in computer science that had no connection with the early evolution of information science, but have addressed information problems similar to those in information science. Among others, these include works on expert systems, knowledge bases, hypertext, and human-computer interaction.

More recently, this involves research and development on digital libraries, a "hot", financially heavily supported area by a host of government agencies in the U.S. and many other countries. Bolstered by heavy support, interest in digital library research exploded on the scene in 1990s, attracting the attention of computer scientists from a wide variety of streams, as well as people from many other disciplines. These areas have a significant informational component that is associated with information representation, its intellectual organization, and linkages; meta-information, information seeking, searching, retrieving, and filtering; use, quality, value, and impact of information; evaluation of information systems from user and use perspective; and the like-all traditionally addressed in information science.

Conversely, these streams of computer science research and development provide a different outlook, framework, and approach, and even a different paradigm, not only for information science research and development, but also for its academic and continuing education. Again, as with librarianship, the issue is not about turf. It is about paradigms, theoretical foundations, and pragmatic solutions; and ultimately, it is about their appropriateness to human information problems.

EDUCATION

That education is critical for any field is a truism that hardly needs to be stated. In particular, research lives by education, it cannot be better than the education that researchers receive and then extend and plow back into education. Unfortunately, education in information science has not received the attention that it deserves. This may explain the many difficulties in the field that I have discussed. Educational models that evolved differed to a degree or even substantially from country to country. I am concentrating here on the U.S. models only.

In the United States, two educational models evolved over time. I call them the Shera and Salton models, after those that pioneered them. Both have strengths and weaknesses. Jesse H. Shera was a legendary library school dean from the 1950s until the 1970s at Western Reserve University. Among others, he was instrumental in starting the Center for Documentation and Communication Research in 1955. Shortly thereafter, the library school curriculum started to include courses such as "Machine Literature Searching" and several other more advanced courses and laboratories on the topics of research in the Centre.

The basic approach was to append those courses, mostly as electives, to the existing library school curriculum, without modifications of the curriculum as a whole, and particularly not the required core courses. Information science became one of the specialty areas of library science. The base or core courses that students were taking rested in the traditional library curriculum. Information science education was an appendage to library science. A few attempts to spin off information science as an independent degree and curriculum were not followed widely. But Shera's model was. Library schools in the U.S. and in many other countries imitated Shera's model.

They used the same approach and started incorporating information science courses in their existing curriculum as a specialty. Out of this was borne the current designation "library and information science." Shera's model is still the prevalent approach in schools of library and information science. The strength of the Shera model is that it posits education within a service framework, connects the education to professional practice and to a broader and user-oriented frame of a number of other information services, and relates it to a great diversity of information resources.

The weakness is a lack of a broader theoretical frame-work and a total lack of teaching of any formalism related to systems, such as development and understanding of algori-thms. The majority of researchers in the human-centered side, as I described earlier, came from or are associated with this educa-tional environment. Gerard Salton was first and foremost a scientist, a computer scientist, and the father of modern IR.

As such, he pioneered the incorporation into IR research a whole array of formal and experimental methods from science, as modified for algorithmic and other approaches used so successfully in computer science. His primary orientation was research. For education, he took the time-honoured approach of a close involvement with research. Salton's model was a laboratory and research approach to education.

As Shera's model resulted in information science educa-tion being an appendage to library science education, Salton's model of IR education resulted in it being a specialty of and an appendage to computer science education. Computer science students that were already well-grounded in the discipline, got involved in SMART and other projects directed by Salton, worked and did research in the laboratory, completed their theses in areas related to IR, and participated in the legendary IR seminars.

They also published widely with Salton and with each other, and participated with high visibility in national and international conferences. From Harvard and Cornell, his students went to a number of computer science departments where they replicated Salton's model. Many other computer science departments in the U.S. and abroad took the same approach.

The strength of Salton's model is that it:

- "Starts from a base of a firm grounding in formal mathematical and other methods, and in algorithms, and
- Relates directly to research.

The weakness is in that it:

- Ignores the broader aspects of information science, as well as any other disciplines and approaches dealing with the human aspects that have great relevance to both the outcomes of IR research and the research itself, and
- Does not incorporate professional practice where these systems are realised and used. It loses users.

Consequently, this is a successful, but narrowly concen-trated education in IR as a specialty of computer science, rather then in information science. Not surprisingly, the researchers in the systems-centred approach came out of this tradition. The two educational approaches are completely independent of each other. Neither is connected to the other. Neither reflects fully what is going on in the field. While in each model there is an increase in cognizance of the other, there is no educational integration of the systems-and usercentered approaches.

The evident strengths that are provided by Shera and Salton model are not put together. Their weaknesses are perpetuated. It is high time for communities from each model to try to integrate education for information science. It is an open question whether the human-and systems-centered approaches can fruitfully work together as urged in all those calls for human-centered design until an educational inte-gration occurs.

While library education receives formal attention from the *American Library Association* (ALA), and education for computer science from ACM, no such formal attention is paid by any professional/scientific society to education for information science, or for IR in particular. Neither ASIS nor SIGIR, as primary homes for information science, have been involved to any great extent in educational matters, such as setting of standards or devising model curricula. Clearly, there is a need and an opportunity for more substantive involvement by both organizations in educational issues.

2

Research in Library and Information Science

INTRODUCTION

The roots of research in our profession are not very deep. Research in library science is a twentieth century occurrence ushered in by the library school of the University of Chicago in mid-1920s. The visionary efforts of the Chicago School bore abundant fruit and offered leadership to the world in library science research.

The pace of library research is picking up everywhere today due to social pressure as well as inspiration. In justifying the Ph.D. programme in our profession, it has been urged that "if librarianship aspires to become a profession, it should depend upon research to develop its knowledge base and its theoretical framework".

THE INDIAN CONTEXT

In India following British tradition and American precedent as established by Asa Don Dickinson, Librarian, Panjab University, Lahore, 1915-1916, library schools for advanced professional education have remained attached to universities. The growth of universities in Independent India ensured their constant growth. In a university, apart from teaching, a teacher is expected to do and guide research. The third function of a university, namely service and consultation, has always remained weak in India despite many newly established universityindustry linkage programmes.

RANGANATHAN'S WORK

The credit for the formal institution of the doctoral degree programme in library science in India goes undeniably to Dr. S.R. Ranganathan. In 1951, he started one at the University of Delhi surmounting many difficulties and facing personal ridicule. The University of Delhi awarded the first de jure degree in library science in 1957 to D.B. Krishan Rao who worked on a faceted classification for agriculture. Doctoral research remained in the wilderness when Ranganathan shook the Delhi soil off his feet in 1955. The *Documentation Research and Training*

Centre (DRTC) in Bangalore, founded by Ranganathan in 1962, is technically not empowered to award the Ph.D.

Therefore, for the rest of his life, from 1962 to 1972, Ranga-nathan only advocated solo and team research with stress on quality, relevance and basics. No big research projects were taken up at DRTC though individual teachers and students maintained both the quality and the tempo of research. Since the death of Ranganathan almost the entire DRTC faculty has earned Ph.D.s from other Indian universities on topics of research relevant to DRTC. Now the DRTC teachers are approved Ph.D. guides in many Indian universities, and they have already produced many Ph.D.

GROWTH OF DOCTORAL RESEARCH IN INDIA

Elsewhere in India other individual librarians and library science teachers eager to earn doctorates were hampered by the non-existence of programmes. In the 1960s and 1970s some doctorates on library-related topics were earned by library professionals from some other faculties such as sociology, history, law, economics, management, and the like.

The mantle of reviving and furthering doctoral research facilities was assumed by J. S. Sharma, then the university librarian and head of the library science department of the Panjab University, Chandigarh. Under his guidance the second *de jure* Ph.D. in library science was awarded in 1977 after a gap of full two decades. Thereafter, there was no looking back. Many universities followed with mostly individual efforts and enthusiasm. Doctoral research got a fillip in the 1980s. India maintained its Third World leadership in library research as well as in library education and literature. Ph.D. programmes have rather mushroomed even despite the lack of facilities or adherence to standards.

FACILITIES FOR RESEARCH

A conscientious university teacher is always in a dilemma over how to divide the time between teaching and research. Teaching is a primary compulsive and urgent duty to be performed. Students expect their teachers to give them time and personal attention. There may be appreciation in good teaching but the rewards lie in research. The university expects its teachers to do research for its prestige and fame lie therein. But when it comes to supporting of research many universities in India are neither generous nor unambivalent.

Ordinarily piecemeal research, especially in social sciences, is not supported financially. Internal support for research trickles through a tedious and off-putting bureaucracy and political manoeuvring. Colleagues are unsupportive. They are unappreciative, intolerant and jealous. Library facilities are poor. Thus most of the teachers are driven to the passivity of guiding doctoral research instead of doing postdoctoral work.

THE DETERIORATION OF STANDARDS

The University Grants Commission (UGC) preconditions for faculty employment and promotions have prompted many library professionals to acquire Ph.D. degrees, though many may not have the aptitude and the intrinsic ability to do research. Standards have not only been diluted but have been kept at abeyance. Supervisors and the examiners have become obligingly compromising. The cut-off date of December, 1992 for obtaining the Ph.D. degree to get an exemption from the national level test for teaching jobs in universities/colleges has done incalculable damage to research standards. An eminent academician has corroborated the ill effects of this policy:

> "They were required to submit their theses before the deadline regardless of the date of registration. Some of the candidates on whom Ph.D.'s were conferred were not fully acquainted with the contents of their dissertations. In some cases even the supervisors were innocent of any knowledge of what the theses were about. The incitement came from the UGC".

Programmes for Ph.D. research have been introduced and expanded mindlessly. As a result, there has been a bit of doctoral boom – a spectacular rise in Ph.D. awarding universities and awardees – though many institutions lack utterly the resources of people or material or both. A 1987 bibliography listed 41 Ph.D. theses written from 1957 to 1985. In a recently published bibliography of doctoral dissertations in India from 1950 to March 1997 about 340 titles have been listed. This record of 340 dissertations, though not wholly authentic, is reliable by and large. In productivity the Panjab University, Chandigarh, led up to the mid-1980s. Thereafter, it lost the number game to the universities of the south. The universities that have so far awarded up to ten degrees are ranked below:

- Karnatak University, Dharwad 44
- Jiwaji University, Gwalior 27
- University of Rajasthan, Jaipur 26
- Andhra University, Visakhapatnam 25
- University of Delhi 17
- University of Pune 16
- Gulbarga University 15
- Utkal University, Bhubaneswar 11
- University of Burdwan 10

The universities in Bangalore, Banaras Hindu University in Varanasi, and Nagpur University are picking up in research.

THE CONTRIBUTIONS MADE BY RESEARCH

Contrary to expectations, dissertations are not fountain heads of the rest of the literature to grow and mature. These primary sources of information are distanced from relevance. The National Social Science Documentation Centre systema-tically procures one copy of each research dissertation in social sciences to preserve and make them available to researchers for consultation within the premises of its library. Retro-spective bibliographies of LIS dissertations in India are available.

The latest information on theses awarded, Ph.D. degrees and Ph.D. research in progress is available in the featured column of the weekly University News of the Association of Indian Universities, New Delhi. It is a major source to keep track of the dissertations awarded Ph.D. degrees by Indian universities in all disciplines. In spite of availability, other researchers do not adequately use these dissertations; nor are these works cited or quoted by teachers or textbook writers.

Working librarians rarely use research results to solve their professional problems. There is no precedent of a library inviting a library school to do research on a problem confron-ting them. At the risk of calling attention to a red herring, it is worthwhile to have this idea corroborated from a veteran library leader. Professor P.N. Kaula candidly observed:

- That LIS departments have little or no understanding and cooperation with the central library... The problem is more psychological than academic... Much harm has been done to the teaching of library science by the disharmony....

Librarians go in for local, *ad hoc* and *pro-tem* solutions for their practical problems. Researchers consult a teacher or a fellow researcher for a topic of research rather than a practitioner. It is not only true in India but elsewhere too. Thus research has become divorced from reality–a theoretical exercise at best. This seems a universal phenomenon in our profession. Carl Keren doubting the value of research in information science daringly suggests that "It would be worthwhile to find out how much of it has really contributed to our body of knowledge and to the methods used by practitioners." He himself understands that "As suggested, probably be rather disappointed". American teacher Margaret Steig endorses this notion:

- Research done by library and information science educators seems to receive little respect from professionals, and if they do not find it of value one has to wonder who will.

USE AND USEFULNESS OF E-JOURNALS

We present and collocate the findings of a recent investigation that have been conducted under the Research Starter Fund at University of Madras, a Project that seeks to bring e-journals use and utilisation of the research scholars of the University of Madras. The results of this study bring a comprehensive detailed picture of the use of e-journals by the research scholars. This investigation is probably one of the first of its kinds in the University after implementing the University Grants Commission's Infonet Programme. The main aim of this chapter is to present the outcome of the research project undertaken to examine the use and utilisation of the e-journals by the research scholars of the University of Madras. The increasing move from print collection to digital collections has generated much significant research on scholars' reading patterns and the take-up the use of e-journals.

This project examines about the kinds of people use e-journals and their information seeking behaviour of the sample population. To understand how e-journals forms and functions may evolve, study examines the current role that e-journals play in scholarly work. This may provide some insight as to how e-journals will establish their niche within a broader set of scholarly resources and how they will complement and challenge traditional paper journals. This investigation applied a standard survey method to analyse the use and utilisation of e-journals. This study restricted only to the research scholars and excluded the faculty members, post-graduate students and M.Phil degree students.

REVIEW OF RELATED STUDIES

Many studies tell us that using of e-journals articles has increased during the last decade and has been boosted by the application of Information and Communication Technologies (ICTs) in scholarly communication. More use of e-journals by the scientists than social scientists, however, enthusiasm for e-journals and patterns of use vary even among field of science.

Chemists and physicists use them frequently, while earth scientists and mathematicians see few advantages in using ejournals. Tenopir and King also found these variations that physicists and astronomers to be among the most enthusiastic users of e-journals articles, because of the digital archives and e-journals available and designed specifically to facilitate their natural work patterns.

Dillon and Hahn report the use of e-journals with study conducted at the University of Maryland. More faculty member used e-journals daily or weekly than they did print journals.

This corresponds to the decrease in physical visits to the library by graduate students and faculty, especially in health sciences, sciences and engineering. Business school faculty reported the highest use, while Palmer and Sandler found economics faculty to be the most enthusiastic users of e-journals. Speier and Hahn found that among business faculty, finance and management information systems faculty were more aware of e-journals than those in other fields.

Faculty members for history, education, and the arts have been slower to adopt e-journals. Among the corporate users, investment and banking companies or departments spend a higher per cent of their budgets on electronic products than do other types of business such as pharmaceutical firms, legal services, food services, or telecommunications. Rudner, Miller-Whitehead and Gellamn found graduate students, particularly Ph.D. students are to be heavy users of e-journals, most likely in their role as researchers.

As found in the SuperJournal Project, graduate students may be 'binge' users consulting e-journals extensively for a short period when they are writing a thesis or dissertation. There are some exceptions—under graduates were the most frequent users in an experimental study conducted by American Chemical Society. Different workplaces or types of institutions have varying use patterns as well. Davis examined e-journals users logs in libraries of the Northeast Research Library Consortium and found that each institutions has a unique pattern of use - medical institutions users had higher use of a smaller number of journals, while users at large universities and smaller colleges downloaded articles from a greater variety of journals title. Differences in e-journals use may be attributed to age, status or rank. Speire and Hahn found that young ARL University Business faculty members reported that they use e-journals more often and were aware than were older faculty.

Another study reported that more than half of the faculty members under the age of 40 reported using e-journals as compared with only 14 per cent of those over 40, although more than 80 per cent of the total respondents indicated that would consider using e-journals in the future. Antoir found that older people preferred print articles; Monopoli found that user between age 21 and 34 used e-journals most frequently. Tenner and Yang found that assistant professors are most likely to have used e-journals (44.7 per cent), followed by professors (34.5 per cent) and followed by associate professors (34.2 per cent).

Researchers in other studies found no relationship between age and searching skills, although the researchers observed that younger users are more likely to browse on the computers, while older users prefer print journals for browsing. Tenopir and King also found no relationship between age and reading patterns among astronmers. Monopoli et al studied amongst the staff of the University of Patras, Greece, found that male staff has frequent use of electronic journals than female staff. Dilhon and Hahn found 70 per cent of the faculty wants core journals in both print and electronic form, but the some member wanted non-core journals only in electronic form. Worlock found that articles recommended by colleagues were more often in print than in electronic format.

Tenopir and King found contradictory results that e-mail and listerv make it easier to share recommended articles with colleagues. University faculty members opined that the ability to send articles to their colleagues instantly as being one of the major advantages of ejournals. Use of electronic books is also clearly course driven-books with the highest usage are those required in a class, and most users come to an electronic book collection to use a single title.

Most college students now are computer litreate and they use the web frequently. This does not necessarily correlate with effective use, however, an study found that professors performed newspapers and journal articles significantly better than graduates. The perceptions that e-journals are of lower quality than print is another problem that may be diminishing as a high percentage of peer-reviewed journals are digitised. Reported that they did not perceive e-journals to be of as high quality as paper counterparts.

While more than 70 per cent of the faculty members in a British University believe the quality of articles in electronic journals is the same as in print journals, this same group of respondents cited the top disadvantage of electronic journals as being the impression that electronic publication is not 'real' publication. Tenopir found that more undergraduate students used the web and web search engines frequently, students are mostly unaware of the distinction between materials on the web and peer reviewed journals.

A nationwide survey of students and academics in the Netherlands found that 60 per cent of respondents in the humanities, 78 per cent of respondents in the social sciences, and 82 per cent of respondents in the sciences used the Internet for study or work and nearly all believed they had Internet skills. Waldman found that 97 per cent of psychology students access the Internet at least weekly, about 44 per cent of the time for educational information.

Lack of awareness was one of the contributing factors for non-use of e-journals. Science, engineering and health sciences faculty at the University of Washington favoured cancelling print journals in favour of electronic only, while humanities and social sciences faculty opposed this idea and responded that maintaining the quality of the print collection is their higher priority.

MEANS AND METHODS

A whole range of different methods with different approaches and objectives have been employed to the use of e-journals. Questionnaire surveys and interviews are the common favourite methodologies amongst the researchers. Transactional log analysis studies are not so common, but they are more popular to study the e-journals as well as digital libraries. A survey method would be adopted to carry out this research project.

In the process of surveying, a predefined questionnaire has been used to collect the necessary data. The questionnaire having questions like personal information, computer education, computer use, Internet and World Wide Web aware and use, search engines, browser, skills search techniques, awareness of the e-journals, level of use, purpose of sue, problems of using e-journals, etc. The University Departments are spread into four campuses and located in different places with group of Departments. Social sciences and humanities in Chepauk, languages in Marina, life sciences and physical and chemical sciences in Guindy and basic medical sciences in Taramani. Questionnaires have been distributed with equal proportion based on the number of departments available in that campus.

DATA ANALYSIS

The data collected through questionnaire have been analysed using statistical tool and presented. The total questionnaire admired this study is two hundred and distributed to the research scholars of all the campuses. Only 72 per cent of research scholars responded. Among the respondents, male representation was 69 per cent and female represent 31 per cent under this survey.

The respondents are grouped into two broad categories for sake of convenient into data analysis, *viz.*, arts and science. Science (53 per cent) arts (47 per cent) and disciplines research scholars having same proportion in the sample population. This indicated that questionnaire have been distributed with equal proportion based on the disciplines. Among the researchers, young researchers are more (45 per cent) than the second year (22 per cent), third year (11 per cent) and fourth year (17 per cent). Research scholars can be grouped into full-time and part-time students. Fulltime students are again divided into stipendiary and non-stipendiary candidates. Part-time candidates are also included in the sample. Full-time non-stipendiary candidates are higher (59 per cent) than the stipendiary candidates. Very small number of part-time candidates responded.

This may be due to the non-availability of researchers in the departments during the survey period. Almost all the respondents are below 35years old except 5 per cent of respondents are above 35 years old. This is because sample population belonging to only the research scholars.

The basic qualification for pursuing Ph.D. degree also taken into consideration with view of, is there any factor affecting the pattern of use? Respondents with Post-graduation are higher (60 per cent) than with M. Phil as qualification for pursuing Ph.D. degree programme. While study the e-journals use, access to e-journals requires computer knowledge some extend. Whether the respondents had acquired any formal computer education or not have been asked to correlate with e-journal use.

The level of education was divided into four categories such as level of degree, postgraduate diploma, diploma and certificate course. Amongst certificate course level is more (36 per cent) followed by diploma holder (20 per cent), 7 and 9 percentages of respondents acquired degree and P.G. diploma levels respectively.

The remaining 28 per cent of respondents are having any level of formal computer education. Almost all the research scholars are using computer for one or other purposes, very less number of respondents are not using computer. Nearly half of the respondents are viewed that the computer is being used for purpose of communicate with others. More than half (55 per cent) of the respondents are using computer for their project work. Now-a-day, digital and electronic resources are playing vital role in satisfying the users' requirements. Researchers and students are depending mainly on electronic sources. But the survey shows that less than half of the respondents (45 per cent) opined that computer is using for preparing assignments. Twothird of the respondents (70 per cent) are using computer for their research purpose. Apart from their academic and/ or research purposes the respondents were asked whether computing is being for entertainment purposes, very less segment of the sample population (24 per cent) is using computer for entertainment. Among the respondents, only 36 per cent are having either personal computer or laptop. Surprisingly 2 per cent of the research scholars respond that they are not aware of Internet and World Wide Web (WWW). Remaining respondents are aware and using Internet with varied years of experience. As far as years of experiences is concerned, more than five years of Internet using experience is more (27 per cent) than the other categories.

This was followed by very young users, *i.e.*, less than two years (21 per cent) and between 2-5 years experiences spread equally in three groups. Almost all the respondents are active users of Internet, either they are using daily (33 per cent) alternate days (22 per cent) or once in a week (22 per cent). A small per cent of the respondents are occasional users. The possible places of using Internet are University's Internet Centre (34 per cent), cyber cafes (26 per cent) and home (5 per cent). More than half (52 per cent) of the respondents learnt Internet through self-learning method.

The second position occupy by the through friends (23 per cent), sixteen per cent of the respondents are taken formal training course for Internet access and only 3 per cent of the respondents are through media/ newspapers. The respondents mainly preferred Internet Explorer for browsing web pages. More than 90 per sent of the respondents are preferred this browser and only 4 per sent of the respondents are using other than Internet Explorer.

Google search engine is most preferred search engine among the respondents. More than three fourth of the respondents are using the search engine either often or sometimes. Yahoo and MSN are not in a significant place among research scholars. Only negligible amount of respondents are preferred Alltheweb, Altavista, Askjeeves, Excite, Hotbot, Lycosand and Infoseek. Alltehweb advanced, Altavista advanced, Google advanced, Hotbot advanced are taken into consideration for identify the usage of advanced search engines. Nearly 70 per cent of respondents are using Google advanced search either often, rare or sometimes.

One fourth of the respondents are not using advanced search, no significant numbers using other search engines. The preferred type of resources among the respondents were been questioned, nearly 20 per cent respondents are using databases often. Full-text publications often search by 42 per cent of respondents. In relation to library web sites, half of the respondents are often or sometimes visits to the library web sites.

More than half of the respondents are not having interest to see health related web sites, others are visits rarely (6 per cent), sometimes (19 per cent) or often (17 per cent). Similar range of respondents engaged with job searching and newspaper reading areas. However, recreational web sites gets high position among the researchers (73 per cent). The possible difficulties in Internet access have been identified, *viz.*, language barriers, broken links, instability of network, slow expansion, finding relevant, and information overload. The respondents opined in this survey that language is low degree of problem in searching the Internet. At the same time 16 per cent of respondents are opined that the language barrier is in moderate level. Broken link is also available in moderate level while searching the web. Regarding instability of network, high degree of responses occurs on that. Slow expansion is another problem among the respondents of the Internet users. High percentage of respondents opined that it occurs in moderate level.

Among the respondents, 30 per cent respondents are strongly agreed that Internet resources are up-to-date information. Very negligible number of respondents disagrees or strongly disagrees this and majority of the respondents are opined that that Internet has lot of information. Good accessibility was scored high (60 per cent) from the opinion about the accessibility of the Internet resources. Similarly optioned on accuracy of the resources available in the Internet, but very limited number of the respondents said that sources are excellent.

The opinion about availability, consistency, flexibility and usefulness, respondents gave rated high to good scale in all the attributes. Below 10 per cent respondents are says these attributes are excellent on availability, similar results one could see for other attributes. Internet and Internet resources have positive impact on studying and teaching strongly agreed by the majority of the respondents. One third of the respondents felt that some have had positive impact. The search methods and level of satisfaction on 'content' and 'keyword' search have been asked to determine the search skills of the respondents. Among the respondents, majority of the respondents are not a habit of searching items with content/ topic in which they required. But significant respondents (38 per cent) among them using content/ topic search often. Majority of the respondents use keyword searching often.

Similarly, majority of the respondents are opined that they are using sometimes. In the topical search, the respondents are received moderate level of satisfaction. Only 20 per cent viewed that they have received high level of satisfaction. High level of satisfaction received from the respondents on keyword search. Various search techniques such as Boolean Operators (AND, OR, NOT), nesting, truncation, phrase searching, controls, case sensitive and wildcard have been asked to find out whether users are using these search techniques while search the web. Majority of the respondents (60 per cent) are never using Boolean operators; the remaining respondents are using Boolean operators rarely, sometimes, or often.

Nesting also never used by the two third of the respondents. Only one third of respondents are using the nesting techniques on the other levels. In the text retrieval system, truncation is one of the techniques used to improve the recall in the search. The result shows that the majority of the respondents (70 per cent) are not using truncation method. Similar results arrived for phrase searching also.

The researchers of the Madras University do not have practice of using 'controls' while search the Internet resources. The result of use of case sensitive methods in searching is shows that 67 per cent of them are not suing case sensitive. The use of wildcard method also asked among the respondents. Almost all the respondents are opined that they never use this while searching.

The utilisation of resources such as bibliographic databases, full-text databases, images, audio-video information, e-books and e-journals by the researchers of the University have been ascertained. Among the respondents, 66 per cent of the respondents opined that they never browse the bibliographic databases, others browsing sometimes, often or rarely. Similar set of results are arrived in the case of full-text database also. Images, audio-video type of information also in the list of very often used sources of information by the one fourth of the respondents. E-books are not in their mind among 40 per cent of respondents, others are using often, sometimes or rarely.

Unlike the e-books, 70 per cent respondents are often use e-journals. Now-a-days open sources are dominant in the web resources. It is considered as one of media for scholarly communication. The awareness of the open sources among the researchers is determined, sharply 50 per cent of the respondents are aware of open sources, the remaining are unaware. More than half (60 per cent) of respondents are aware of virtual libraries, other respondents are not aware of virtual libraries. Similar result is arrived for the awareness of electronic libraries (64 per cent). Nearly 40 per cent of respondents are not aware of consortium functioning in India. Among the three major functional consortia in India, UGC's Infonet is one of the aware and using consortia than All India Council for Technical Education's INDEST and CSIR's Consortia. The use and utilisation of e-journals have been assessed with following questions:

- Whether you are using e-journals?
- What mod you are using (consortia or open source)?
- Is e-journals are useful?
- Is e-journals are substitute to the printed form?

Among the respondents, nearly 50 per cent of the respondents are not using e-journals either from open sources or through consortia. One fourth of the respondents (26 per cent) are using e-journals through consortium, remaining respondents are using open sources. Majority of the respondents (82 per cent) felt that the e-journals are useful sources of information. Regarding the substitution of e-journals, two third of the respondents (61 per cent) felt that e-journals are considered as a substitute to the print journals.

The remaining of them opined reverse. The e-journals characteristics such as accessibility, authenticity, availability and usefulness are asked and the results are: half of the respondents (51 per cent) are 'agree' about the accessibility. Nearly 30 per cent of respondents 'somewhat agree' on accessibility of e-journals.

At the same time very few of them opined 'strongly agree'. Only 2 per cent of the respondents have opinion of 'disagree' and 'strongly disagree'. While asking the authenticity of the e-journals, the result is reflecting the same as in the accessibility. Nearly half of the respondents (47 per cent) of the respondents 'agree' about the authenticity of the e-journals.

One-third of the respondents are 'somewhat agree'. Similar result one could see from the results on availability of the e-journals. Majority of them (75 per cent) either 'agree' or 'somewhat agree'.

The opinion of the usefulness of the e-journals slightly differs from the other characteristics. Majority of the respondents (82 per cent) are 'strongly agree' and 'agree' and 13 per cent respondents 'somewhat agree'.

INFERENCES

The following inferences have been arrived and summarised as follows:

- *Sex*: Male respondents are more than female in the sample population.
- *Department*: More or less equal number of distributions of respondents in both Arts and Science disciplines.
- Fresh-hand researchers are more than senior researchers among the sample population.
- Full-time non-stipendiary candidates are more than stipendiary candidates; very less number of respondents belongs to part-time researchers.
- *Age*: Majority of respondents are youngster rather old persons.
- *Qualification*: Post-Graduation qualified research scholars are more than with M.Phil qualified respondents in the sample population.
- *Computer Education*: Two third of the respondents are having formal computer education.
- *Computer Use*: Almost all the researchers are using computer one or other purposes.
- *Purpose of using Computer*: The research scholars are using computer for preparing assignment, project, research and some extend to entertainment rather business purpose.
- One-third of researchers under survey are having own computer system. Others dependent outside resources.
- *Internet and World Wide Web*: Almost all the respondents are aware of Internet and World Wide Web and one third of them having good experiences in using Internet and World Wide Web.

- All the respondents are active users of Internet and World Wide Web. They spent reasonable time in browsing the net.
- The research scholars are not only depending upon the University's Internet Centre's but also Cyber cafes. Only minimum number are using in their home.
- *Internet use Learning*: The researchers are learnt Internet browsing by themselves and through friends. This indicates that the syllabus does not have any course on Internet study area.
- *E-mail*: E-mail communication exists as one of the communication channels among the research scholars of the University of Madras.
- *Internet Browser*: Internet Explorer is popular Internet browser among the respondents. Mozilla Firefax occupies the second position. No other became popular to the research scholars.
- *Search Engines*: Google, Yahoo, MSN are the most popular search engines among the research scholars. Other search engines are rarely using by the respondents. No much use of the advanced search engines, except some respondents are using Google's advanced search engine.
- *Type of sites using*: The researchers mostly preferred full-text publications, Education and Job sites. Recreational, Health, etc are visiting by the researchers sometimes. Newspapers/ Magazine, Travel and Tourism related web sites are least preferred.
- Internet Access Difficulties:
  - — *Language Barriers*: Language is not at all considered as barriers in Internet access.
  - — *Broken Links*: Broken/ dead link problem affect the researchers in the moderate level.
  - — *Instability of Network*: The instability of network also not affects the use of Internet.
  - — *Slow Expansion of site*: Researchers opined that it is in moderate level.
  - — *Relevant Information*: The research scholars are found relevant information while searching the Internet.
  - — *Information overload*: The same opinion of the above could find this case also.
  - — *Internet Resources*: The researchers are strongly felt that the Internet resources are up-to-date and enormous information is available. But somewhat agree on ideal way of communication.
- The University research scholars felt that the attributes such as accessibility, accuracy, availability, consistency, flexibility and usefulness are good rather excellent or poor.
- *Impact of Internet*: The Internet had positive impact on research and academic activities of the research scholars.

- *Search Skills*: Keyword search is preferred search methods adopted by the majority of the researchers rather content/ topical search. The moderate level of satisfaction they acquired through keyword search.
- *Search techniques*: Boolean operators, phrase searching are some of search techniques rarely being used by the researchers. The other techniques such as nesting, truncation, controls, wildcard, etc never being used by the almost all the research scholars.
- Advanced search by restricting type of resources, file format and period never being used by the University of Madras research scholars.
- Type of Resources browsing:
  - — *Bibliographic databases*: It is not a preferred resource for browsing by the research scholars.
  - — *E-books*: Almost all the researchers are not having the habit of using e-books.
  - — *Audio-Video*: Rarely it being used by the researchers.
  - — *Full-text databases*: Full-texts databases are preferred areas of interest of most of the scholars.
  - — *E-journals*: The majority of the research scholars often use e-journals.
- *Open Sources*: The researches are aware of 'open sources' in the Internet and World Wide Web.
- *Virtual and Electronic Libraries*: They have knowledge about 'virtual library' and 'electronic library'.
- Consortia:
  - — University of Madras is one of the member institutions in the UGC's InfoNet Programme. The researchers are aware of it. But the other major consortia such as AICTE's INDEST and CSIR's Consortia are not aware of by the researchers.
  - — The researchers of the University do not often use UGC's InfoNet. Science discipline research scholars fully aware about the programme and using, whereas Arts discipline researchers are not aware and used.
- E-journals:
  - — E-journals are using by the research scholars of the University. Among the researchers, Science discipline researchers are using open sources as well as consortia.
  - — Generally the e-journals are useful sources of scholarly communication
  - — Both the opinions are found that Ejournals are considered as substitution to the print journals and not.
- E-journals characteristics:
  - — Accessibility of the e-journals is easy than printed journals.

— Though authenticity is one of the criticisms when the 'open sources', e-journals are considered as one of the authentic sources of information. Lot of e-journals is available in an electronic form, which made available through open sources and consortium.
— Digital information has an attribute of manifestation. e-journals are considered as useful resources.

RESEARCH IN ELECTRONIC JOURNALS MODELS

There are four Ithink models of electronic journal production and delivery. The first is a model of a non-commercial electronic journal with traditional economic characteristics. In this model, costs are recovered from sales of subscriptions and individual articles.

A "Traditional model" is presented first to facilitate easy comparison with journal production and delivery in a print environment. The second model is based on the economic model proposed by Harnad and Hemus and is hereinafter described as the "Harnad model". The third is a 'market' model based on Fishwick *et al.*'s eLib supporting study on the economic implications of different models of publishing scholarly electronic journals and is hereinafter referred to as the "Fishwick model".

The fourth model is an alternative model, proposed by the authors, which is informed by the other three models. The Traditional model is presented first and assumptions informing different elements in the model are explained.

The Harnad model, the Fishwick model, and the authors' alternative model are then described. Where elements and assumptions in these models differ from those in the Traditional model these are documented.

The values of several elements in each of these models were varied and the models run to monitor the effects. The costs and benefits for different stakeholders of manipulating model elements was established and model sensitivities were identified. The results are described.

Model Simulations

The overhead rate applied to production costs and the journal rejection rate are varied and the effect on submission fees is monitored. The results are recorded below. If the overhead on production costs is 120 per cent, at a 10 per cent rejection rate the submission fee is £878.90.

This figure falls to £97.66 for a 90 per cent rejection rate. If the overhead on production costs is reduced from 120 per cent to 60 per cent the submission fee is reduced and ranges from £639.21 for a rejection rate of 10 per cent to £71.02 for a rejection rate of 90 per cent. For a 10-page article, a fee of £639.21 represents a page charge of £63.92. If the submission fee were £639.21 the page charge for a 20-page article would be £31.96 but for each of those 20-page papers the model requires two corresponding 5-page articles, submitted at a cost of £127.84 per page. If the overhead on production costs is reduced to 30 per cent, the submission fee is further reduced and ranges from £519.36 at a rejection rate of 10 per cent to £57.71 for a rejection rate of 90 per cent. Clearly, submission fees are reduced in line with reductions in the overhead rate applied to production costs. We argue that an overhead rate of 120 per cent is realistic.

Thus, if the overhead rate is reduced, the remaining overhead must be covered by the host institution as a subsidy. Presumably, this could be justified with reference to the kudos gained from producing a reputable peer reviewed journal and only if journal production responsibilities were spread across the HE sector.

However, even at an overhead rate of just 30 per cent, fees are not reduced to within the range that Harnad would expect. He suggests that fees of tens of dollars a page rather than hundreds of dollars a page would be acceptable and estimates that it would cost approximately $400 to produce a 20-page article. This converts as approximately £250 for 20 pages, *i.e.* a page charge of £12.50.

In the model, a page charge of £12.50 would not cover the production costs of any journal with a rejection rate below 80 per cent. If an overhead of 120 per cent were applied, a page charge of £12.50 would cover publication only if the rejection rate were 88 per cent or more.

If an overhead of 60 per cent were applied, a page charge of £12.50 would cover publication only if the rejection rate were 84 per cent or more. If an overhead rate of 30 per cent were applied, a page charge of £12.50 would cover publication costs only if the rejection rate were 80 per cent or more.

Nevertheless, fees are reduced to a level close to that charged for submission to many US journals. The latter also charge subscription fees which the Harnad model avoids. Thus, although costs are not reduced to the level anticipated by Harnad, cost recovery by author submission fees is a viable model.

Clearly, in this model, rejection rate is a key factor determining viability as submission fees are much higher for papers submitted to journals with high rejection rates. This effect would make submission fees in the natural sciences much more expensive than those in the humanities. In the former, rejection rates tend to be around 10–20 per cent and in the latter, they tend to be around 80–90 per cent.

This may appear to be reasonable as research in the natural sciences is more likely to be funded by substantial grants, so it may be argued that natural scientists can better afford to pay high submission fees. However, the difference between disciplines of the cost of submitting a paper for publication is misleading.

Most academic papers are published even if they are rejected by the first or second choice of journal. In disciplines where the rejection rate is high, presumably authors often have to submit the same paper to several journals before it is eventually accepted for publication and thus, they would be required to pay several submission fees.

Ultimately, the total cost to scientists and humanities scholars would be similar. It may, however, be argued that in these circumstances cost would regulate quality. In other words, authors would not go to the expense of constantly submitting (and paying submission fees) a paper they knew to be inferior.

This argument, whilst valid, is countered by the argument that rejection rates in the humanities do not simply reflect an abundance of poor-quality material. Humanities subjects are characterised by debate rather than the scientific method.

Quality assessment in these subjects is more subjective than in the sciences. Thus, material that is rejected by referees selected by the editor of one journal may be commended by referees selected by the editor of another journal. It is likely, therefore, that the majority of authors will persist with their articles. As expected, in this model the cost to users of journals is very low.

Thus, any HE subsidy for journal production and development could be offset by savings in acquisitions costs. A library providing 4880 Harnad-modelled titles to its users could expect to pay only £11 956 in fees to an information broker.

Compared with subscribing to an average journals collection at the average price (£103.71) for a total cost of £506 104 this represents a huge saving for the library.

New Journal of Physics

Working examples of the journals modelled by those who seek to change the economic characteristics of the scholarly information delivery chain are rare. Many journals available in electronic form are published in parallel with print and the price mechanism is traditional. Many other journals that are produced only in electronic form are grant funded and recover costs neither from authors nor from users.

A new electronic journal, *The New Journal of Physics (NJP)* is published by an established publisher of peerreviewed scholarly journals, the Institute of Physics Publishing (IoPP). The *NJP* is published only in electronic form and is no doubt intended to cover its costs; this it does from its authors.

Thus, to a degree, it exemplifies the Harnad model. However, whereas Harnad suggests that costs be recovered through submission fees, the IoPP seeks to recover the cost of publishing the *NJP* through acceptance fees. Presumably, fees paid by authors of papers that are accepted for publication must cover the cost of all papers submitted.

The IoPP charges $500 for production of an accepted paper in the *NJP* and the journal is available to access free of charge over the Internet. This suggests that the *NJP* can be published for $60 000 per volume (based on a volume of 120 accepted papers).

The IoPP encourages authors to submit only papers that are of the highest quality and of wide appeal which suggests that they wish to keep the rejection rate as low as possible. It is common for physics journals to have rejection rates of approximately 10 per cent.

The Ithink model produced to test Harnad's theory was revised to simulate the characteristics of the *NJP*. This revised model was run and the results show that if the overhead rate on production costs is 120 per cent, the total production cost for a volume of the *NJP* consisting of 120 10-page papers ranges from £114 000 at 2 per cent rejection rate to £115 000 at 10 per cent rejection rate.

If overhead is applied at a rate of 60 per cent, the cost is approximately £84 000. If the journal were to recover these costs through a submission fee then, at an overhead rate of 120 per cent the fee would range from £958 to £882 for rejection rates of 2 per cent and 10 per cent respectively. If an overhead of 60 per cent were applied, the fee would range from £697 to £641 for rejection rates of 2 per cent and 10 per cent respectively.

The submission fee decreases as the rejection rate increases. However, if costs are recovered through an acceptance fee, as proposed by the IoPP, then at an overhead of 120 per cent, fees range from £958 to £960 for rejection rates of 2 per cent and 10 per cent respectively.

If an overhead rate of 60 per cent is applied, fees range from £697 to £698 for rejection rates of 2 per cent and 10 per cent respectively. The fee increases with the rejection rate. Hence the desire of the IoPP to keep the rejection rate of the *NJP* low. These figures suggest that production of an electronic journal costs a great deal more than a sum that can be recovered from acceptance fees of about $500 (£311).

Presumably, over the longer term, the IoPP expects to recover costs from some other sources. It will be interesting to monitor the success of this new journal.

Fishwick Model

The Fishwick model is significantly different from either of the other models in that it introduces 'normal' market feedback mechanisms into the academic information delivery chain. Both submission fees and subscription fees are used to recover costs as Fishwick argues that both users' requirement for reading material and authors' requirement for publication create demand.

The financial cost of producing a Fishwick journal is much higher than the cost of the other journals modelled because the editor and referees are paid for their contributions. Again, the entire editorial process is conducted electronically and journals are delivered in electronic form. Libraries are free to obtain subscriptions/individual articles directly from publishers or to obtain them from an information broker. It is assumed, if the library chooses the former, that terms will be negotiated between the library and the publisher.

Content Origination

In this sector manuscripts are submitted to the editorial office for publication and authors are required to pay a submission fee. Only authors of papers which are refereed are charged a submission fee. Thus, the 2 per cent of authors whose papers are rejected immediately do not contribute to publication costs.

Fishwick *et al.* propose that a submission fee should contribute to refereeing, editorial and production costs. Thus, all authors submitting a paper for publication contribute to production costs regardless of whether or not the paper is accepted.

The alternative would be to charge a submission fee which covers only editorial and refereeing costs and, on acceptance, charge an additional publication cost. However, this would incur an additional administration cost. The contribution of editors and referees is the same in this model as in the traditional model. However, both referees and editors are paid for their work at an hourly rate of £50 including overhead and any other related employment costs.

The submission fee consists of the total cost of editorial, refereeing and editorial office work on the manuscript plus a contribution to publisher costs. Fishwick *et al.* do not suggest an appropriate rate at which authors should contribute to publication costs nor do they suggest a suitable rate at which authors should be paid royalties on sales of their papers. In the model, authors contribute 10 per cent of the production cost and receive royalties at a rate of 5 per cent of usage fees.

Generally, authors, their employers, or their funding sources will pay the fee but a small number of papers will be submitted by authors who cannot pay the fee. In these cases, the editorial office will apply, on behalf of the author, for publication assistance from public/charitable bodies. Any royalties accumulated from publication of these papers will be paid to the body which funded publication.

Publication

Production costs in the model vary with the overhead rate applied. It is assumed that overheads cost 120 per cent but a rate of 60 per cent is also tested. As in the traditional model, a profit margin varying from zero to 20 per cent is applied. Fishwick *et al.* suggests that the basic product be simple unedited text and that a more sophisticated product be available at a higher price. Research suggests that users and librarians expect electronic journals to have additional functionality and would not consider it worthwhile learning how to use a system simply to access text which they would then print. It is assumed in this model that users would subscribe only to a more sophisticated product, *i.e.* that the minimum requirement would be hotlinks to cited papers.

Production costs are based on this assumption and consist of the two part-time staff members described above with reference to the Traditional model. Authors contribute 10 per cent towards production costs and the remaining 90 per cent is recovered through subscription/individual article fees.

This journal would be more expensive than the others to administer because of the additional tasks associated with unfunded papers. As well as manuscript management administration, the cost of the following tasks would be incurred:

- Receiving applications for assisted publication;
- Applying to funding bodies on behalf of those applying for assistance;
- Administering receipt of submission fees;
- Administering royalty payments.

It would cost £19 500 to employ a part-time secretary on a pro-rata salary of £15 000 if the overhead applied were 120 per cent. If the overhead were 60 per cent, it would cost £14 400. A cost per-paper is required for the model.

It is assumed that the cost of applying for assistance with publication costs would be spread across all papers and that the secretary could administer 600 papers per annum. This would be the number received by a journal with an 80 per cent rejection rate. Thus, the cost per paper is £32.50 (£19 500/600) if the overhead rate is 120 per cent and £24 (£14 400/600) if the overhead rate is 60 per cent.

Fishwick *et al.* suggest that published papers be sold to users either by subscription to the publisher's whole list, by subscription to specific parts (*e.g.* within a specific subject areas), by a two-part tariff which consists of a reduced subscription price combined with reduced transaction costs relating to individual articles, or simply on a pay-per-use basis. These different pricing mechanisms are different risk-sharing schemes. When the publisher shoulders most of the risk in a pay-per-document model the price is higher but when the library shoulders most of the risk by subscribing to a whole database from which users may select only a small proportion of the content, the price per paper is lower. These different pricing mechanisms were not modelled. To include them in the model would be to introduce too many variables and thus, simulations would reveal economic factors that apply only in very specific circumstances. Only subscription and individual article fees are included in the model. Subscription fees vary with level of use as in the Traditional model. It is assumed that the journal is an ongoing concern, *i.e.* that journal start-up costs need not be amortised

Information Brokerage

Assumptions informing the role of the information broker were the same in this model as in the Traditional model.

HE Library Function

Assumptions informing the HE library function were the same in this model as in the Traditional model.

SUBMISSION FEES

The submission fee covers the cost of the editorial process and contributes to publisher income for use in the production process. However, it is not informed by subscription price or any of the elements affecting price and thus, it is not affected by the profit margin applied by the publisher.

It varies only with rejection rate and the rate at which overhead is applied. The latter alters the submission fee because the fee includes the cost of administering the manuscript which is not insignificant in this model.

If the overhead is applied at a rate of 120 per cent, submission fees will range between £446.56 for a journal with a 10 per cent rejection rate to £368.44 for a journal with a 90 per cent rejection rate.

If the overhead is applied at a rate of 60 per cent, submission fees will range between £413.92 for a journal with a 10 per cent rejection rate to £357.10 for a journal with a 90 per cent rejection rate.

These fees fall within the range charged by many US journals and thus, are not entirely unacceptable.

Unlike the Harnad model however, they contribute little to a reduction in costs for the user.

SUBSCRIPTION PRICE

The subscription price does not vary with rejection rate because it is determined by the cost of producing the 120 papers published in the journal.

It does not include the editorial process which is covered by the submission fee.

If the overhead is applied at a rate of 120 per cent and the profit margin is 20 per cent, the subscription price if 200 subscriptions are sold is £728.66. The subscription price if 500 subscriptions are sold is £291.46.

The subscription price if 1000 subscriptions are sold is £145.73. The subscription price if 2000 subscriptions are sold is £72.87 and the subscription price if 20 000 subscriptions are sold is £7.29.

If the overhead is applied at a rate of 60 per cent and the profit margin is 20 per cent, the subscription price if 200 subscriptions are sold is£529.93. The subscription price if 500 subscriptions are sold is £211.98. The subscription price if 1000 subscriptions are sold is £105.99.

The subscription price if 2000 subscriptions are sold is £52.99 and the subscription price if 20 000 subscriptions are sold is £5.30. If the overhead is applied at a rate of 120 per cent and the profit margin is 10 per cent, the subscription price if 200 subscriptions are sold is £667.94. The subscription price if 500 subscriptions are sold is £267.18. The subscription price if 1000 subscriptions are sold is £133.59.

The subscription price if 2000 subscriptions are sold is £66.79 and the subscription if 20 000 subscriptions are sold is £6.68. If the overhead is applied at a rate of 60 per cent and the profit margin is 10 per cent, the subscription price if 200 subscriptions are sold is £485.77. The subscription price if 500 subscriptions are sold is ££194.30. The subscription price if 1000 subscriptions are sold is £97.15. The subscription price if 2000 subscriptions are sold is £48.58 and the subscription if 20 000 subscriptions are sold is £4.86. If the overhead is applied at a rate of 120 per cent and the profit margin is zero, the subscription price if 200 subscriptions are sold is £607.22.

The subscription price if 500 subscriptions are sold is ££242.88. The subscription price if 1000 subscriptions are sold is £121.44. The subscription price if 2000 subscriptions are sold is ££60.72 and the subscription price if 20 000 subscriptions are sold is £6.07. If the overhead is applied at a rate of 60 per cent and the profit margin is zero, the subscription price if 200 subscriptions are sold is £441.61.

The subscription price if 500 subscriptions are sold is ££176.64. The subscription if 1000 subscriptions are sold is £88.32. The subscription if 2000 subscriptions are sold is £44.16 and the subscription price if 20 000 subscriptions are sold is £4.42.

AUTHOR ROYALTIES

Author royalty is based on income from subscriptions and sales of individual articles, *i.e.* it is based on the price of subscriptions and individual articles. It is not affected by the rejection rate because editorial and associated administrative costs are covered separately by submission fees. Nor is author royalty affected by the number of subscriptions sold.

Subscription price varies with the number of subscriptions sold so that journals/individual articles may be delivered to users at the cheapest rate possible; this a non-profit initiative.

The royalty is affected, however, by the overhead applied to production costs and by the profit margin applied by the publisher as both of these things vary the price of the product. If overhead is applied at a rate of 120 per cent, a profit margin of 20 per cent is applied, the mean royalty received is £24.03.

If overhead is applied at a rate of 60 per cent, a profit margin of 20 per cent is applied, the mean royalty received is £17.48. If overhead is applied at a rate of 120 per cent, a profit margin of 10 per cent is applied, the mean royalty received is £22.03. If overhead is applied at a rate of 60 per cent, a profit margin of 10 per cent is applied, the mean royalty received is £16.02. If overhead is applied at a rate of 120 per cent, a profit margin of zero is applied, the mean royalty received is £20.03.

If overhead is applied at a rate of 60 per cent, a profit margin of zero is applied, the mean royalty received is £14.56. Individual articles are priced at double the rate of a paper sold as part of a subscription. However, prices of papers and subscriptions vary with the number of subscriptions and individual articles sold, *i.e.* with income from sales. Thus, although a single paper may sell well on an individual article basis, the mean author royalty will be static.

The royalty is included in Fishwick's model as an incentive to publish only high-quality material. A very successful paper could recover the submission fee through royalties such as these.

For example, the royalty for a journal produced when an overhead of 120 per cent and a profit margin of 10 per cent are applied is £16.02. In this case the submission fee is £413.92. To recover the submission fee, the author would be required to attract 22 per cent of the royalty funds available for that title in a single year.

The Fishwick model is expensive. Submission fees are not insignificant and, primarily, they pay for work that is unpaid in other models.

Furthermore, although authors contribute 10 per cent to production costs, the effect on subscription fees is small. Thus, in financial terms the model does not compare well with the others. Nevertheless, like the other models, subscription fees generated for this model are modest compared with fees of commercial publishers.

Alternative Model Proposed by Authors

Like the Fishwick model, the alternative model proposed here recovers costs through a submission fee and a subscription fee in recognition that both authors and users create demand for publication of scholarly articles.

However, this is not a market model and does not introduce payment for editors and referees. The model differs from the standard non-commercial model only in that a proportion of the production cost is recovered from submission fees.

3

Library Application in Encoding Methodology

An essential component of any library application is an encoding methodology that allows computers to process characters and symbols used to represent language information in written form. For years the encoding mechanism was not developed under a unified umbrella nor did it reach various languages equally. Without a standard unified character code, users have to use different software and terminals to display or enter data in different languages, especially when dealing with more than a few scripts. The international library community began developing large multilingual digital libraries in the 1990s. Language representation is a particular concern for major research libraries, whose collections may include materials in as many as 400 written languages. Standards for record structure and character sets were established long before either Unicode or the Internet was created.

Hundreds of millions of bibliographic records exist around the world in variations of the MARC format, although in multiple character-set-encoding formats and multiple forms of transliteration. USMARC was implemented with the *American Library Association* (ALA) character set, which extends the English language keyboard to include diacritics from major Roman-script languages. The ALA character set is used by *Online Computer Library Center* (OCLC), the largest bibliographic utility in the world, and by most American library applications; languages not included in the ALA character set tend to be transliterated. The increasing interest in adapting USMARC and other forms of MARC to Unicode reflects the fact that other systems will have to accommodate the huge quantity of MARC records that already exist in other character-set formats.

The Library of Congress – which contributes its records in digital form to OCLC, to RLG and to other cooperatives in Europe and elsewhere – has done original-script cataloguing for the JACKPHY languages since the early 1980s. RLG pioneered the ability to encode the JACKPHY languages in their original-script form for bibliographic records, using available script specific standards.

The Library of Congress, OCLC, RLG, and other bibliographic utilities around the world exchange records encoded in full-script form. Libraries took a long-term view of their data, capturing and representing non-Roman characters in their fullest form many years before search and display technologies were widely available. Full vernacular script in these records can be printed on catalogue cards, but until very recently scripts could only be displayed on computers with special equipment.

Even though JACKPHY records from OCLC, RLG, and other sources are loaded into the online catalogues of individual libraries, most applications only support searching the transliterated forms. Integrated library automation software that supports Unicode is becoming more widely available, thus allowing records in non-Roman scripts to be displayed on most terminals and computers. The Library of Congress has implemented a new integrated library system that incorporates Unicode, enabling them to display their JACKPHY records on public terminals in full form.

Previously, these records were viewable only through other systems outside the Library of Congress. The international library community is more and more concerned about multilingual, multi-script data exchange as new regions of the world come online. The European Union is promoting Unicode and is funding projects to support Unicode implementation in library automation. In the mid 1990s, Borgman conducted a study of six countries in Central and Eastern Europe each with its own national language and character set, found that a variety of coding systems were in use. More than half of the research libraries in the study used Latin2, one used Unicode, and the rest used a national or a system-specific format to encode data; none used the ALA character set.

ACADEMIC LIBRARY STRUCTURES

Organisational structure can be defined as "one of the interrelated components that define any organisation referring to the definition of individual jobs and their relationship to each other as depicted in organisational charts and job descriptions." It clarifies how information is distributed, and jobs are organised. For decades the hierarchical structure of management was regarded as the most efficient way of managing an organisation. This system worked well in and environment where the future was predictable and librarians were in the driving seat. Hierarchies were not designed to foster creativity and lead workers to self-fulfilment.

It is therefore very difficult to introduce fundamental change within hierarchical structures which are naturally resistant to change. In an effort to bring about reorganisation within organisations institutions try to either modify the existing hierarchical structure or replace it with something else. Deming as cited by Mullins states that management systems still prevalent today have had a destructive impact on people. According to Deming "people are born with intrinsic motivation, self-esteem, dignity, curiosity to learn... " Qualities such as these are undermined by a management style that reward top achievers and punish those that do worse. Managers that exhibit such management styles use disapproval as a negative control measure. This approach leads to a climate where staff performance is primarily directed at pleasing their superiors and that inevitably lead to average performance.

According to researcher managers have a natural tendency to maintain the status quo. They would instinctively fall back on models and practices that worked in the past. The volatile nature and unpredictability of information services is forcing managers to adopt new management styles. It is beginning to dawn on people that the bureaucratic way of management is becoming outdated and that change will be more effectively achieved through education, sharing, motivation, teamwork and coaching.

Moran states that unprecedented change has forced managers to re-evaluate structures. Customary practices designed to maintain organisational stability are being questioned. To cope with change, organisations have started flattening structures to induce more flexibility within those organisations. These new structures being adopted have decreased levels of hierarchy, increased flexibility and resulted in diminishing boundaries between departments.

Issues to Consider when Introducing New Structures

Management theorists are very reluctant to prescribe to a particular structural model but advise that structure should rather be designed to meet organisational needs and goals. Organisations should try and learn as much as possible from others who have implemented organisational change. They should never introduce a structure simply because it is being used elsewhere but always to meet specific organisational needs. Of cardinal importance is to determine how people within the organisation will adopt the new structure. Researcher shares the following points learnt from a process of restructuring:

Before implementing a process of restructuring it is important to have clear vision, goals and objectives with the focus on service delivery. It is useful to establish a core team to lead the restructuring process. It is vitally important that senior management support the process, *e.g.*, a deputy vice-chancellor. It is important to involve the entire staff component, listen to their inputs and concerns since ownership by the staff is vital for successful change implementation. Staff development programmes should be part of the process to prepare staff for new functions or roles they may be involved in.

After implementation it is important to critically analise the performance of the academic library within the new structure. Managers often do not adapt easily to the flatter less bureaucratic structures that are generally being adopted. Even staff members at lower levels experience this problem. Generally it is very difficult to introduce change that goes against prevailing organisational culture. Proper planning is needed to take the organisation from the existing structure to the new one.

Employee input in developing such a strategy is crucial. Research indicates that organisational transformation had been most successful in scenarios where employees had maximum input. Finally evaluation is necessary after change implementa-tion to determine its success. In reorganised libraries structures are always flatter resulting in manager's roles reverting from directing to coordinating. The prime purpose of reorganisation is to create a more effective organisation. Reorganisation results in academic libraries becoming learning organisations.

The learning organisation is characterised by staff empowerment, is team based, decentralised, practices participative management and information sharing. In the learning organisation the person closest to a problem has the responsibility and authority to deal with it. Tom Wilson as cited by Moran states that the academic library is in bad need of reconstruction. To Wilson academic libraries were essentially designed to manage physical artifacts. The rise of the Internet has completely transformed the way information is created, distributed and accessed.

The e-journal is a typical example. Johansen and Swigart as cited by Moran states "we had outlived the usefulness of models from the Industrial era but don't yet have robust organisational models for the information era". It is therefore of paramount importance that academic librarians continuously re-evaluate current structures and through an experimental process adopt new models.

Moran states that for people who advocate restructuring there is good and bad news. The good news is that people understand that technological change will compel fundamental organisational change. The bad news is that there is a lack of urgency. Generally organisational change appears to be incremental rather than radical.

IMPACT OF ICT CHANGE ON ACADEMIC IBRARIES

The Internet has made information access and retrieval both simplistic and complex. Information retrieval systems are being designed to suit the needs of end users and therefore try to simplify the process. Simultaneously however the user is overwhelmed with so much information resources and choices that the process becomes complex.

This creates a situation where the users need skills and knowledge in terms of search strategies and conceptualisation. Herrington is of the opinion that information literacy instruction at the point of need can be very effective. Wood and Walther is of the opinion that unlike popular believe the Internet will not completely replace the skills of professional librarians but rather make them indispensable.

Changes in the Job Description of Academic Librarians

An overview of the core competencies required by academic library and information workers gives one an idea of how dramatically information and communications technology has changed the library profession. Cheng identifies the following core competencies needed by the future librarian:

- Good communication skills.
- Should be more than just computer literate and should have a good understanding of ICT and its relation to information resources.
- Should have an in-depth understanding of organisational and user needs that is research based and should organise library resources to satisfy those needs.
- Competent in Web publishing techniques.
- Skilled in manipulating metadata to organise digital information.
- Skilled in training users in the use of e-resources.
- Skilled in filtering, evaluating and appraising Internet information.

Researchers identifies another quality required, an in-depth understanding of what information resources are available on the Internet, as well as insight in terms of its reliability and scope.

The Changing Nature of the Academic Library

ICT is busy transforming the nature of academic libraries. A variety of terms such as hybrid, digital and virtual library are used to refer to the academic library. A digital library can be defined as "a managed collection of information, with associated services, where the information is stored in digital formats and accessible over a network".

The virtual library has been defined as "remote access to the contents and services of libraries and other information resources, combining an on-site collection of current and heavily used materials in both print and electronic form, with an electronic network which provides access to, and delivery from, external worldwide library and commercial information and knowledge sources". Hybrid libraries are libraries that provide access to both electronic resources and paper-based resources.

From the definitions it is clear that most of today's academic libraries fall in either the hybrid or virtual category. The library of the future is unlikely to be a physical entity as we know it but would probably be a Web portal providing access to information.

The emphasis will be on access to information rather than physical ownership. Akeroyd supports this view and states that as a physical space entity the library, as we know it is unlikely to prevail in a digital environment. One reason for this is that because of Web access the digital library is accessible from anywhere.

Changes in the Information Seeking Behaviour of Users

Academic librarians have a good understanding of the tremendous value of printed and electronic resources available to students at academic libraries. Academic library users do not necessarily share this insight. New generation academic library users have a preference for Web resources rather than visiting the library.

Research done on undergraduate engineering students in 2004 revealed that they would turn to the Internet as the primary resource for information for their projects. Moyo refers to a scenario where users were asked what they expect from an academic library service. They responded as follows:

- All resources should be available in full text and be printable.
- The library service should be fast and easily accessible.
- 24/7 availability of a virtual reference service.
- Wish to do all library transactions online.
- Web resources that is easy to use and Web search engines that meet information needs.

What is clear is that new generation academic library users prefer the convenience of digital access above reliance on assistance from librarians. This preference for the Internet poses a serious challenge to the academic library which has to move from a paradigm of the library as a physical entity to a library where the users do not have to come to physically to make use of it's services. Electronic access to information resources does have many advantages, *e.g.*:

- Multiple access which implies more that one user can access a resource simultaneously.
- Lots of resources are available in full text.
- 24/7 access which means users can access resources remotely, *e.g.*, from off campus or from dormitories.

One of the disadvantages of remote access from an academic library point of view is that users are not always aware of the fact that they are using library resources. One user stated: "No, I don't need to use the library, I use Internet resources". Despite the apparent preference for digital content the need for access to high quality digital content remains constant. Greater cooperation between library and faculty is necessary to develop ways to connect users and high quality digital materials.

IMPACT OF ICT ON COLLECTION MANAGEMENT

Collection development can be defined as the selection and acquisition of library materials based on current and potential user needs. Collection management goes beyond this. It is concerned with managing the utilisation, storage and accessibility of a collection. Collection development can thus be seen as a subdivision of collection management. Academic librarians find themselves in an era of unparalleled access to information.

The latest edition of Uhlrich's has indicated the availability of more than 1,72,000 journal titles. Although this appears to be a most ideal situation it is not because the financial resources available in acquisitions departments have not necessarily increased. The sheer volume of information available also makes selection of the most suitable information a complex task. The impact of electronic resources has made collection management a very complex and challenging task. There are budgetary constraints, numerous formats, ever changing user needs. Collection management implies involvement in tasks such as analysis of needs, negotiation of contracts and evaluation of resources. There was a time when the size of an academic library collection determined its stature. At that time the library's resources were generally adequate to meet most of its users needs. Since then the academic library has exchanged the ownership model for an access model where physical location becomes completely irrelevant.

Access versus Ownership

Information and communications technology has had a fundamental impact on library collection development policies. Academic libraries had traditionally applied an ownership or just-in-case approach to collection development. The premise was that users would need the material and make use of it. Having the material available in the library would also provide immediate access to it than having to borrow it from a third party. The cost of maintaining collections and increased demands for more information had forced academic libraries to reconsider the ownership model and adopt another model. Unparalleled price increases and shrinking budgets had ushered in a new model called access or just in time where the focus is to give the user the information that they need when they want it.

Cost

Technically it is more cost effective to produce an e-resource, for example an electronic journal, because the first copy costs are reduced. There is also savings in terms of packaging, delivery and storage. In practice these savings have not lead to reductions in the cost of e-journals. It has been suggested that the academic library adopts a pay-as-you-use approach. This make sense according to research done in 1997 that indicated that 22 per cent of science articles published in 1984 were never cited for the next 10 years. In the social sciences this figure goes up to 48 per cent.

Storage Space

With the access model there is no need for storage space, *e.g.*, back copies. Moahi cites Cooper who states that the storage cost per single copy is between \$25 and \$40. Calculations to determine JStor pricing lead to the conclusion that the cost per single volume was between $24 and $41. When costs for re-shelving and maintenance were included, the estimated cost rose to $45 per title per year for a core journal and $180 per title per year for a large research library.

Enhanced Access to Information

One of the benefits of ICT is enhanced access to library services and resources. The academic library can expose its users to a much larger collection than it can house physically because users can access information remotely. With online access it is possible to accurately measure utilisation of e-resources and that is invaluable in determining which resources to purchase. It is easier to search e-resources and access speed is greatly enhanced. Other advantages are that users can simultaneously access the same resource, and there are no incidences of lost copies or mutilated issues. Singh is of the opinion that a paradigm shift is taking place within the academic library as more academic librarians are doing collection management rather that collection development. The focus is rather on interpretation of information rather than selection. Librarians are becoming knowledge managers rather than collection managers.

Digital Preservation of Data

One of the major costs facing the academic library is the cost related to the conversion and preservation of information in digital format. The cost of this process amounts to $1 per page. This does not include the cost relating to the annotation for indexing purposes and the cost of conversion of audio-visual material. One of the problems with converting records into digital image is the fact that the technology used to store these pages as a digital photograph results in large files which have storage implications and place demands on band-with. Funding allocated to preservation of digital material is generally inadequate. This has to do with expectations that the costs of digital preservation over length of time might be very high. It is also difficult to forecast cost in terms of how long to retain digital material in an archive and computer architectures needed to access material. Preservation of digital materials poses many challenges. It is further complicated by the fact that computer technology changes at an unprecedented rate.

There are concerns that changing interfaces, standards, formats and operating systems will render it impossible to read today's computer discs at some point in future. The implication of this is that one needs migration strategies to move data to new operating systems and structures or have scenarios where computers can simulate data structures and operating systems of previous eras. This scenario will make digital preservation prohibitively expensive. A great deal of current research into digital preservation is based on overcoming the technical issues to ensure long-term preservation of digital content. The issue of digital preservation initially came to the fore as an impending crisis. Fears were expressed that large portions of our cultural heritage were in danger of disappearing forever. Examples were cited of Web sites available today that might be gone to-morrow.

Although digital materials are more fragile by nature than analog materials the risk varies within different categories of digital materials. Although it is true that a Web site currently available may disappear overnight, the same does not apply to electronic journals. This realisation has transferred the focus from the immediate rescue notion to an approach that sees digital preservation as part of a carefully planned digital access management process. One way academic libraries can deal with digital preservation is through cooperation. Through cooperation various institutions can share costs. Another advantage would be that it would reduce redundancy. Because of the fragile nature of digital materials libraries cannot put off decisions to preserve digital information *ad infinitum*. Time is of the essence.

Unlike a book that can be repaired or rebound, once a digital file becomes corrupt it may be impossible or prohibitively expensive to restore the data. Another problem facing the academic library is the long-term preservation of digital information. There are questions concerning the long-term stability of digital information stored on disks and tapes. There is the potential of these media deteriorating over a period of time. Another way digital preservation is approached is by letting the vendors do the preservation. These days there are also escrow repositories, *e.g.* Elsevier has agreed to provide the National Library of Netherlands with a copy of Science Direct which the National Library will maintain and make available should Elsevier be unable to do so.

ELECTRONIC RESOURCES

ICT has fundamentally changed academic library collections. Forever gone is the era when an academic library's physical collection determined its stature. In the modern networked technological era the emphasis has shifted from ownership of physical resources to access to electronic resources that are globally accessible.

Internet Information

There are huge amounts of unedited information on the Internet. There are countless Web sites and no single listing of them all. There is also the phenomenon of Web sites disappearing overnight that create problems in terms of access.

The Invisible Web

Academic library users make use of search engines such as Google and Altavista to find information on the Web. As a result they are only exposed to a small portion of the Web called the 'Publicly Indexable Web' These students are only exposed to Web pages accessible via hyperlinks. Search engines do not index Web pages that requires authentication or Web pages behind search forms. The Web consists of two components namely the 'Publicly Indexable Web' also referred to as the visible Web and the invisible Web. The invisible Web refers to all those information resources available yet not indexed by conventional search engines yet accessible via the Web.

Masses of information available via the invisible Web are found in subject databases. Most of the databases that academic libraries make available to their users resort under the invisible Web, *e.g.* EbscoHost and Eric. Conventional search engines can find databases such as EbscoHost but cannot access them. Search engines can only find content that was indexed by their software called spiders or crawlers. The problem is that they only index Web content available in formats such as HTML and PDF. Michael K. Bergman in year 2000 in a paper on the invisible Web for an Internet Search Company called Bright Planet suggests that the invisible Web is 500 times larger that the visible Web with approximately 550 billion documents.

The Issue of Quality of Resources Available on the Visible Web

The Internet had become a very important research tool for academic endeauvour. Slaouti as cited by Stapleton notes that the relevance and importance of the Web as a research tool should not be underestimated. There is a stark contrast in the way resources are published on the Web versus traditional publishing. In the traditional print environment publishing generally was done by a publisher hence a controlled environment that impacted on quality as well as the scope of the audience being reached.

The open nature of the Web, the development of sophisticated search engines, browsers, Web creation and publishing software and easy access to networks via low cost connectivity has developed the Web into a tool that can be easily utilised by the masses for publishing purposes, people who were formally shut out of the publishing process.

This has lead to a flood of Web publications of variable quality. During the 1990's library scholars recognised this dilemma and suggested criteria to evaluate Internet resources, *e.g.*, authority, purpose, coverage and objectivity and accessibility. These days a single search can yield hundreds of thousands of items.

The unfiltered nature of Web resources has made evaluation of these resources essential. One often finds that unlike in traditional printed media, e-resources found on the Web often lack important criteria such as author or date. Web pages because of its non-linear textual nature has added new effects to the search process such as sound, videos and access to thousands of items by clicking a mouse. These new elements imply that new sets of skills are required on the part of the researcher.

Reference Works

According to Moyo reference statistics in academic libraries are plunging. At the same time electronic access of these resources are increasing. This tendency can be ascribed to the fact that users can access these resources remotely via the Internet. Internet connectivity and e-resources had become absolutely essential for the new reference service paradigm. One of the key elements of e-reference service success is that the service is available at the point of need. The tremendous growth in the use of online reference works has created a need within the academic library to develop services to support this type of service.

Academic libraries are turning to on-line real time reference tools also referred to as ORR to support students remotely. The Pen State University library has more than 300 databases that students may access. On-line real time reference support is used to assist students at the point of need. E-reference works share all the benefits of e-resources, *e.g.*, 24/7 remote accessibility, concurrent access for multiple users and the potential for online updating to keep content up to date.

Electronic communication had become the primary mode of communication in e-reference services. Online chat had become the method of choice. Some e-reference application providers have added *Voice over IP* (VOIP) to their products which enable voice dialogue with the library user. E-reference services have many advantages, *e.g.*:

- Availability via the Internet.
- Service at the point of need.
- Easy for people who are unable to come to the academic library, *e.g.*, the physically disabled.
- 24/7 availability.

Moyo cites Stormont who states that online real time reference support is very labour intensive. In order to cope academic libraries have adopted a distributed staffing model where the load of the service is shared among various libraries.

E-Journals

The e-journal can be defined as "a version of the traditional print or paper-based journal which is disseminated electronically in some form or other directly to the end user." Although e-journals had been in existence since 1976 it became prominent during the 1990's. Since it's inception in 1665 the printed journal remained the primary vehicle for communication among academics and researchers. The advent of the Internet transformed publishing radically as it made it possible to publish cheaply. Internet also made access universally available. Because of the Internet academics and researchers became more creative and productive.

Cost Factors

There had been major increases in the cost of journal subscriptions during the last two decades. According to researcher between 1986 and 1996 the average increase per journal subscription had been a whopping 147 per cent. This state of affairs had been laid at the door of the commercial publishers. Moahi states that simultaneously there had been a significant increase in the number of science and engineering journals published. Because of ever decreasing budgets academic libraries are unable to purchase the titles they deem necessary. Falk cites McCabe of Georgia Institute of Technology stating that publishers offer libraries bundled packages of e-journals under the pretense that it is cheaper but these deals actually inflate prices.

Moahi is of the opinion that a consequence of these bundled deals is that academic libraries end up with titles they do not want or need. Despite the fact that publishers have substantial cost savings on first copy production of e-journals and also save on distribution costs, these savings are not passed onto their customers. Cost of e-journals tend to be similar or higher that their printed counterparts. What further complicate matters are the fact that provision has to be made for connectivity and desktops, which means additional costs. Aggregate publishers also tend to drop titles without prior consultation with academic librarians.

Academic Library's Response to Publishers

Despite general expectations that e-journals should be cheaper than printed versions publishers maintain the status quo by maximizing profits. Publisher's attitudes have forced academic institutions to take a tougher stance against them. Recently the Senate of the University of California instructed the library to sever all ties with Elsevier, *e.g.*, cancel subscriptions and cease submission of research papers if negotiations with them fail to obtain a reduction in the price of subscriptions. Harvard University has cancelled their Elsevier subscriptions of bundled journals. The Senate of North Carolina State University urged that excessive prices from publishers be resisted.

Four North Carolina universities had signed a deal for a bundle of 1300 journals in 2003 with the proviso that no titles are dropped. When these institutions wanted to renew subscription for 2004 the price was so exorbitant that they all cancelled the deal. Cornell University and the University of Missouri also cancelled subscription with Elsevier for the same reasons. Three North Carolina universities have drafted policies to only forward research to publishers whose journals are reasonably priced and widely accessible.

In the event of this not being possible they will include an "authorisation to publish' clause in contracts that empower the author to retain copyright to reproduce research for academic and research purposes. Kansas University includes a clause in their contracts that give them permission to use their research for teaching and research purposes and retain the right to make it available on public accessible Web sites.

Open Access Journals

The open access initiative is aimed at making scholarly research freely available via the Internet. Open access journals are journals available on the Internet for academics, researchers and the general public. The open access journal philosophy received a tremendous stimulus with the birth of the *Public Library of Science* (PLoS). At its conception 30,000 scientists promised their support in terms of submitting research. The first open access journal to emerge was PLoS Biology in the year 2003 which was received with great enthusiasm. In the publishing arena the Biomed Central publishing house embarked on free access to peer-reviewed journals. Recently the *Directory of Open Access Journals* (DOAJ) made open access journals available covering different languages and subjects.

Open Access Archives

Many leading universities are setting up electronic archives as depositories for their research output and are granting access to it. There are plans in progress to use theses archives as a platform to provide open access journals. The *Massachusetts Institute of Technology* (MIT) has made software freely available for managing electronic archives. Currently there are approximately 140 universities that have established open access archives. The number of journals held in these archives have increased from 20,000 in 2001 to 1.3 million in 2003. Although this is still fairly insignificant compared to the 2 million peer reviewed journals printed annually it nevertheless sends out a clear warning signal to commercial publishers of what is to come. In Europe the Open Archives Forum was established. The goal of this forum is to establish electronic archives and make it globally available.

e-Books

There are various definitions for e-books but e-books are essentially published books and reference materials that were digitised and are distributed electronically. In the year 2000 e-books were heralded as the new publishing revolution. One market research company predicted that by 2005 there would be 1.9 million users. Forrester Research predicted that income generated from e-book sales would increase from $9 million in 2000 to $414 million in 2004.

Unfortunately e-book popularity never rose to expected heights. Despite the negativity surrounding e-books it had not demised completely. There are still some companies dealing with e-books that are profitable and experiencing growth. One of the first commercial e-book services, NetLibrary, was established by OCLC in 1998. The NetLibrary collection has since grown to over 400 000 titles. The shortcoming in the NetLibrary system is the fact that an e-book can only be used by one user at a time. Questia, another commercial e-book service went live in 2001. Their target market was students and they employed librarians to manage collection development. By 2003 Questia had more than 400 000 titles from more than 200 publishers.

Advantages of e-Books

E-books have numerous advantages. There are no printing, storage, warehousing and shipping costs. Consequently e-books can be published at costs much lower than conventional books. Additional advantages are online availability, keyword-searching capability, cross-referencing, adjustable fonts, electronic bookmarks and imbedded audio. Updating e-books will be easier than re-editing conventional books.

From an academic library point of view benefits would include cost savings in terms of shelving, binding, circulation, overdue notices and management of fines. All needed would be a person to maintain the collection and a person to manage user accounts. Print collections in academic libraries are very expensive to acquire and maintain. E-books are also environmentally friendly in the sense that no tree pulping is necessary to for its production. The flaws in current e-book technology will be overcome. When that day dawns e-books being much cheaper to produce and publish than printed books as well as economies of scale will tip the balance in favour of e-books.

Disadvantages

The devices needed to read e-books are relatively expensive, *e.g.*, hand held devices, PC's and laptops. In order to minimize piracy publishers use proprietary hardware devices and software platforms. This lack of universal standards is a problem. The question many ask is whether e-books pose a threat to libraries. Can it eventually put libraries out of business. Although e-books did not take off as well as expected within the public domain, the use of e-books at schools, colleges and universities are rapidly increasing.

Use of e-Books

Falk refers to research done by Forrester that indicated that 4 million e-books were sold at campus stores in year 2000. Forrester forecasted that by year 2005 e-book sales should have increased to 140 million. Research indicates that students are developing a preference for e-books above printed books. At the University of Rochester Rush Rhees Library course reserve section students were exposed to printed books and their e-book equivalents. Statistics compiled on a weekly base indicated a three to one preference in favour of the e-books.

RESEARCH PYRAMID IDENTIFICATION PROCEDURES

Based on the properties of publications and characteristics of RPs, next we propose two offline research pyramid identification procedures, namely, the link-based (LB) and the proximity-based (PB) RP identification procedures. Both procedures start by choosing a candidate root node for an RP, called the cornerstone paper. The paper that is located at the root of a research pyramid receives more citations than others as other publications within the research pyramid are 'motivated' by it, and directly or indirectly cite it. Thus, our approach is to identify papers with high in-citations as cornerstone papers (*i.e.*, the roots) of RPs to be constructed. The link-based procedure locates research pyramids by identifying pyramid-like structures in the citation graph of the publication set.

In summary, within an individual RP, publications are topically related and motivated by each other and we use the four properties to identify citations within RPs—as summarised next. In AnthP, the average number of citations to a paper, denoted by CI, is 2.066. Note that, in our experiments, we consider only the AnthP citations that are completely within AnthP; any citation from a paper within AnthP to a paper that is not in AnthP is removed. Using Property 3 and RP-Property 1, we limit RP heights to 3. Thus, the expected number of papers within a research pyramid RPP with paper P as the root and with height 3 is |RPP| = 1 + CI + CI2 + CI3 H' 15. Of course, the actual identified RP sizes vary.

Some RPs may deal with active research topics, and, in such cases, the number of in-citations of publications are noticeably higher than CI, leading to noticeably higher RP sizes as well. Figure presents the link-based LB-IdentifyRP procedure. The proximity-based PBIdentifyRP is similar, except that the function call to LB-FormRP is replaced by the function call PB-FormRP. The procedure LB-IdentifyRP:

a. Selects a cornerstone paper P from the existing publication set as an RP root, by simply picking the current most-cited publication;
b. Calls LB-FormRP to locate the RP set RPP of P; and
c. Eliminates RPP from the current publication set CurrAnthP, and repeats (a)-(c) again, until no more publications are left in CurrAnthP.

Note that our approach in this chapter is to create distinct and non-overlapping research pyramids. An alternative approach, not reported here due to space limitations, is to allow overlapping research pyramids as follows: Do not to eliminate any papers from the original publication set; instead, simply colour each selected publication, and continue until all publications are coloured, meaning that, when the algorithm ends, each paper belongs to at least one RP set, and possibly more.

The two main functions of the link-based LB-IdentifyRP procedure are ChooseRoot and LB-FormRP. ChooseRoot chooses publications that are cornerstone papers, or roots of research pyramids. The function LB-FormRP forms the RPP of a root publication P by adding direct citers of P into RPP, and indirect citers of P at a level up to the LMax; in experiments, we choose LMax as 3, by following the property 3. The function Citers(P, l, CAgeMax-Topic-Decay) returns the set of publications that cite P at a level l (which is at most LMax) where the citation age of the citing paper with respect to P is less than the maximum citation age CAgeMax-Topic-Decay. In more detail,

- Paper-id pidP of root P along with its level 0 is inserted into RPP and the queue Q, which holds paper-ids for future expansions and their distances to the root paper P.
- Two-tuple <Pi, A > in Q is dequeued, and expanded by locating direct or indirect citers of Pi so long as their levels with respect to P is at most LMax-TopicDecay and their citation age with respect to P is less than the maximum citation age CAgeMax-TopicDecay. All expanded publications and their level info with respect to P are inserted into the queue Q.
- The above two steps are repeated until Q is empty; then RPP is returned.

```
proc LB-IdentifyRP(AnthP, RP-Sets)
{
RP-Sets:= Ø;
CurrAnthP:= AnthP;
while (CurrentAnthP = Ø)
{Root:=ChooseRoot(CurrAnthP);
RPRoot:=LB-FormRP(Root,LMax-TopicDecay);
RP-Sets:=RP-Sets U RPRoot;
CurrAnthP:=CurrAnthP-RPRoot;
}
}
```

(a) Procedure LB-IdentifyRP

```
funct ChooseRoot(CurrAnthP)
return TopCitedTopicDecay(CurrAnthP);
```

(b) Function ChooseRoot

```
funct LB-FormRP(P, LMax)
{Set RPP:={P}; Queue Q;
Q.Enqueue({P},0);
while(Q is not empty)
{<Pi, A>:=Q.Dequeue;
if(A<LMax)then
{CiterSet=Citers(Pi, A, CAgeMax-TopicDecay);
Q.Enqueue(CiterSet,(A+1));
RPP = RPP +CiterSet;
}}}
```

```
Return RPP}
(c) Function LB-FormRP()
Funct PB-FormRP(P, LMax)
{Set RPP={P}; Queue Q;
Q.Enqueue(P,0);
while(Q is not empty)
{<Pi, A>:=Q.Dequeue;
if(A<LMax) then
{CiterSet(Pi):=Citers(Pi, A, CAgeMax-TopicDecay)
TopSimSet:=TopSim(Pi,|CiterSet(Pi)|, CAgeMax-TopicDecay);
Q.Enqueue(TopSimSet, A +1);
RPP= RPP+TopSimSet;
}}
Return RPP}
(d) Function PB-FormRP()
```

Fig. Functions of LB-and PB-IdentifyRP Algorithms.

The function PB-FormRP of the proximity-based approach utilises a graphbased proximity measure, namely SimRank to compute similarities between publications. It captures RPP of the root publication by locating publications that are most similar to P and yet:

- Are linked to P with a citation path length of at most LMax-TopicDecay; and
- Have a citation time distance less than CAgeMax-TopicDecay. SimRank iteratively computes similarity scores between nodes in a graph G following the rule that "two nodes are similar if they are linked with similar nodes".

In other words, the SimRank similarity between two nodes a and b, S is iteratively computed using the formula:

$$S(a,b) = \left[C/|I(a)|\ |I(b)\ | \right] * \sum_{i=1}^{|I(a)|} \sum_{j=1}^{|I(b)|} S\left(I_i(a), I_j(b)\right)$$

where I(a) and I(b) are sources of in-links of a and b, respectively. C is the decay factor between 0 and 1. We choose C=0.8. If |I(a)|or|I(b)| = 0 then S(a, b)=0 by definition, in the case where a=b, S(a, b)=1. The space complexity of the naive SimRank algorithm is O(N2) where N is the graph size. We prune as in by considering node pairs that are near each other in the range of radius r. We choose r=6, which is twice the value of the expected research pyramid height. PB-FormRP receives as input the root P, the maximum level LMax from root, and utilises the maximum citation age CAgeMax-TopicDecay and returns the RP set RPP of publication P following the same main steps of LB-FormRP with one main difference: the way the twotuple <Pi, t > dequeued from Q is expanded, as follows:

- Top |Citers Pi, A,CAgeMax-TopicDecay| similar papers, based on SimRank, to Pi are identified. The number of citers of Pi is used to capture the density of the RP being identified, and thus to expand RP at Pi accordingly;
- The identified similar papers are added to RPP and also enqueued to Q for further expansion, this time with the level increased by 1. Similar to LB-FormRP a maximum level of LMax-TopicDecay is employed.

Advantage of PB-FormRP over LB-FormRP is that it successfully captures co-existing members of RP as well as those that are not reachable through any citation path from RP's root. We give an example.

Example

Figure shows two RPs; RP1 and RP2. RP1 contains two co-existing roots A and B. Such a case occurs when two researchers work on the same problem simultaneously. At some point of our RP identification process, A will probably be recognised as a root of a new RP, say RP3, as it has more in-citations than B. And, since, B is not reachable through any path from A, LB-FormRP will fail to identify B as a member of RP3. PB-FormRP will succeed to place both A and B into RP3 in this case as B is very similar to A.

A similar problem will be observed with paper C that is not reachable through any path from the root. Furthermore, LB-FormRP may incorrectly identify F, that probably 'uses' a technique proposed in A, as a member of RP3 when F is really a member of RP2 which co-exists with RP3. PB-FormRP successfully repels F from RP3 as F is not similar to A or any of RP3's members, based on SimRank. We observe here that PB-FormRP may capture pyramid-like structures, but not exactly pyramid structures.

SimRank computes similarity between two papers P1 and P2 by averaging the similarity of the citers of both. However, note that similar papers to a member of an RP will be the other members of the same RP since, members of an RP are usually cited by each other.

Improved Publication Scores Via the RP-Model

In the authors have applied the two RP-identification algorithms on the AnthP set. After that, they normalized publication scores within the research pyramids identified. The authors observed that, for RP-based scores, the observed skew values range in the RP-based scores. In comparison, the original scores showed highly skewed values that range between 8.12 and 13.04, which mean that they are sharply left-skewed. They also observed that, for RP-based scores.

In comparison, in the case of globally normalised scores, Kurtosis values range between (113.28) and (291.10). The enhancement of score distribution comes from the fact that publications are being compared to their peer groups, *i.e.*, publications that belong to the same scope, and thus have the same chances of receiving new citations.

Here we report only PageRank-related results as we have observed that PAuth and PPgRank scores are highly correlated with a correlation coefficient of 0.98, and the correlation between PPgRank and PCitCnt is 0.74. The authors in have also performed multiple searches and manually evaluated the accuracy ranking publication via the RP-Model. They observed that research-pyramid-based scores resulted in 16 per cent-25 per cent more accurate search outputs than the PageRank-based quality scores. Accuracy was measured for the top-k publications in the result sets, where k is 10.

Section Summary and Conclusions

The Research-Pyramid model proposed in used to solve the separability and accuracy problems of publication score functions. We showed that:

- Normalising publication scores within their research pyramids provides more accurate and less skewed scores, moreover;
- Ranking search results by these scores promises to give higher accuracy compared to ranking by globally normalised publication scores due to reduction of topic diffusion effect.

However, as noticed by citation-based measures compute popularity of publications based on the 'current' state of a citation graph that continuously changes and evolves. Thus PageRank is effective in capturing the popularity of publications based on the current citation-graph in-hand. We show that PageRank may assign inaccurate popularity scores for both old and recent publications.

And thus PageRank cannot be used to rank OLDL search outputs. We therefore need effective techniques to order search results based on their importance and relevance to users' interests.

GROWTH AND DECAY PHASES OF PUBLICATION POPULARITIES

In the field of literature digital libraries, citation analysis is employed to evaluate the impact of publications and scientific collections. It is also employed to order digital library search outputs. Examples of citation-based measures are citation-count and PageRank.

However, as noticed by citation-based measures compute popularity of publications based on the 'current' state of a citation graph that continuously changes and evolves. Next we present two scenarios where usage of such popularity scores becomes problematic.

Page Quality and Webpage Popularity Evolution Model

Cho via a simple user-web model, developed a formula for the popularity growth of webpages, and then used the formula to estimate page quality.

Publication quality, based on the web-user model, is defined as the popularity of the publication given that all possibly interested authors are aware of it and those who like it have cited it. After getting published, a paper goes through two main phases:

- A popularity growth phase where its popularity increases as more authors become aware of it and cite it. After some time, the publication's popularity reaches to a certain value. During the growth phase of the publication;
  — Researchers develop awareness of the publication, *i.e.*, more authors get to know it; and,
  — Research problems inspired by the paper get studied by authors. This means that the longer the growth phase of a paper, the better the quality of the paper; and
  — The authors who like the paper cite it in their works.
- A saturation phase: after the transient growth phase, the publication's PageRank score settles at a certain value, and minimally changes.

Definition:

- The growth region of a publication is the time interval during which the publication popularity grows.
- The saturation region of a publication is the time interval that starts at the saturation point; and, afterwards, the publication usually does not receive new citations.
- The popularity function p (p, t) of publication p, is a function that computes the popularity of p at time t.
- Publication quality Q (p) is the intrinsic and (saturation-time popularity) quality of a publication.

Remark

The popularity of a publication p at time t is estimated as the p's PageRank score based on the citation graph at time t. Also, the quality of publication p is estimated as the PageRank score at saturation phase. The remark forms a bridge between the PageRank score change curve and Cho et. al.'s popularity growth model base their model on the fact that the quality of a page is time-invariant and does not change overtime. Thus; Q (p) is assumed to be a constant estimated at any time as the sum of:

- The current popularity or PageRank score of p, and

We argue that we need to distinguish between two measures of quality for a publication:

- The first measure represents the scientific value of that publication. This value is time-invariant and is represented by Q (p).
- The second measure represents the value of the paper to the user at the time s/he is searching the digital library. This value, in contrast

to Q (p), is time-dependent, especially in fast-moving fields of study. We refer to this quality measure as the Publication Quality with Aging Factor.

We show that publications go through the popularity growth phase during which publications gain awareness and thus popularity. We empirically show the popularity growth curves conform to the 'sigmoidal' evolution pattern derived.

Properties of Publication Citation Graphs and Research Pyramids

In this section we validate Cho et. al.'s popularity growth phase by:

- Using PageRank as a popularity indicator; and
- Utilising the research-pyramid model of research evolution to show that popularity scores of publications converge to a steady-state value that can be estimated by equation.

We first note one difference between a publication citation graph from a web citation graph: Publication citation graph evolution behaviour is to some extent more controlled than web graphs and can be anticipated.

A webpage that has been on the web for a relatively long time may still receive new links; old publications, however, are rarely cited. Consequently, publication citation graphs are highly unlikely to face structural changes around relatively old publications.

This special characteristic of publication citation graphs allows for developing accurate mathematical models for changes to publication's PageRank scores, and thus better estimation of publication quality. In contrast, a web graph may face abrupt structural changes at any time in any part of the graph. Studies show that, every week, around 8 per cent web pages are replaced and that about 25 per cent new links are created.

Next we describe the research-pyramid (RP) model of publications that also suggests time-dependent growth patterns in publication citation graphs. The RP-Model is based on the observation that citations between research publications produce multiple, small pyramid-like structures, where each pyramid represents publications related to a highly specific research topic.

A research pyramid is defined as a set of publications that represent a highly specific research topic, and usually has a pyramid-like structure in terms of its citation graph. The RP-Model suggests that publication citation graphs evolve in a time-controlled manner through the stimulation of most-specific research topics from one another as follows.

A publication that deals with a new specific research problem appears, and proposes the first solution for it. More publications appear after that publication, addressing the same problem and proposing enhanced or refined solutions to that problem.

RELEVANCE OF RESEARCH

In a developing country like India, there could not be a dearth of research problems to be investigated. But there seems a lack of perception to visualise and identify valid problems for research. A cursory glance of the topics worked on will at once reveal that the topics chosen do not have a problem or hypothesis but merely survey the state of the art or the existing conditions. The popular areas for research have been, in order of popularity: university libraries, bibliometrics, library use and user studies, information seeking behaviour, information systems, classification and indexing, special libraries, library history, reference service and sources, and library science education.

Document selection and procurement, cataloguing, and experimental designs in library management are the least popular topics — though these seem practical and relevant to present day needs. That basic research is the most neglected area is endorsed by other surveys of doctoral research. Library automation, library software, networking and information technology are just emerging. There is need to revive research in classification especially in context of OPACs, information networks and the electronic information environment in general. The Curriculum Development Committee (CDC) on Library and Information Science of the University Grants Commission rehashed the importance of research, though it did not dwell at length on this aspect in its report. The blue document listed some areas for research, which are no less broad than the current courses being taught at the Master's level:

- Structure and development of knowledge.
- Classification, cataloguing and indexing.
- Infometric studies.
- Computer applications.
- Historical studies.
- Social and economic aspects of librarianship.
- Library and Information management and systems analysis.
- Applications of techniques of library and information science to evaluate other disciplines.

The list could have been more specific. Though not much revered, the report rightly lays emphasis on standards in research. It uncompromisingly asks for a clear declaration from Ph.D. candidates that the "work is based on the discovery of new facts by the candidate or the new relations of facts... and how the work tends to the general advancement of know-ledge". While it is normally expected of every completed piece of research, yet it rarely happens. The evaluation process, however formal, is easily manipulated without qualms. Examiners are obliging on a reciprocal basis.

In a small profession like ours this interplay of mutual usability comes in easily. It is often said jocularly that the degree is recommended more for the supervisor than for the candidate. We must admit that the library profession has failed to lure the best brains and even more to retain them. Mediocrity thrives; hypocrisy reigns. But this is not to overlook the genuine research and researchers. Apart from not so relevant topics, theses have contributed little towards pushing the frontiers of knowledge; few are models of methodology. Indian library research seems to have no moorings in the prevailing realities.

Topics are ideal, superficial and bookish. Even experi-enced librarians keen on earning the Ph.D. degree rarely come with an important problem for research. The supervisor who shies from controversial topics usually suggests the topic. Criticising individuals in formal black-and-white mode or exposing harmful tendencies of a class are not for them. Even a mild and healthy criticism is not tolerated in India. Feudal norms still lie deep in the Indian social ethos.

In addition, there is a dire paucity of data archives and reference works. Collecting data and information is considered a satisfactory end to the job — the goal of the research exercise. It is very difficult to collect data by questionnaire in a vast country like India. Each researcher has a bag full of woeful tales to tell. Library associations at all levels seem to have washed their hands of the research responsibility. These do not even collect and compile statistics of the professional activities pertaining to their areas. Their libraries are poor. They have no research budget. For quite a time professionals have been talking, writing and conferencing about library education and research in India.

Every year the Indian Association of Teachers of Library and Information Science (IATLIS) holds a seminar on topics of library education and research. That it is the most popular topic with the teachers and librarians can be gauged from the fact that the FID/ET seminar was the largest of all the 49th FID pre-conference seminars held in India. The literature on library education and research is enormous, though repetitive and inflated. We have given lip service to the change of curricula and the raising of standards of research. But the needed change has not come through. The blame is wholly put on the lack of infrastructure and unavailability of funds. That is not the entire reason. The lack of effective collective efforts to safeguard the standards seems no less major cause.

DIGITAL LIBRARY OF INDIAN BIOMEDICAL JOURNALS

Digital Library of Indian Biomedical Journals medIND has many functional and process components.

Selection of Journals

The scope of the Collection development policy is well defined to include only those Indian Medical Journals that are either indexed in IndMED or in PubMed database. The selection policy of IndMED is to include peer reviewed journals having at least published on time for the last three years. At present, IndMED covers 77 Indian biomedical journals. All the articles are assigned metadata using data input worksheet based on Common Communication Format of UNESCO. These articles are indexed using controlled vocabulary 'Medical Subject Heading (MeSH) list of US National Library of Medicine.

It is being updating on an ongoing and timely basis can be accessed at <http://indmed.nic.in> which is searchable through web interface. The securing of intellectual rights has been easier due to rapport existing with the publishers of these journals. To remove any ambiguity and to reach clear understanding with the publishers, a formal Memorandum of Understanding (MOU) was signed with the journals [represented by their editors] to make available their contents for the medIND project.

At present, 37 Indian biomedical journals have signed a formal MOU with NIC. The aim of this understanding is to provide a rights framework under which cooperation is established between NIC and joutnals to provide their full content to the end user free of cost. The journal publishers provide the content and NIC does all the other activities like conversion, organization, hosting and providing access to the end users. The salient features of MOU are given as below:

- The resulting materials will be stored and hosted on NIC server;
- No fee will be payable to either party for providing content to NIC or converting into digitization;
- On termination of the agreement, NIC shall provide continuing access to the digitized completed up to the date of such termination;
- The copyright of the data would remain with the respected Editors.

Acquisition of Source Materials

The acquisition of material is the important part of project management. The content is of three types - printed version, born digital, and online existing journal archives. This heterogeneous material is converted into homogenous digital content as given below:

Converting Existing Print Media into Digital Format

Bulk of the archival and back volume content received is in form of printed copies of the journals. Each article, editorial and case study is scanned and stored as PDF (multi page) files. The files related to issue of a journal is put in a separate folder. File names are assigned as per a file naming policy that is based on bibliographic properties of content. The journal's content page of each issue is scanned, OCR and converted into HTML file. The content page in HTML format has all the links to the respective PDF files holding the articles.

Converting "Born Digital" Journals

These days, it is common to find journals being composed in DTP packages like PageMaker before they are printed. For such journals, the composed material is acquired with the cooperation of the editors/publishers of the journals. This is directly converted into the PDF files without the need of scanning. The quality of such PDF files is of much better quality. The name of the files is converted in accordance to the file naming convention. The content page of the issues is converted into HTML format and links are provided to the PDF files containing the full text articles.

Archives of On-Line Journals

There are few Indian journals that are already available on-line on the web. However since they are presently hosting on commercial web servers, it may not economical for them for continuing hosting back-volume of the journals. In such cases the archive can be moved to medIND after suitable conversion according to the policy of file names and file organization. This would ensure unique and persistent address for the contents in such archives.

File Naming and File Organization Policy

Unique and persistent URLs for each article are most desirable for such a project. To achieve this there has to be suitable policy for file names and file organization. Such a policy was formulated and adopted.

This formed the core on which cross linking between references in IndMED and their corresponding full text file under medIND has been done. Salient features of the policy is as follows:

Directory Structure

The directory structure is as follows: <http://medind.nic.in>/Journal Folder/.../Year-Folder/.../Issue Folder/...Article Files .../Article Folder/

Journal Folder

There is a folder under the site domain for each journal. The name should be unique for each journal folder. A unique three alphabet code has been created for each journal under MedIND called as MJID. This folder contains Year-Issue Sub-Folders and default (index.html) and other html files constituting the home page for the journal.

Year (Sub) Folder

This folder contains the issue subfolders. The Year folder is of three character format 'cyy' whereas c is for century and yy stands for last two digit of the year. For example, Year 2002 would be t02.

Issue (Sub) Folder

This folder is named as "Inn" format having at least two character long. Each Issue folder contains a table of content html file with same name as folder name.

Article File Naming Policy

The file names of articles are given as per the format given below: *<MJID><Century-Year><Issue No.><Pagination> <DOT><File Extension>*

- <MJID>: It is a unique identifier for each journal in IndMED and MedIND. It is of three alphabetical characters.
- <Century-Year>: It represents the year of publication and of three characters. The first character represents the century and is an alphabet. Next two characters are numeric representing the year (first year would be taken if it is a block year).
- <Issue No.>: A variable length of characters, starting with "i" followed by numerical characters represent the issue number.
- <Pagination>: A variable length of characters, starting with "p" followed by numerical characters represents the starting page number of the article. In case more then one articles starts on the same page then a alphabetic character is suffixed to qualify each article sequentially.
- <DOT>: The name portion of the file ends with a dot (.).
- <File Extension>: Three character extensions are suffixed after the dot to represent the common file types.

DIGITIZATION

Thirty-seven journals have signed MOU till now and given the consent for putting their contents under medIND project. The content is being received in hard as well soft copies formats. Each format requires digitization process. These processes are described below:

Conversion from Hard Copies

Steps Involved in OCR to PDF document

- Scanning the document: Resolution has been fixed for text as 300 dpi whereas for table and image, the resolution is 600 dpi;
- Each table is marked as an image as OCR most often distorts table;
- The remaining document is OCRed and saved as Word Document;
- Necessary corrections are performed such as spellings, special characters, colour changing, layout of the text and references;
- Quality checks: Each document is verified and passing quality test, is converted into PDF using Acrobat.

Steps in creating Table of Contents from scanned document

- Scanning the content pages of a journal, OCR and save in Word;
- Necessary corrections are performed such as spellings, special characters in the Word document;

- To design table of content in the same layout as given in the journal, it is designed in HTML format and saved as per naming convention. Hyperlink is given to each article;
- Quality Checks: Each link is being checked for correctness.

Conversion of Born Digital Contents

Steps in converting born digital contents to PDF document

- Content is being received in the form of Page Maker format;
- Converting from Page Maker format to pdf document and save it as pdf file as per the naming convention adopted;
- Checking the completeness of the document;
- In case, image or page(s) are missing, these are scanned locally for completeness.

DESIGN OF DIGITAL LIBRARY MEDIND WEB SITE

The medIND project is having its own domain name at the Internet (http://medind.nic.in). It has pneumonic value and stands for Medical Journals on Internet [from India]. Home page gives details of the project listing of the participating journals.

This listing is hyperlinked to each participating journal home page at the medIND web site. The site provides two approaches to access the journal articles.

Browsing

Journals are hyperlinked and arranged in alphabetical order. Such hyperlinked list leads to pages giving details of selected journals such as editors, instructions to authors, contact address, parent body etc.

Further, this leads to listing of issues of the journal by years/volume wise. The content page provides hyperlinks to the individual article.

Searching

The searching is being provided through the bibliographic database IndMED. Each record of the IndMED has been linked to the individual article in the MedIND site. The searching of the articles can be achieved through from http://indmed.nic.in as well as from http://mednic.nic.in web sites.

The references will display icons indicating the availability of the full text. In developing digital collection, issues of intellectual property rights have been dealt to strengthen the cooperation between editors and content service provider to facilitate access to digital content through Internet to end users in the area of biomedicine on non-commercial basis. The design of digital collection should be usable, flexible and simple enough to accommodate future changes and also enables other applications to utilize data for development of future applications. The naming convention of digital collection is acted as bridge between metadata base and full text of content. This project fulfills the demand of providing full text of documents to health professionals free of cost throughout the world.

It serves as a model for the development of similar collections in others S&T areas, medIND is a step in the process of making it as an open archive source where Indian journals covered in Medline database as well in IndMED database will be stored and will be provided access free of cost to health professionals throughout the world.

This will give enough visibility and exposure to Indian biomedical journals and demand for Indian literature would be met through the medIND project. In future, more visibility to articles included in medIND journals would be provided by adopting and exposing metadata in OAI-PMH and RSS protocols.

4

Research on Quantitative Aspects of Library Science

Two studies by Grignetti deal with quantitative aspects of representations of information in digital memories. The first study concerns the average length of representations of descriptions of documents or, in greater generality, the average length of representations of 'terms'. The second concerns the informational measure 'entropy' - or, to look at it the other way around, the redundancy - of English text considered as a string of _ words. Thus both studies bear upon the amount of memory required to store library information: the first with indexes, the second with actual text.

ON THE LENGTH OF A CLASS OF SERIAL FILES

From one point of view, the over-all organisation and concept of a library or of a pro-cognitive system is a more important thing to grasp, or to improve, than is the efficiency of a low-level 'detail' function. On the other hand, a few functions that appear from one point of view to be mere details, to occupy low levels in the over-all system, are seen from another point of view to be both basic and ubiquitous. One of these functions that looks like a technical detail from one standpoint and like something very basic and general from another is the encoding of elements of information for storage in a digital memory. Let us, for the purposes of this discussion, adopt the point of view from which it seems important.

As soon as we do that we may be prepared to examine subcategories, and one of the most conspicuous of these is the subcategory that includes catalogues and indexes. The study to be summarised deals with such files of information. Perhaps the best schema to keep in mind while thinking about this problem is the schema of an index consisting of the names or numbers of the documents in a collection and, associated with each name or number, a list of terms or descriptors that characterise the corresponding document according to some coordinate indexing system. The problem under consideration is how to encode the terms. The object is to be economical in the use of storage space and, at the same time, to make it easy for a computer to decode the representation and determine the names or numbers of specified documents. One of the most widely used techniques for representing terms is simply to spell them out in full or to record readable abbreviations of them. The direct way to encode such representations for storage in digital memory is to assign a binary code to each character in the character ensemble and to store the binary code patterns.

That technique has the disadvantage of using much more memory space than is necessary. A technique that is more economical of memory space is to number all the terms that may be used and to represent in memory in association with each item, not the corresponding terms themselves, but the numbers that were assigned to them. Since there are sometimes several terms per document, it is important not to let the numbers that represent different terms run together in such a way as to preclude subdivision of the over-all representation into its parts. The encodings of the sets of terms associated with different documents must also be kept separable.

In the past, people have kept codes separable either by using special characters as separators or by adding enough leading zeros to the short codes to make all the codes the same length. The prevailing opinion has been that the use of separators leads to more compact files than the use of fixed-. length codes.

The first thing Grignetti did was to analyse that comparison. It turned out that, on the average, and under certain reasonable assumptions, the fixed-length code is actually shorter than the variable length code plus separator. If one thinks about this question with simple, schematic examples in mind, he is likely to doubt this conclusion of Grignetti's and to agree with the prevailing opinion that Grignetti finds incorrect.

However, Grignetti's conclusion becomes quite obvious as soon as attention is focused upon large filing systems in which the list of legal terms is long. Consider, for example, that, of a list of nearly 1000 terms, almost 90 per cent would be represented by three-digit codes. About 9 per cent would require one leading zero, and about 1 per cent would require two leading zeros to bring them up to the 'fixed' length of three digits.

In his work on coding efficiency, Grignetti also examined the notion that products of prime numbers might provide the basis for an effective coding system for the purpose we are considering here. In such a system, each term would be assigned a prime number, and the set of terms associated with a particular item would be represented by the product of the prime numbers associated with the members of the set.

Grignetti was able to show conclusively that the prime-number code is an inefficient code, less good than either variant of the elementary system considered in the foregoing paragraphs. The preliminary enquiries just described led Grignetti to look for a truly efficient coding system for terms. He found one. He calls it the 'combinational code.' It is fairly easy to construct a combinational code. First, one has to decide the maximum number of terms that will be associated with an item, say, five. Second, he examines the list of legal terms, numbers the individual terms, and makes up all the possible combinations of term numbers, taken five or fewer at a time.

Third, he orders the numbers corresponding to the terms of each combination in a sequence of increasing magnitude. Fourth, he reorders the list of combinations according to a criterion that takes into account primarily the magnitude of the largest number in the subset but also, secondarily, the number of numbers in the subset.

Finally, he assigns integers in increasing sequence to the members of the reordered list. Grignetti gives an analytical procedure for encoding and decoding. He points out that the procedure does not have to be changed, and that existing code numbers do not have to be altered, when new terms are added to the list of legal terms. Finally, he shows that the combinational code is the shortest possible code.

ENTROPY OF WORDS IN PRINTED ENGLISH

Grignetti's interest was attracted to the question of the representational efficiency of direct encodings of the strings of *words* that constitute text by the consideration. That storage of the body of knowledge in processible memories will be an important basis for pro-cognitive systems. In order to estimate the representational efficiency, it is natural to compare determinations of the number of bits required to store a typical segment of text with estimates of the actual information content of the text. The classical estimate of the information measure of a typical word of text is the one made by Shannon in 1951 on the assumption that the frequency of occurrence of word types is sufficiently approximated by Zipf's famous law. Shannon's estimate of the information measure, or entropy, was 11.82 bits per word.

However, Berner using roughly the approximation that Shannon used, calculated that words could be stored, on the average, in 10.76 bits of memory space - with the aid of a compression code that was obviously not optimal. That led Grignetti to examine Shannon's results closely.

By a method slightly different from Shannon's, a method that seems straightforward and in which no flaw has been detected, Grignetti found the information measure to be 9.7 or 9.8 bits per word. From one point of view, the difference, which is only 2 bits per word, does not seem likely to have much practical significance. From another point of view, however, the important question is whether or not further work on encoding of text seems to be intellectually attractive. If it seems attractive, then it is possible, and perhaps likely, that a coding scheme will be found that is highly efficient in use of memory space and, at the same time, economical in respect of processing. On the other hand, if further work is not intellectually attractive, there is not likely to be an increase in either the efficiency of the use of space or the economy of encoding and decoding. Perhaps the 2 bits per word will have a stimulating effect. Clearly, the point on which study should now concentrate is the simplification of encoding and decoding.

A MEASURE OF THE EFFECTIVENESS OF INFORMATION-RETRIEVAL SYSTEMS

To some information-retrieval systems, a particularly simple schema is appropriate. The system is a 'black box' that contains a collection or set of items and that, from time to time, either spontaneously or in response to a request, offers a subset of its contents to one of its subscribers and withholds the complementary subset. An item may be thought of as a document. A subscriber may be thought of as simply a criterion: to the subscriber, an item is either pertinent or not pertinent. If one considers a single item of the collection and focuses his attention upon a particular occasion—a particular request from a subscriber or a particular spontaneous offering by the system.

Note that only two of the relative frequencies are independent, for the sum over the four categories must be unity, and the fraction of the items that meets the subscriber's criterion of pertinence is assumed to be fixed. Note, also, that there has to be some way to ascertain the pertinence or non-pertinence of withheld items. Investigating the problem of evaluation of effectiveness, Swets found that eight of the ten studies that met his criterion of pertinence reduced the analysis to two-by-two contingency tables.

However, in none of the studies was advantage taken of the fact that evaluative procedures have been developed for, and found useful in, other fields of application in which performance may be summarised in two-by-two contingency tables. Swets therefore adapted some of the apparatus of statistical decision theory to the information-retrieval context and proposed a measure of merit, a measure that quantifies the ability of the system to maximize the expected value of a retrieval trial, *i.e.*, of an offering or withholding of an individual item on a particular occasion.

The measure takes into account the relative frequency and the utility of each of the four categories in the two-by-two table. We shall not review here Swets's explanation of its derivation.

Let it suffice to say that an assumption of normality of distribution is involved, that the measure is based on maximum-likelihood statistics, and that, given the relative frequencies of hits and false drops in a particular sample, one can read the value of the measure from an available table or graph. The measure is simple, convenient, and appropriate. It gives definite meaning to the concept, the 'basic discriminating power' of an information-retrieval system.

The measure clearly separates discriminating power from mere willingness to yield output, thus avoiding a confusion that has been rife these last several years and that appears to be at the root of many informational difficulties. Moreover, the measure brings with it a well-developed system of procedures that facilitate analysis and interpretation of data. We expect Swets's measure to prove useful in evaluation of information systems. The main obstacle may lie in determination of the pertinence of withheld items. That obstacle is wide. It causes trouble for all the approaches to evaluation of performance in retrieval of information from large collections.

KINDS OF INFORMATION SERVICE

Information service, in the most general sense, is the process of assisting library users to identify sources of information in response to a particular question, interest, assignment, or problem. Sometimes referred to as reference service, the *Reference and User Services Association* (RUSA) of the American Library Association defines reference transactions as "information consultations in which library staff recommend, interpret, evaluate, and/or use information resources to help others to meet particular information needs". These reference transactions can take place in person or via the telephone, e-mail, or virtual reference technologies.

Librarians are also creating Web sites, answer archives, and links to answers to "frequently asked questions" all designed to anticipate user questions and help people find information independently. Traditional reference desk service continues to be highly valued by library users in many settings, but the newer forms continue to grow in popularity. Consequently, it is all the more important that librarians understand the range of enquiries that can be expected, allowing them to provide a full and ready answer, regardless of the form in which the query arises.

ANSWERING REFERENCE QUESTIONS

In light of the immense diversity and range of possible questions, being approached by a patron with a reference need can seem like a daunting prospect. Indeed, much of the difficulty of information services arises from uncertainty about the kind of service or breadth of information called for by a given question. Categorizing reference questions by type is a useful way to make sense of such concerns.

Three common types of information service are ready reference questions, research questions, and bibliographic verification. *Ready reference questions* such as "Where was Abraham Lincoln born?" "Who won the 1992 World Series?" "What is the capital of Nicaragua?" or "Where can I find a copy of the United States' Declaration of Independence?" can be readily answered using one or two general reference sources. The librarian may be tempted to tell the user the answer to simple ready reference questions. Yet here the old saying that "giving a man a fish feeds him for a day while teaching him to fish feeds him for a lifetime" is proven true. No matter how simple they seem initially, ready reference questions provide the possibility of teachable moments. Whenever possible, librarians should lead users through the process of looking up the information rather than simply providing the solution.

Librarians who assist users with ready reference enquiries on a regular basis sometimes choose to create a "ready reference" section of the most commonly used resources either in print or on the library's Web site to answer quick questions. Typically, such sections include a general all-purpose encyclopaedia, dictionaries, almanacs, and handbooks. Care must be taken to keep the sources uptodate and to avoid depending so heavily on this subset of the collection that other sources are overlooked by library users and librarians.

Librarians may find that ready reference questions have diminished due to the ease of answering basic questions through online information portals such as Google. Nevertheless, ready reference remains a cornerstone of information services, and librarians should be primed to provide it at any time. *Research questions* are more complex, may take much longer to answer, and typically require multiple sources of information. These questions often require the user to consider a variety of sources and viewpoints and to subsequently draw conclusions.

Sometimes questions that initially seem like ready reference questions are far more complex as previously hidden facets of the user's enquiry are revealed. Here, the variety of possible sources increases with the complexity of users' questions. Librarians should, for example, guide the user in the use of bibliographic sources, citations, and the back-of-the-book bibliographies. Likewise, users with complex questions may need to be taught how to find or request the full text of articles for which only citations are given in a search of electronic databases, allowing them to move beyond cursory surveys of the literature.

Research questions, especially if the user is unable to fully articulate the nature of his or her query, require librarians to ask questions of their own, trying to get at the nature of the request before setting out to help the patron answer it. The librarian may, for example, have to determine how much information is needed, what level of information is needed, and what other sources have already been consulted. Information services call for mutual engagement, especially with more complex questions.

Reference librarians should never be passive participants, pointing the way to an answer. Instead, they should play the part of dynamic guides, joining users on their journeys to knowledge. Naturally, the extent of such engagement may vary from one circumstance to another. Different types of libraries tend to have their own standards for how long librarians should spend with users on research questions. Many public libraries recommend that users be given five or ten minutes of personal assistance and then asked to return if more help is needed.

A university library may have a similar standard, or depending on the institution, may be able to invite the user to make an appointment for more in-depth research assistance. Some libraries may suggest that users call or e-mail ahead of their visit so the librarian can be prepared to offer the best possible assistance. Other libraries, including special libraries, may only be able to provide a basic level of help during the first visit. Libraries may refer users to other libraries with more specialized materials in the area of the user's research or may offer to call back if additional information is found.

Finally a library user may seek *bibliographic verification* when he or she has already obtained the information needed but must verify the sources. Sometimes this service is a matter of fact checking, whereas on other occasions users may have completed their research but lack full citation information. As users increasingly depend on electronic databases for information, compiling and formatting bibliographic citations becomes easier. Verifying and citing material found on Web pages is more difficult since the information needed for the citation is not always easy to find.

READER'S ADVISORY SERVICE

Reader's advisory service, sometimes considered a type of information service, is the quest to put the right book in the hands of the right reader. Librarians are increasingly expected to provide an answer to the dreaded question, "Can you help me find a good book?" Fortunately, as demand has increased, so too has the ease of providing this service. Although there is no substitute for one's own knowledge or experience, many new technologies serve to make the reader's advisory far easier than it was in the past. Many online databases, for example, have functions that automatically recommend other books for those who like a given title. Others have searchable lists of works by genre, helping readers match their favourite books to others like them.

As always, however, remember that reader's advisory, like other reference work, is predicated on the interaction between librarian and library user. Asking directed questions, listening carefully to the users' responses, and tailoring assistance accordingly is the basis of excellent, truly helpful service. The reader's advisory service is generally associated with public libraries and tends to be employed primarily by those looking for fiction. In academic libraries, it is far less common as users rarely come in searching for a mystery to read. Even so, reader's advisory may be needed to help lay researchers looking to deepen their knowledge of a particular field.

A patron who has read and enjoyed Stephen Ambrose's *Undaunted Courage*, but is troubled by allegations about Ambrose's questionable accuracy and academic honesty, may want to know the titles of books about the Lewis and Clark expedition that are both reputable and engaging. Successful reader's advisory librarians are skilled at asking users questions that enable them to assess users' reading level, language, or educational background. They must know a great deal about various genres of fiction and non-fiction and be intimately familiar with their library's collection. Significantly, it is important that they be able to convey their expertise in a friendly and conversational manner.

INFORMATION LITERACY

User instruction, which is now usually referred to as *information literacy*, may range from showing an individual how to use the library's online catalog and basic print reference sources to formal classroom sessions about conducting research in the library. The basic component of information literacy includes demonstrating how, when, and why to use various reference sources in an integrated way that will capture the user's attention at the teachable moment. In today's educational settings, the ease of using electronic resources often results in a failure to teach more traditional research strategies. While finding superficial information has grown easier, in-depth information has become increasingly obscure for many students.

In the library too, approaches to instruction may vary and librarians often question whether to simply answer questions posed by users or to teach users how to employ the available resources. This may be contingent on the mission or purpose of the library. Academic institutions may call on their librarians to help students understand how to engage effectively and independently in the research and information evaluation process. Public librarians, by contrast, may try to teach users about reference sources in a more informal manner as they lead users to the answers they seek.

Thus, while instruction is always an important part of reference work, the degree to which they go about providing it is highly contingent on the circumstances. In any case, all reference librarians must be skilled at helping users find information and answers quickly and be ready to teach users how to use the reference sources that are available. The best reference librarians develop an intuition for when to be information providers and when to be bibliographic instructors. In some libraries, only specific, designated librarians are charged with conducting library instruction courses.

Nevertheless, an increasing number of librarians are required to participate in their libraries' bibliographic instruction programme, and library school graduates are expected to be capable of teaching basic classes on the use of library resources. As should be clear, even those librarians not charged with providing formal instruction have the opportunity to teach those they serve.

LIBRARIES AND QUESTION ANSWERING SYSTEMS

Marill's Report, 'Libraries and Question Answering Systems,' laid the groundwork for subsequent research on question-answering systems. The report consists of three parts:

- Two Concepts of a Library,
- Question-Answering Systems and
- Semantic Nets: Informal Introduction.

The first of the 'two concepts of a library' is a schematisation of a present-day library. In the schema, the library consists of the collection of documents, the 'tag' system, and the retrieval system that makes use of the tags to retrieve desired documents. The contributions that technology can make within this first concept are acceleration of document handling, automation of the process of 'tagging' and improvement of the retrieval process.

Marill argues that this first concept, instrumented on a modest scale, would yield unsatisfactory results, and that, carried to its logical limit, it would be absurd. The second concept of a library is one in which the primary function is to provide not documents but information. The 'system' of the second concept will be able to 'read' and 'comprehend' the documents themselves and not merely their tags. It will have a high capability for organising the information internally. It will be able to accept questions worded in natural English. If it has the requisite information available, it will answer the questions in natural English. Thus Marill advocates a very sophisticated pro-cognitive system. He is concerned that people may believe the goal unreachable because it will be thought to require that inanimate mechanisms 'think.'

Marill refers to the question-answering system called 'Baseball' to forestall that misconception. In his discussion of question-answering systems, Marill defines the primary concepts: the corpus, the question, and the answer. The corpus consists of a set of quantificational schemata and their attendant predicate definitions, one definition for each predicate in the corpus. Thus Marill immediately seizes upon a predicate calculus as the formalism for representation of the information in the body of knowledge. There are two kinds of questions: questions satisfied by yes-no answers, and questions that require sentence answers. Answers, therefore, are also of two types: yes-no answers and sentence answers. The answer to a yes-no question is 'yes' if the question can be deduced from the corpus - if there exists a deduction that has the sentences of the corpus as premises and the question as the last line. The answer is 'no' if the negation of the question can be deduced from the corpus. There is no answer if neither the question nor its negation can be deduced from the corpus.

A sentence qualifies as a sentence answer if the sentence can be deduced from the corpus and if the schema of the sentence is the same as the schema of the question when the question is in statement form. There can be only one yes-no answer, but there can be any number of sentence answers. Marill's treatment of semantic nets is an extension and formalisation of the discussion of relational networks given in Part 1. Marill takes the view that the proper structural analysis of a sentence is given by the quantificational schema of that sentence, as understood in symbolic logic. To this, he adds the view that the meaning of a one-place predicate is identified, ultimately, with the set of objects of which the predicate is true, and the meaning of a two-place predicate is identified with the set of all ordered pairs of objects of which the predicate is true, and so forth. Finally, he adds the notion that the meaning of an object is identified with, first, the set of one-place predicates that are true of the object, and, second, the set of two-place predicates that are true of it and something else, and so forth.

The sets with which meanings are identified are extremely large. The machine cannot be required to prove its 'understanding' of a meaning by producing all the members of the sets. Marill maintains that it is enough for the machine to produce a convincingly large sample. The usual representation of a quantificational schema has the form of a string of symbols. Marill views the semantic net as an alternative notation, equivalent to the string notation, but more promising for computer exploitation. To demonstrate the relation between semantic nets and string-form schemata, Marill starts with three simple statements in string notation and transmutes them, by degrees, into diagrams in which lines tie together the several instances of a variable. The elements of a semantic net in Marill's exposition are the following:

- *Rectangles*—which represent the truth functions corresponding to logical operators and their arguments. Each rectangle has one terminal for each argument.
- *Diamonds*—which represent quantifiers. There are two types, corresponding to 'some' and 'all.'
- *A triangle with point down*—which represents 'sentence.' This triangle contains an 'S.'
- *A circle*—which represents a predicate. The circle has as many terminals as there are places in the predicate.
- *A triangle with point up*—which represents an individual.

Mariu gives six rules governing the combination of elements and the formation of semantic nets. The rules are:

- Connecting a predicate to a sentence symbol forms a sentence.
- Inserting a negation rectangle between the sentence symbol and the predicate negates the sentence.
- To connect two sentences, divert their predicates to a two-place truth-function rectangle and connect it to a single sentence-symbol triangle.
- To add a quantifier to a sentence, insert it in the line between the sentence symbol and its nearest neighbour.
- To terminate an unterminated predicate, attach an individual object to the unused terminal, or connect that terminal to a quantifier that is already in the diagram of the sentence.
- To merge two or more networks into one: for each individual, overlay all the triangles that represent the individual, retaining all the lines

that are attached to any of the triangles; associate all the occurrences of the same predicate by connecting them with 'association lines.'

In 'Semantic Nets: An Informal Introduction,' Marill presents diagrams to illustrate the rules and to demonstrate the interpretation of moderately complex semantic nets. Marill's diagrams and discussion make it clear that the semantic net is formally equivalent to the conventional representation of a system of statements in predicate calculus. Marill believes that semantic nets afford a promising path into computer representation and processing of complex systems of relations.

STUDIES OF COMPUTER TECHNIQUES AND PROCEDURES

The following studies are concerned with early steps along the course from present digital-computer system to future pro-cognitive systems. Let us consider the studies in the order of their locations along that course. The first ones were intended merely to make it convenient to carry out some of the functions that are required in research on library and pro-cognitive problems or in the efficient use of large collections of documents. The last ones in the sequence were intended to explore functions that we think will actually be involved in future pro-cognitive systems.

AN 'EXECUTIVE' PROGRAMME TO FACILITATE THE USE OF THE PDP-1 COMPUTER

One of the first needs of the study was a computer programme to facilitate the programming and use of the laboratory's digital computer. The computer is a small but excellent machine, Digital Equipment Corporation PDP-I, specialised to facilitate interaction with users who work 'on line.' The PDP-1 has an oscilloscope display with light pen, several electric typewriters, a set of programmable relays, an analogue-to-digital converter, and an assortment of switches and buttons. Its primary memory is small but it is capable of transferring information rapidly between the primary memory and a secondary drum memory that holds about 90,000 eighteen-bit words.

Associated with the computer are two magnetic-tape units. With the computer, it is possible to implement, in a preliminary and schematic way, several of the functions that were described in Part I as functions desirable in a pro-cognitive system. One encounters two main difficulties in trying to do, with the PDP-1 computer, research oriented towards a future period in which information-processing machines will have more advanced capabilities.

First, although the machine is reasonably fast, and although its secondary and tertiary memories make it possible to work with significantly large bodies of information, the machine is not capable of performing deep and complicated operations on really large bodies of text with the speed that would be desired in an operational system. The result is that it may take 30 seconds or a minute to get something that one would like to have almost instantly, that the display flickers on the oscilloscope screen, and so forth. Second, there is not available, at present, on any machine, either a programming language or a man-machine interaction language that makes it easy to do, or possible to do rapidly, many of the things envisioned in the discussion of pro-cognitive systems in Part I of this report. Our approach, during the study, was simply to put up with, and make allowances for, the shortcomings of the hardware system. It was easy to do that in informal experiments conducted by members of the research group; it was not realistic, however, to hope that all the observers of demonstrations would make the necessary allowances, and the shortcomings of the equipment effectively precluded formal experimentation.

Nevertheless, the equipment situation was at least tolerable, in terms of absolute assessment, and it seemed superb when we compared our man-computer interaction situation with any but two or three of all the others with which we were acquainted.

The unavailability of highly developed languages and, of course, the interpreter and compiler programmes that would be required to make them useful - was, however, a seriously inhibiting factor. During the period of our study, two good programming-language systems came into being: DECAL, which is a quite elegant and powerful language and compiler of the ALGOL type, suitable for a small computer, and MACRO, which is an ingenious language and assembler system that incorporates several of the features that DECAL lacks and lacks several of the features that DECAL incorporates.

However, neither DECAL nor MACRO was designed for on-line programming, and neither was designed particularly to handle the problems that seem likely to present themselves to users of pro-cognitive systems. Those considerations led to the effort, which was never quite completed, to develop a composite programme oriented and user-oriented system to facilitate our research in man-machine interaction.

The system is called 'Exec,' which stands, of course, for 'executive program'– and thus expresses something about the mode of operation: statements of the input language, coming into the computer, are examined by the executive programme, and, depending upon whether or not they fall into the class requiring interpretation, are either interpreted and executed with the aid of a set of subroutines associated with the executive programme or simply executed as machine instructions. Exec was written originally in the symbolic language called 'FRAP' and had, as its main function, simplification of the preparation of programmes and subroutines to be translated and assembled by FRAP.

When DECAL became available, Exec was rewritten in DECAL, and slight modifications were made to facilitate the use of Exec in the preparation of programmes and subroutines to be translated and compiled by DECAL. The original intention - to develop Exec to the point at which it could operate as an on-line language as well as an adjunct to a programming language—was not accomplished. One of the main themes in the work on Exec was to simplify and regularise the 'calling' and 'returning' of subroutines. In most computer-programming systems, and especially in the computer-programming systems that will be required in the implementation of plans of the kind, a computer programme is a complex arrangement of parts. The highest echelon of the structure does little more than represent the chapter headings of the general plan.

The actual work—the detailed processing of data - is handled by subprograms or 'subroutines' that break the task down into successively simpler sub packages at successively lower levels of detail until, finally, there is nothing left for the lowest-echelon subprograms to do but to perform simple, explicitly defined operations upon the few codes or numbers that are supplied to them. In this process of successive delegation of responsibility, the transactions that appear repeatedly are the 'calling' of a lower-echelon subroutine by a higher-echelon subroutine and the 'returning' of control from the lower-echelon subroutine to the higher-echelon subroutine. Calling usually includes transmission of instructions, and also the designation of the arguments upon which the lower-echelon subroutine must operate, from the calling subroutine to the called subroutine. The transmission of information down the line we shall call 'briefing'. Transmission of results up the line we shall call 'debriefing.' In the conventional way of handling calling and returning, a subroutine eventually returns control to the subroutine that called it, but it may first call one or more lower-echelon subroutines. Fortunately or unfortunately, depending upon one's point of view, there are many different ways in which subroutines can be called and briefed and in which they can return control and do their debriefing. As indicated, one of the main purposes of Exec is to simplify and regularise this whole process.

In order to simplify the process of calling and returning, Exec is interposed between the calling subroutine and the called subroutine at the time of calling and between the called subroutine and the calling subroutine at the time of returning. With each subroutine is associated a compact code, that provides Exec with a description of the needs.of the subroutine. Exec can therefore handle in a systematic, centralised manner several of the functions that would otherwise have to be handled by each subroutine.

In taking a burden off the routines, Exec takes a burden off the programmers who prepare them. The arrangements in Exec for calling and returning are set up in such a way that the chain of subroutine calls can be recursive. That is to say, it is possible for subroutine *A* to call subroutine *A*, or for subroutine *A* to call a subroutine *B* which, directly or through one of its minions, called subroutine *A*.

To permit recursive operation, one must handle 'temporary storage' - storage of the scratch-pad jottings made by each subroutine during its operation - in such a way that results written by *B*, for example, do not destroy results that *A* calculated before calling *B* and will need to use after *B* returns control. The functions just described have been implemented in a few programming systems - notably in the systems called IPL and LISP. In IPL and LISP, however, one either works wholly within the system or does not use the system at all. Exec extends the basic programming language and provides the new capabilities and conveniences within the structure of DECAL. In implementing the handling of subroutines, we made use of the technique of the 'pushdown list'. A pushdown list is an arrangement for storing information that resembles the spring-supported tray on which plates are stored in restaurants. If one puts a plate onto the top of the stack, it pushes all the others down, and if one then takes the plate off the top, the others pop up again. Exec, itself, employs one pushdown list.

Another pushdown list is available to the programmer or user through simple commands. He has only to give the name of the entity to be stored into the pushdown list or returned from it and to say whether he wants to push it down or pop it up. In the process of handling a call to a subroutine or a return from a subroutine, Exec examines the subroutine's heading code – determines whether or not, and how, to fulfill each of a number of functions, and then carries out those required. These functions include protecting contents of certain special registers of the processor against destruction during the running of the subroutine, finding the arguments needed by the subroutine and displaying them for its use, accepting the results obtained by the subroutine and communicating them to the calling routine, and protecting the contents of various temporary storage registers and 'flag' registers against modification by the called subroutine.

Exec protects information by putting it into the pushdown list. A second general purpose of Exec is to provide the advantages of generality and the advantages of specificity both at the same time and within the same system. If a computer programme is written in such a way as to make it useful in a particular situation. On the other hand, if the programme is written so that for example, it alphabetises or orders any kind of strings of alphanumeric text in any file or table, then he has to communicate to it, or have the routine that calls it communicate to it, that it should operate on words and that it should alphabetise according to a specified alphabet. In Exec, an effort is made to accommodate very general subroutines and to make it maximally convenient to communicate to them the information required to prepare them for specific applications. This is done by setting up and maintaining a description of the prevailing context of operation. In the terms of the example, his description may contain a specification that the currently prevailing string class is the class of 'words.'

It contains the specification that the *x,* in any subroutine prepared to operate upon 'Table *x,*' should be interpreted as 3. The subroutine, therefore, automatically performs on the operation intended by the programmer, despite the fact that the programmer was thinking in terms of abstractions and not in terms of the particular present task. With arrangements of the kind just suggested, Exec makes it possible to use a subroutine that contains the expression, 'next string,' for example, to operate on the next character, or the next word, or the next sentence, or the next paragraph, or the next section, or the next chapter, and so forth. Exec keeps track of three 'string classes' simultaneously, class *u,* class *v,* and class *w.* At any time, the programmer can set anyone of the string classes to anyone of seven levels. He can write, for example, '*SSCU* word,' meaning to *set* the string class *u* to have the value, *word.* From that time on, until the instruction is superseded, all the subroutines that deal with the string class hierarchy *u* will consider the *u* strings to be words.

The procedure for designating tables is similar to that for designating strings. If the programmer would like to have programmes written in terms of Tables *x, y,* and *z* operate on the contents of Table zones 2, 5, and 7, he writes '*ntox* 2, *ntoy* 5, *ntoz* 7.' * When Exec sees those instructions, it does more than merely substitute 2 for *x,* 5 for *y,* and 7 for *z.* It finds the descriptions, in its file of table descriptions, that characterise the three numbered tables, and it substitutes these descriptions for the pre-previously prevailing descriptions of Tables *x, y,* and *z,* respectively. When a subroutine operates on the contents of the table, it examines the table's description and controls its processing accordingly. This makes it possible to accommodate diverse formats and conventions. Inasmuch as the adjustments are made 'interpretively' during the running of the programme, the user can change his mind and reprocess something in a slightly different way without having to go through extensive revision and recompilation of his programmes. This is an advantage that the present technique has over the technique, based on the 'communication pool,' that has been developed in connection with the programming of very large computer systems—systems programmed by teams so large as to discourage the effort to enforce the use of a single, standard set of conventions and formats.

The part of Exec that we have been describing is approximately an interpretive communication pool. The third set of functions with which Exec is concerned has to do with the display of alphanumeric information on typewriters and on the oscilloscope screen. Although these are very simple functions, they involve enough detailed programming to be a nuisance unless they are handled in a systematic way. Exec makes it convenient to separate specification of the information to be displayed from specification of the equipment through which it is to be displayed. It uses standard programmes to handle strings that are long enough to be considered messages or texts, but it provides special arrangements to facilitate preparation of labels, headings, and the like.

For example, the programmer can call for the typing of any particular character *x* on whatever typewriter is currently specified to be typewriter *b* simply by writing *'type x.'* If the programmer wants the character to appear upon the screen of oscilloscope *a*, he writes *'scpa x.'* With the aid of Exec, the programmer can define in equally short instructions the size of the print, the vertical position at which the text should begin, and other parameters of the visual display.

Exec's arrangements for displaying capital and lower-case letters on the oscilloscope are primitive, but it is a step in the right direction to have both capital and lower-case letters. At present, a 'lower-case' letter is simply a small capital letter. We settled for that stopgap solution only in the interest of economy. The fourth and final set of functions handled by Exec has to do with display, by the computer, of what the computer is doing. One technique developed for this purpose, a technique called 'Introspection,' because it was developed as a separate project. The arrangements described here are integral to Exec. One of the main causes of difficulty in man-computer interaction is that the computer does not give the man any good clues about what it is doing until it completes a segment of processing and spews forth the results.

When the computer is running, its lights flash so fast that they are scarcely interpretable. It seems important to provide a way of having the computer give a running account of its processing. A part of Exec called the 'Reporting Subsection 'an optional part - is brought into play each time a subroutine is called and each time a subroutine returns control to its caller. When the reporting subsection is brought into action, it examines the list of things that it should do. This list can be changed while Exec and other programmes are running. Ordinarily, the first thing on the list is to give the address, and, if it is available in the directory, also the name, of the subroutine that is being called or that is returning control to its caller. Since the subroutines operate very rapidly, the names and addresses would appear to be presented simultaneously, one on top of another, if they were shown in a fixed location on the screen.

Therefore they are displayed in a format corresponding to that of a conventional outline. If a chain of subroutines is called, each one operating at a level just lower than its caller, the names and addresses appear on successive lines of the display with increasing indentation. Then, as the subroutines return control, each to its caller, the names and addresses are displayed again in such a way as to redisplay the outline pattern from bottom to top. To the display just described can be added, at the option of the operator, a display of the contents of the active registers of the computer. In addition, the operator may see the contents of whatever parts of the computer's memory he wants to examine. He designates the various parts of memory to Exec by typing on the typewriter while the programme is running. He can change his prescription at will. The current version of Exec allows him to specify nine different sectors of memory, either symbolically or in terms of absolute addresses. When he indicates that he wants to see 'the subroutine,' Exec interprets 'the subroutine' to mean the particular subroutine that is being called, or that is returning control to its caller. That will, of course, be one subroutine at one moment and another at another moment. When the operator wishes to examine a table or a programme in detail, he touches the space bar of the typewriter. That causes the system to pause in its progression through the sequence of things to be displayed, and to hold the current display until the operator releases it by touching the tab key. The Reporting Subsection provides a few additional conveniences - minor ones introduced from time to time on an *ad hoc* basis - but the foregoing will suffice to give an idea of the existing arrangement. Let us mention a few of the steps not yet accomplished, however. It seems worth while to connect to the Reporting Subsection the 'Introspection' programmes that will be described later.

It is necessary to complete the arrangements that associate the tables that reside in the primary memory to corresponding structures in secondary and tertiary memory and, in the manner of the Atlas computer system, to arrange it so that information structures are automatically shifted up through the memory hierarchy whenever they are addressed. It is necessary, also, to expand the mechanism that associates symbols with machine addresses. That mechanism is only a simple table-searching system, but it is inherently capable of effecting the translation required to make conveniently readable the reports of 'what is currently going on in the computer.' We found it useful to distinguish, in Exec, between 'intrinsic' and 'extrinsic' subroutines. Exec is highly 'subroutinised' and has the partly hierarchical, partly recursive, structure that we have described as essential for pro-cognitive systems. Each sub-function of Exec that appears to have any likelihood of proving useful in future applications is separated out and set into the form of a subroutine. In the process of writing subroutines to handle substantive problems - subroutines that made use of Exec but were not at first intended to be part of the Exec system - we encountered repeatedly several sets or clusters of functions. By associating with Exec the subroutines prepared to handle those functions, we were able to build up a system of considerable convenience and power. The part of the system not intrinsic to Exec was too extensive to be held in primary memory at all times. However, it was clearly desirable to bring parts of it into primary memory - coherent clusters of it corresponding to major functions - whenever required in the execution of a programme. The easiest way to accomplish dynamic storage and transfer of subroutines, and to handle the associated bookkeeping, was to take care of it automatically through Exec's ability to examine calling sequences and subroutine headings. We did not make much progress towards that end during the course of the study.

However, we did work with the problem enough to see the great convenience and power that reside in a coherent structure of computer subroutines and a largely automatic arrangement for calling them and transferring information among them. Evidently, the more sophisticated the arrangements, the larger the fraction of the subroutines that will be intrinsic to the arrangements. We visualise a system in a continual process of development, with a set of intrinsic subroutines, a set of extrinsic subroutines, and a continual flow from the extrinsic set to the intrinsic set as more and more functions are brought within the scope and capability of the system.

ON-LINE MAN-COMPUTER COMMUNICATION

'On-Line Man-Computer Communication' by Licklider and Clark discusses several problems in, and several steps towards the improvement of, interaction of men and computers. These include problems and developments in the use of computers as aids in teaching and in learning and as a basis for group cooperation in the planning and design of buildings. The part of the paper that stemmed from the present study was the development of a pair of programmes, referred to earlier as 'Introspection,' that are closely connected with the last described major function of Exec. The two programmes of 'Introspection' were designed to demonstrate that, although present-day computers are opaque and inscrutable, of all the complex organisms and systems in the world, computers are, in principle, the most capable of revealing the intricacies of their internal processes. We consider this to be an important problem calling for much research. Our two programmes constitute only exploratory steps. The two parts of Introspection are 'Programme Graph' and 'Memory Course.' Programme Graph displays, in the form of a graph relating that quantity to time, the contents of any specified register or registers of the computer.

Memory Course displays the progression of control from one memory register to the next during the operation of a programme. With the aid of these two programmes, the operator can see what is happening, as it happens, within the processor and the memory of the computer. These programmes give him at once both a global view and a considerable amount of detail. They let him see relations among parts of the over-all picture. No longer is he constrained, as he has been with conventional procedures, to peek at the contents of one register at a time, and to build up the over-all picture from myriad examinations of microscopic details. To provide a rough impression of the operation of Programme Graph, it may suffice to describe how it operates when it is set to display the contents of the register of the computer that is called the 'programme counter.' The programme counter contains the address of the memory register that contains the instruction that is being executed. In the absence of 'branching' or 'jumping,' control proceeds from one register to the next, and the contents of the programme counter increase by one, each time an instruction is executed. When a 'branch' or 'jump' occurs, the number in the programme counter changes by some integral quantity different from one, and often the increment or decrement is rather large. Programme Graph plots the graph relating the number in the programme counter to the time. The display presents about a thousand individual quantities simultaneously to view. From the graph, it is easy to recognise the upward-sloping line segments that correspond to non-branching, non-jumping stretches of programme.

When the programme 'loops,' as it often does, branching backward and repeating a sequence of instructions over and over, the display shows a saw toothed waveform. When the programme calls a subroutine, the jump to the subroutine, the loops within the subroutine, and the return from the subroutine are all clearly evident. When Programme Graph is used to display the contents of the accumulator, the input-output register, or one of the memory registers, the interpretation of the graph is, of course, quite different. In general, however, its main value lies in its presentation of a large quantity of information in such a way that relations among parts are easy to perceive. The other Introspection programme, Memory Course, displays only the course through memory followed by the programme under study.

It shows that course as a succession of circles connected by a heavy line against a gridlike background representing the primary memory of the computer. The grid upon which the display of Memory Course is shown consists of 4096 dots, arranged in 64 squares of 64 dots each, and representing one bank of memory. A register is represented by a very fine light dot if the instruction and the address it contains are both zero. The dot is a little heavier if the instruction is not zero. The dot is a little heavier still if the address is not zero. If both the instruction and the address are not zero, the dot is heavy. From the grid, therefore, the user can see which parts of memory are occupied and which are not. In addition, after he has gotten used to the display, he can make out which parts of memory are used to store programmes, and which parts are used to store data. When Memory Course is used to display the 'trajectory' through memory followed by an object programme, the object programme itself is not run in the usual way. Instead, the object programme is operated by Memory Course, which 'traces' the progress of the object programme and displays it on the oscilloscope screen. Each time an instruction is executed, a circle is drawn around the dot that corresponds to the location of the instruction in the computer memory. When a programme 'loop' is traced, the line is set over slightly to one side of the circles it has been connecting. That keeps it from retracing its path backwards and helps it represents the cyclic nature of the course. Memory Course represents loops, as just suggested, by tracing out a closed course. When the programme transfers control to a subroutine, a line jumps out from the dot that corresponds to the call and leads to the dot that corresponds to the beginning of the subroutine.

Thus, Memory Course provides a simple, maplike representation of the programme structure. One can see where the various subroutines are, how long they operate, when they receive their calls, and when they return control to their callers. If an error occurs, either in the computer or in the programme, control is very likely to be transferred to an inappropriate location. If the user knows the structure of his programme, either from having programmed it or from experience operating it, he sees that something unexpected has happened.

He then looks back to the beginning of the unexpected line and determines precisely the location of the register within which the error originated. Having done that, he typically reruns the programme, following its course very carefully as it approaches the critical point. If the error recurs, he reruns the programme once more, this time stopping it at various points ahead of the critical one and using other means to examine the instructions, addresses, and data associated with those points.

A FILE INVERTER

The project to be described next was aimed, like Exec, at increasing the convenience and effectiveness with which the computer could be used in the study of library and pro-cognitive problems. This project, however, had a much sharper focus than Exec. Its aim was simply to implement the operation called 'file inversion.'

A direct file is ordered with respect to its 'items', and usually several terms are associated with each item. An inverse file is ordered with respect to its 'terms,' with several items usually associated with each term. Obviously, both the direct file and the inverse file are aspects of a more general structure consisting of items, terms, and associations between items and terms.

The 'File Inverter' is a computer programme, written in DECAL by Grignetti, that accepts a direct file and produces an inverse file. Since there is no difference in abstract format between a direct file and an inverse file, the programme produces a direct file if it is presented with an inverse one. The file-inverting programme includes a subprogram that alphabetises the entries. If it is used to invert a file consisting of terms associated with alphabetised items, it yields a file of items associated with alphabetised terms.

If the items consist of the bibliographic citations of documents, and if the terms are the key words of the titles of the documents, then the result obtained by applying the file-inverting programme is a kind of 'permuted title index.' Grignetti's programme includes a subprogram that facilitates the selection of key words from titles. The subprogram selects from a string of words all those that do not appear upon a list of words to be excluded. The list of words to be excluded ordinarily contains the 'function' words and, also, words that have been found not to discriminate.

AN AUTOMATED CARD CATALOGUE

Using parts of the file-inverting programme, Grignetti prepared a programme that automates some of the functions involved in using an ordinary card index. The kind of card index towards which the programme is oriented is not precisely the kind used in most libraries. It differs mainly in assuming that each card will contain a series of descriptive terms.

Such card indexes are found more frequently in documentation centers that specialise in laboratory technical reports and reprints than in libraries of books and serials. The 'Automated Card Catalogue' is a DECAL programme for use in exploration of card catalogue problems.

The user sits at the computer typewriter and presents his retrieval prescription to the computer in the form of a Boolean function of the terms in which he is interested. A person interested in non-digital simulations of neural processes, particularly including studies made under the heading, 'perception, ' but also other studies in the field of artificial intelligence, might type:

- (Artificial intelligence or perception or neural simulation) and not digital

Using the terms of the Boolean function as retrieval terms, the programme searches a magnetic tape containing the 'card' file. Whenever it finds one of the terms, it looks further within the entry to determine whether or not the function is satisfied. If the function is satisfied, the programme displays the entire contents of the 'card' on the oscilloscope screen for examination by the user.

Grignetti's programme makes it convenient for the user to correct his retrieval prescription, to reinitiate a search, to find out just where he stands at any point in his study, and to save 'cards' for future reference.

The programme 'knows' the rules for regular pluralisation and considers the search for a term to be satisfied if either the singular or a calculated regular plural or a given irregular plural of the term is found. In addition, the programme works with a simplified system of spelling, as well as with literal spelling, and is therefore often able to find the desired term on a 'card' even when the term is misspelled in the prescription. In such an instance, it displays, for example,

- Do you mean 'intelligence'?

The user then types y for 'yes' or n for 'no.' The programme remembers this answer and does not bother the user again with the same question. That may be convenient when the user is dealing with names he does not know very well, but it leads to complications that will have to be settled through further programming. Probably it will be better to correct the prescription than to perpetuate the indiscrimination.

A SYSTEM TO FACILIT ATE THE STUDY OF DOCUMENTS

The two programmes described in the preceding sections are related to, and are intended for incorporation into, a system to facilitate the retrieval and study of documents. The 'study' part of the over-all system is described in a report by Bobrow, Kain, Raphael, and Licklider.

The study system, called 'Symbiont' because we hope to develop it into a truly symbiotic partner of the student, displays information to the student via the typewriter or the display screen. It is intended as an exploratory tool, for use mainly by students who are at the same time experimenters, and it does not yet have the perfection or polish required for realistic demonstration or practical application. However, it does make available, in a single, integrated package, several functions that prove quite useful to a student who wants to examine a set of technical documents, take notes on their contents, compare or combine graphs found in different papers, and so forth. Among the functions provided by Symbiont are the following:

- Present for examination a document specified by any sufficiently prescriptive segment of its bibliographic citation.
- Turn pages, forward or backward, in response to the pressing of a key.
- Permit designation of a passage by pointing to the beginning and then the end with a light pen.
- Accept labels from the typewriter and associate them with passages of text.
- Record as a note, and preserve for later inspection, any designated passage.
- Append bibliographic citations to extracted passages.
- Accept retrieval prescriptions from the typewriter.
- Accept from the typewriter coded versions of specifications of such operating characteristics as, 'Consider a neighbourhood to be five consecutive lines of text,' or 'Consider a search to be satisfied when any two of the three elements of the search have been satisfied.'
- Carry out retrieval searches and display passages in which the retrieval prescriptions are satisfied.
- Compose graphs from tabulated data and present the graphs, against labeled coordinate grids, on the oscilloscope screen.
- Set two graphs side by side to facilitate comparison.
- Expand or compress the scales of graphs, under control from the light pen.
- Change the number of grid lines or the calibration numbers associated with the lines, or both together, and recalculate and redisplay the calibration numbers when grid lines are added or deleted.

The search routines used in finding desired passages of text operate with three sets of retrieval terms. The user specifies the terms of each set initially through the typewriter. All the terms of a subset are considered equivalent during the search, and the search is satisfied insofar as that subset is concerned if anyone of the terms is encountered in the text. The user can specify whether he wants to find a passage in which at least one of the terms of one of the sets occurs, or a passage in which at least one of the terms of each of two of the sets occurs, and so forth. Even though this implementation is primitive, it is evident from preliminary experiments with Symbiont that automation of the function of searching for 'ideas' will be a very powerful aid in technical study. Machine aid in manipulating graphs will also be very helpful.

ASSOCIATIVE CHAINING AS AN INFORMATIONRETRIEVAL TECHNIQUE

Most of the information-retrieval systems that have actually been developed, and even most of those that have been subjected to intensive research, retrieve unitary elements of information, such as documents, paragraphs, or sentences. A basic point in Marill's paper is that for many purposes the retrieval of a unitary part of the corpus is inadequate, and that what often is needed is an answer to a question that may have to be derived through deduction from elements of information scattered throughout the corpus.

When the relation between two items is direct, they are said to be connected by a first-order chain. When the relation between two items can be established only through the intermediary agency of a third item, the first two items are said to be connected by a chain of second order, and so forth. In a report on 'Associative Chaining as an Information Retrieval Technique,' Clapp describes the idea of chaining as a general schema, then shows the correspondence between the chaining schema and certain schemata of graph theory, and finally discusses a programme that traces chains of relevance through corpora consisting of files of sentences.

Chaining, as a technique, is particularly simple and easy to discuss when it is separated from the problem of the nature of relevance. In Clapp's work, the two things - the technique and the concept of relevance - are well separated. For purposes of simplicity and convenience, Clapp considers two sentences to be directly associated if they have one or more words in common. Thus, the sentences, 'The cat is black,' and 'Black is a colour,' are directly associated. They have two words in common, 'is' and 'black.' There is no direct, first-order association between the first two of the following sentences, but only a second-order association through the third sentence:

'The cat is black,' 'Feline animals move gracefully,' 'A cat is a feline animal.' It is obvious, even at the outset, that something has to be done to inhibit associations based on the common occurrence of frequently used verbs and function words. In Clapp's approach, however, whatever is done about that is a separate matter from the development of the algorithm that traces out the chains. Clapp's computer programmes are divided into two sets. The first set of programmes facilitates the preparation of a machine-processible file of information units, such as sentences, paragraphs, or documents. It then prepares, from the file, a series of concordances.

Finally, with the aid of the concordances, it determines the set of all first order associations. The second set of programmes operates upon a retrieval prescription plus the set of first-order associations. The retrieval prescription is a set of words drawn from the vocabulary of the corpus.

The first thing that the chaining algorithm does is to find all those elements of the corpus that contain all the words of the prescription. This is what a 'conventional' information retrieval system would do. Then, however, the chaining algorithm goes on to trace higher-ordered chains through the corpus and to retrieve the information elements that are involved in higher-ordered chains up to some cutoff order specified by the operator.

The programme has been tested and demonstrated only with a corpus consisting of sentences. Except for minor considerations having to do with delimiters - the clues that mark stopping points such as ends of sentences or paragraphs - the chaining programmes are not sensitive to the distinctions among sentence, paragraph, document, and so forth, and it is obvious that the chaining operation can be carried out on textual strings of any class. However, pursuing the technique of chaining based on the common occurrence of words beyond a level of the sentence does not seem to offer much promise.

It is evident that every book would be directly associated with almost every other book if the criterion were a word in common and it is equally evident that almost no book would be associated with any other book if the criterion were a verbatim paragraph in common. For the technique of chaining, ordinary sentences seem to be approximately the optimal length. Fortunately, the sets of descriptive terms used in coordinate-indexing systems are of approximately the same length as sentences. The notion of association based on inclusion of common terms is quite appropriate for them. It is in that domain that we think it most likely that the chaining technique, and the chaining algorithms developed by Clapp, will find practical application. In his exploration of the relations between graph theory and associative chaining, Clapp developed the chaining schema in considerably more depth than is reflected in this summary. For example, his development uses the number of parallel links as well as the order of the links in the chain of association. Some of his ideas recognise gradations in the strength of association.

That seems important because, intuitively, one thinks of relevance as capable of variation in degree. The next step in the development of the concept of associative chaining, we think, should be an attempt to define the fundamental relatedness or relevance on which the 'association' is based. Associative chaining has a natural connection with the relational networks and with the semantic nets and question-answering systems studied by Marill and Black. The next step may, therefore, take the form of merging the chaining concept with the concepts underlying the relational and semantic nets and the question-answering systems.

TWO QUESTION-ANSWERING SYSTEMS

Marill's short paper on question-answering systems, described earlier, initiated a series of studies that involved a meld of symbolic logic and computer programming. Most of these studies were carried out by Black, who described them in a series of memoranda and a report. The memoranda and the report share with the corpora of the question-answering systems a tight, terse, logical quality that makes them attractive to the logician and difficult for the non-logician to understand. Following is an effort to summarise, without gross distortion, two of the principal accomplishments of the work on question-answering systems in a freer and less formal exposition. One might justify this aim by quoting a paragraph from Black's 'Conclusions on QAS': A string of words cannot be rephrased without significant loss of facts or ideas relevant to some area. However, if we limit ourselves to certain areas, then the string of words can be rephrased without loss of facts or ideas *relative to those areas*. In the final paragraph of the same memorandum Black goes on to say: Before we can rephrase a string of words without significant loss, we must define our interests precisely.

If we are interested in everything, then we cannot rephrase the string at all. Let us say, therefore, that we are interested in assessing the possibility, and also the technical feasibility, of:

- Representing large parts of the body of knowledge, as well as questions relating to the body of knowledge, in a formal language amenable to processing by a computer and
- Developing a system that will, by processing the questions and the stored corpus, deduce and display COrrect answers.

Black's results attest to the possibility of doing those things. However, Black's programmes take a long time to determine the answers to fairly simple questions. That fact suggests that economic feasibility is dependent upon greatly increasing the processing efficiency of the question- answering system or the processing speed of the computer, or both.

The prediction made in Part I that it is unlikely that there will be great increases in speed in the same computers that have a greatly increased memory capacity, may not bear very heavily on this problem. It may be that as suggested, use procedures that are fast, but not very deep, to retrieve parts of the corpus that are rich in statements germane to a particular question, and then turn to deeper and slower procedures for the derivation of the answer from the rich informational ore.

The first of Black's two contributions to be summarised, the memorandum, 'Specific-Question-Answering System,' February 8, 1963, describes Version III of a system written in the LISP language for the IBM 7090 computer. In this system, the corpus consists of statements that are strings of ordinary words, symbols representing variables, and parentheses. The use of the ordinary words is highly constrained - so constrained that nothing can be said that could not be said equally well in the shorter, but less widely readable, notation seen in books on logic. The only variables are *Xl, X2, X3, what, when, which,* and *how.* The parentheses have the effect of forcing the system to consider as a unit the string within the parentheses.

The 'questions' asked of the Specific-Question-Answering System may be either statements, in which case they are confirmed or denied by the system, or ordinary questions containing the variables, *Xl, X2, X3, what,* and *when,* etc. The answer elicited by a 'yes-no' question is 'yes,' 'no,' or 'no answer.' The answer to any other question is a list of items that constitute a correct and reasonable reply, or 'no answer'.

The system seeks answers to questions by processing the questions and the corpus in a very straightforward, rigourous way.

It looks through the corpus for a statement that is the same as the statement that constitutes the question or that can be transformed into the question by removing a 'not.' If it finds a match, the answer is 'yes'.

If it finds a negated match, the answer is 'no.' If it finds neither, it looks for a conditional statement in the corpus in which the consequent matches the question. If it finds such a statement in the corpus, it undertakes to determine an answer to the subsidiary question, whether or not the premise of the conditional statement is true. Proceeding in this way, it tries every possibility of deriving the question or its negation from the statements of the corpus. The procedure for processing of questions containing variables is a little more complex than the procedure just described.

It is necessary, in seeking an answer to a question containing a variable, to keep track of all the individuals that can be values of the variable. The process amounts, approximately, to determining the list of individuals that meet all the conditions that are imposed upon the variable. The system is capable of answering not only simple, single-variable questions, but also multiple questions, conditional questions, and even questions containing the names of LISP computer programmes.

In the latter case, there is a rigid format that must be followed in giving the name of the programme and its arguments. All the foregoing structures mentioned as acceptable question forms are also acceptable as forms for statements in the corpus. In the corpus, a programme name may occur even in the antecedent of a conditional statement.

We mention these things to indicate that the system has the capability of expressing complex relations and of deriving answers to complex questions. To see approximately what the system does, let us consider a few oversimplified examples and one more complex example. Suppose, first, that the corpus consists merely of two statements:

- Mercury is (a planet) if (Xl is a planet) then (Xl is a planet of the sun)

The question asked of the system, in statement form, is:

- Mercury is a planet of the sun

To that question, the system says, simply:

- Yes

Suppose, for the second example, that the corpus consists of only one sentence:

- Earth is smaller than jupiter

The question asked of the system and the foregoing rudimentary corpus is:

- Jupiter is smaller than earth

The answer given by the system to that question is:

- No Answer

But now suppose that a second statement is added to the corpus. The corpus now consists of the two statements:

- Earth is smaller than jupiter if (XI is smaller than X2) then (X2 is not smaller than XI)

The question is still:

- Jupiter is smaller than earth

The system is now able to determine an answer. It says:

- NO

The question asked of the system and this corpus is:

- What is a major planet

The answer provided by the system is:

- Neptune
- Uranus
- Saturn
- Jupiter

This last example would be more impressive than it is if the corpus contained a large number of irrelevant statements in addition to the statements shown. The presence of irrelevant statements would increase the length of time required by the computer in answering the question, but the computer has the great advantage, in operations of this kind, that it does not tend to forget the relevant facts already found while it is examining the irrelevancies.

For a human being, on the other hand, a problem of the present kind that is difficult but nevertheless within one's scope of capability becomes entirely hopeless as soon as a large amount of irrelevant material is introduced. That fact, we believe, is significant in its bearing on the problem men face in drawing answers from the body of knowledge that is now held in libraries and document rooms.

The other paper of Black's that we shall discuss here is 'A Question-Answering System: QAS-5'. This paper describes in detail the operation of a later generation question-answering system, a descendant of the Specific-Question-Answering System that we have been discussing. The main advances made in the interim between the two papers were advances in the handling of quantification and advances achieved by formalising the language approximately in a way suggested earlier by McCarthy. The advance in quantification makes it possible for the system to deal with problems involving 'some' and 'all.'

The formalisation of the language makes it difficult for the uninitiated reader to understand what is being done, but it reveals the flaws and pitfalls to the veteran in a clearer way than the more readable language does, and, moreover, it suggests what to do to correct or avoid them. We consider the formalisation, therefore, to be a step more in a right direction than in a wrong one - a step that must be taken in order to reach a position from which it will be possible to move forward to simultaneous readability and formal effectiveness.

The mode of operation of QAS-5 is similar in basic principle, though somewhat deeper and more complex, to the mode of operation of the Specific-Question-Answering System. Some of the flavour of the method is given by the following protocol:

- Step 1: The system finds the first match for question 1 in statement 6.
- Step 2: The system forms the backward transform of question 1 and statement 6, giving a new conditional (7) - at (desk, *y)*, at *(y,* country) at (desk, country).
- Step 3: The system sets up the first antecedent of (7) as a new question (2) - at (desk, *y).*
- Step 4: The system finds the first match for question 2 in statement 2.
- Step 5: The system forms the transform of question 2 and statement 2, giving the answer to question 2 - (I) at (desk, home).

The latter would be read, as one might possibly guess, 'I am at my desk at home.' The problem to which Black's QAS-5 report is wholly dedicated is a problem posed by McCarthy in 1958 and hitherto not solved by any non-human system. It is a well known problem in artificial-intelligence and heuristic-programming circles and is called the 'airport problem.'

The problem, stated here informally, is fairly simple: I am at my desk, at home. My car is in my garage, which is also at my home. I want to go to the airport. The airport is in the same county as my home. I can walk from any point that I would call 'at my home' to any other point that I would also call 'at my home,' because, of course, the dimensions of the area subsumed under 'home' are not very great.

I can drive from any point in my county to any other point in my county. What should I do? The answer to the question, or the solution to the problem, is said to be:

> I should go from my desk to my garage on foot and get my car, and I should then drive my car from the garage to the airport.

Having stated the problem and given the solution, we should perhaps repeat that, although the answer is obvious to any adult human being who understands English, no one had succeeded in devising a wholly automatic system that would derive the answer from the description of the situation and the statement of the question. Black's report gives a step-by-step account of the procedure used by QAS-5 in solving the problem. In addition, it displays, point by point, the minor differences between the notation suggested by McCarthy and the notation employed by Black. The conclusions that we draw from our experience with question-answering systems are summed up in the assertion that the achievement of Black's programme in solving McCarthy's problem is simultaneously a signal advance in automated question answering and a commonplace performance for a moderate intelligence. In greater detail, the conclusions are:

- Clear progress is being made in bringing logical deduction within the scope of automation.
- In the process of programming a system to accomplish a feat such as the one described, one begins to see how extremely deep and complex are the intellectual processes that one accepts as commonplace and undemanding of intelligence when those processes are carried out by people.
- In the running of such programmes, one begins to sense the magnitude of the gulf that separates a demonstration of the type just described from an economically feasible operating system. As the problems become more complex, and as the corpus becomes larger, the amount of time required for processing goes up steeply. This is a discouraging counterpoise to the pattern of growth of the information-processing technology.
- At the same time, one sees, even at this stage, many ways in which processing can be made more efficient, and one senses that there are - waiting to be discovered ways of formulating the procedure that are much more powerful than the ways thus far employed.

In short, it appears to us that the domain of question-answering systems is an intellectually deep and technologically demanding area for research and development. As suggested, there is an extremely long way to go before useful answers can be deduced from extensive information bases at reasonable cost. On the other hand, it may well be that, in this area, each basic conceptual advance will be a long stride towards the pro-cognitive systems we envision for man's future interaction with the fund of knowledge.

AN APPROACH TO COMPUTER PROCESSING OF NATURAL LANGUAGE

This final project was pursued intensively during the first year of the study, but, for reasons not related to its degree of promise, it lay dormant during the second year. Although the project does not appear to be worth continuing in its present form, the following description may prove useful. The approach selected at the outset - to try to mirror in computer programmes the ontogenetic development of the human ability to generate and understand language - was quite different from the approach, then more popular, based upon syntactic analysis. The approach adopted paid more attention to semantics than to syntax.

However, many of the investigators who earlier had concentrated on syntactic analysis have directed their efforts towards semantic analysis, and what seemed to us at the outset to be an unpopulated field is rapidly becoming crowded. That fact, together with our sharpening awareness of the very great difficulty and even greater extent of the task, account for the negativeness of our thoughts about reactivating 'Ontogeny.' At the beginning of the project, it seemed to us to be a good idea to start with 'baby talk' and to try to recapitulate, as closely as possible, the development of the human language process. Recognising the importance of the 'verbal community' in each individual's development of language process, we set up a situation in which an operator at the typewriter played the role of the verbal community and, acting as stimulator, instructor, reinforce, umpire, and protector, presided over the 'shaping up' of language behaviour in the computer.

It was necessary, of course, to provide the computer with basic structures and capabilities corresponding roughly to those that would be inherited by a human being. It was necessary also to set up some domain of discourse that would be potentially 'meaningful' to the computer, as well as to the operator, and that would provide an analogue to the 'environment' in which human beings behave and with reference to which most of their language - that is not about themselves - is oriented. One part of the internal mechanism - of the system of computer programmes - seems worth describing despite the fact that its nature does not in any direct way determine the nature of the over-all system. This part of the programme is concerned with the representation, in the computer memory, of the words and phrases communicated between the operator and the computer. In the input and output equipment, the words and phrases take the form of strings of characters or character codes.

The codes are the so-called 'concise' codes for alphanumeric characters employed in the PDP-1 computer. Each code is a pattern of six binary digits. Representation of words, phrases, and so forth, as strings of coded characters is inconvenient and uneconomical for many information-processing purposes. In a computing machine that has registers of fixed length, it is inconvenient to have words and phrases of variable length. We were at the outset not so much concerned with economy of representation as with convenience of processing, and we adopted an approach designed mainly for convenience. We represented each word, or phrase, or sentence, or string of any recognised class, by a 36-bit code. The code was made up of a 30-bit main code and 6 bits of auxiliary information, which included designation of the class to which the string belonged. A 36-bit code can be stored conveniently in two consecutive registers of the PDP-l memory. The rule for representing incoming words in the computer memory was the following. If the word consisted of five characters or fewer, the concise-code representation is the computer representation; if, on the other hand, the word contained more than five characters, then the computer representation consists of the concise codes of the first three characters, the six auxiliary bits, and, in addition, a 12-bit 'hash code' calculated by a rather complicated procedure from the concise codes of the remaining characters. This representation is capable of discriminating among about 4000 different words with the same three leading characters.

Because the calculation of the hash code is carried out by a procedure akin to the generation of 'random numbers,' one cannot be entirely sure that two different words will not yield the same code. Nevertheless, he can make the probability of a 'collision' as low as he likes by selecting a sufficiently long representation. In the initial stages of the work, we were not much concerned about accidental confusion of one word with another. Children certainly confuse words. Indeed, we were attracted by the hypothesis that some of the confusions that arise in human communication and thinking are attributable to something like a hash-code process in neural representation. The agent that converts strings of text into hash codes is, of course, a computer programme.

First it divides a string of text into words and determines a code for each word. Then it combines the words into phrases, using punctuation as a guide, and determines a hash code for each phrase from the codes for the words within the phrase. Then it determines a hash code for each sentence from the codes for the phrases within the sentence, and so forth. Thus, for each word, for each phrase, for each sentence, there is a 36-bit representation. After the conversion to this internal code has been effected, and until a stage is reached at which it is necessary to generate a response in the form of a string of alphanumeric characters, all the processing is carried out with the internal 36-bit codes. It is easy to transform alphanumeric text into internal codes. To do that, it is necessary only to apply the transformation programmes that calculate the codes. However, to transform in the other direction - to go from the internal code representation to a string of alphanumeric characters - is another matter. Because information is sometimes lost in the forward transformation, it is not possible simply to calculate the reverse transformation. It is necessary to employ a 'table-searching' procedure. However, it is certainly neither necessary nor desirable to store every string of characters received in order to have it ready to type as a response. If one is to respond in a natural way, he must be able to generate sequences of words that he has never received. Moreover, there are too many strings of words to consider storing them all in a computer memory.

The procedure adopted, therefore, is to associate with each internal word code, but not with the code for any string of any class other than word, its complete concise code, *i.e.*, the string of concise codes corresponding to the characters of the word. The association is achieved in the following way. All the internal codes, for words, phrases, sentences, and so forth, are kept together - along with other information - in a table called the 'Hash Table'. One of the entries in the Hash Table, for each word represented in that table, is the address of the register in the Vocabulary Table in which the corresponding concise-code representation begins. That makes it possible, given the internal code corresponding to a word, to find the corresponding concise code and to have the word typed on the computer typewriter.

For those internally represented strings that are not merely words, there is still another table, called the 'Sub address Table'. The entry in the Hash Table that is associated with a sentence the way the Vocabulary Table address is associated with a word, is the address of a register in the Sub address Table. At that address in the Sub address Table, one finds the beginning of a list of 'sub addresses' that are addresses of registers back in the Hash Table. In those registers in the Hash Table are the entries for strings of the next lower class. With each hash code for a phrase is associated the address of another register in the Sub address Table. Going back to the Sub address Table with that address, one finds addresses of registers in the Hash Table.

Finally, in the designated registers in the Hash Table are addresses of registers in the Vocabulary Table. In the Vocabulary Table, of course, are the concise codes of the words. The procedure just described is implemented by programming, so no effort of thought is involved after the programme has been perfected. The programme runs much more rapidly than the typewriter can type, and there is therefore no observable delay. With the system, one can start out with a 36-bit hash code and wind up with a long typewritten sentence. If the initial code is the code of a paragraph, indeed he winds up with a paragraph. We have checked the system to that level of operation. Obviously, nothing stands in the way of representing an entire book with a 36-bit internal code. However, one cannot uniquely represent the individuals of any set of sise approaching $2n$ with hash codes n bits in length.

Our selection of 36-bit codes, and our compromise in the direction of readability by man as well as by machine, was conditioned by the fact that we were working with a 'young' language mechanism that would not be expected to develop a very large vocabulary for some time. It is now doubtless evident that a description of computer programmes in ordinary language encounters serious problems of exposition and endurance. We shall, therefore, not describe the entire Ontogeny programme in as great detail. Let us, nevertheless, explain how the system is designed to keep track of the properties of the various words and phrases and the entities and operations for which they stand. The repository for factual information, in Ontogeny, is a table called the 'Property Table.' One of the entries in each section of the Hash Table is the address of a corresponding section in the Property Table. For convenience, the Property Table records the corresponding Hash Table address and also the internal code of the string with which the properties are associated. The properties themselves are represented by internal codes. When it is necessary to determine the meanings of the property codes, one has to find the codes in the Hash Table and go on from there in the way just described. The structure within which properties are represented in the Property Table is a simple hierarchy, an 'outline.'

The rules for listing properties are loose. In the main, they were made up as problems arose, and indeed a certain amount of care was taken *not* to create a sharp, formal, rigid system. Syntactic and semantic properties are mixed indiscriminately. In the basic system, there is not even any distinction between the symbol and the thing for which it stands. That is to say, under 'table' we might record the property of being used mainly as a noun, the property of being used sometimes as a verb, and the property of usually being made of wood. However, the system would be expected to function without great difficulty if, through happenstance, the arrangement were set up as:

We did not reach the point at which programmes actually operated with that kind of irregularity of format, but we did have search programmes that examined the 'next level down' if they did not find a satisfactory property on the level initially assigned.

From the description thus far, it may be evident that the Property Table is, by nature, full of circular definitions. Everything is defined in terms of something else - except for a relatively few primitives that are associated with subroutines. One of the properties of 'move,' for example, is that move is often used as a verb. Another is that, when it is so used, it is to be implemented by executing a subroutine that is capable of taking arguments that answer 'what', 'by whom', 'from where', and 'to where'. Some of the properties of 'pencil' refer to its capability of serving as an argument. A pencil is 'movable', 'takable', 'bringable', and so forth. We are now almost in a position to turn our attention to the procedure through which an incoming message is processed and responded to by the computer. One more part of the system must be described, however, before that can be done conveniently.

This remaining part is the one that has to do with the 'domain of discourse' mentioned earlier. The domain of discourse is a model room equipped with a few items of furniture. The room has a door that can be opened to various degrees, a window that can be opened or closed, a table that can occupy any otherwise unoccupied position within the room, and a chair subject to the same constraint. There are a book and a pencil, to be manipulated, an active agent called 'Comp', and another active agent called 'Oper'. The discourse involves Comp and Oper and is actually carried out by the computer and the operator. The room and its contents are represented in the computer memory, of course, and they are also represented diagrammatically by simple line drawings on the screen of the oscilloscope. When the door is opened, the representation of the door in the computer memory changes, and the schematic door on the oscilloscope screen swings. The basic subroutines, corresponding to operations in the domain of discourse, are implementations of 'move', 'go', 'carry', 'bring', 'open', 'close', 'put', etc. These subroutines, together with the subroutines that handle the encoding and decoding, the search for properties and the analysis of input messages, were all that we actually prepared and operated. The plan encompassed two additional classes of subroutines. The first of these was to handle the addition, deletion and modification of properties, under the control of input messages.

The second was to handle the addition and modification of subroutines, again under the control of input messages. If we had been able to carry through to some accomplishments in the first additional category, we should have been able to increase the verbal capability of the system, but only by adding to its knowledge - to its vocabulary and its fund of facts. If we had been able to move on into the second additional category, we should have had within our grasp the capability of achieving almost unlimited restructuring and reorganisation of the system. But we did not accomplish either of those things, and we mention them here only to indicate that the approach had a higher aspiration than merely to move line diagrams about on the screen of an oscilloscope. Now, at last, we come to the procedure employed in analysing the incoming messages and selecting and directing the actions taken in response to them.

The responses were, as suggested earlier, to move things about in the room, to make replies by way of the typewriter, and - in hope but not in actuality - to add to the internally stored knowledge and to the internally stored behaviour patterns. By knowledge, of course, we mean the contents of the several tables mentioned earlier. By behaviour patterns, we mean the set of subroutines available for use in responding. The problem of interpreting an incoming message is, in the approach we have been describing, to select the appropriate subroutine or patterns of subroutines and to find the arguments that they require under the prevailing circumstances. The selection of subroutines is guided by associating subroutines with verbs. The search is carried out by a part of the programme that examines the internal codes that represent the incoming message and a list of roles that the message segments may play. Records are kept in a matrix during the processing of a message. The rows of the matrix are associated with the words of the incoming message.

The columns of the matrix are associated with the possible roles. In the version of Ontogeny that was carried to the point of demonstration, the processing deals only with words. The first step is to look up each word of the incoming message in the Property Table and place a tally in each cell of the matrix that corresponds to a function that the word can fulfil. When this has been done for all the words of the message, the task becomes one of finding an appropriate and consistent assignment of words to functions and, at the same time, a correspondence between the functions and the argument requirements of a subroutine that goes with the verb. The procedure used to carry out this task starts by 'freesing' the rows and columns of the matrix that contain only a single tally. The next step is to prepare simpler matrix patterns in which each of the words at first associated with two or more roles is assigned to a single role. These simpler matrixes are then considered one at a time.

The subroutines corresponding to the word assigned to the verb category in the first simplified matrix are examined. If one of them has a set of argument requirements that match the roles to which words are assigned, then that subroutine is selected, the arguments are supplied to it, and the response is executed. In an effort to get the system into operation quickly, we satisfied ourselves with the first subroutine that met the requirements. If no subroutine met the requirements of the first assignment pattern, the second assignment pattern was used, and so on. As soon as a suitable subroutine was found, supplied with arguments, and executed, the response was considered accomplished. The programme then simply went into a 'listening' mode and waited for the operator to take the next step.

Towards the end of the work on Ontogeny, we were planning a set of subroutines that would operate on higher-echelon strings than words. With this set of subroutines, there was to be associated a subsystem for keeping track, in a primitive way, of the 'situation.' The system was to be capable of asking, on receipt of a message, 'Am I already familiar with this message in this context?' If so, it was to enquire of itself what response it had previously made and how effective the response had been.

If the result had been sufficiently favourable, then-the system would simply have made the same response again and taken notes on its effect. In the likely event that no record existed of previous experience with the over-all message in the prevailing context, then the projected system would work with lower-echelon segments of the message, hoping to find that one or more of them was already 'understood.'

In the absence of usable prior experience at each echelon, the system would drop down to the next-lower echelon until it finally came to words. Failing to understand a word, or failing to understand a phrase given experience with the words of the phrase, it would ask for help. Our experience with Ontogeny left us with five main impressions:

- It seems possible, and even likely, that we could store up enough substantive information in a computer memory to handle the analysis of natural language - semantic as well as syntactic - an analysis capable of supporting 'reasonable' responses, if only the domain of discourse is not very wide.

- It is probably more important to limit the domain of discourse than to limit the length or complexity of the input messages.
- Many so-called semantic properties play roles that are almost indistinguishable from syntactic roles. The distinction between things that are capable of acting with initiative as voluntary agents and things that are not, for example, seems to be approximately as important as the distinction between the active voice and the passive voice of verbs.
- A sympathetic, cooperative, verbal, community is a fundamental essential for the development of a sophisticated verbal mechanism. To develop complex language behaviour in a neutral environment would, we think, take another long-suffering recapitulation of evolution.
- On the other hand, no one seems likely to design or invent a formal system capable of automating sophisticated language behaviour.

The best approach, therefore, seems to us to be somewhere between the extremes - to call for a formal base plus an overlay of experience gained in interaction with the cooperative verbal community.

5

Technology of Academic and Research Library Science

The application of computing to library work in India has a history of at least three decades because since the time the computer entered premier academic institutions and selected R & D facilities, it has been explored for improving information processing and management routines. *Information technology* (IT) enriched library services arrived initially for *science and technology* (S&T) information handling and for the special libraries attached to *research and development* (R&D) centres and academic libraries in higher education institutions.

In comparison to other libraries, academic and research libraries have better infrastructure and skilled manpower in greater numbers, making them able to offer information services comparable to advanced countries. Like qualified teaching and research personnel and well-equipped laboratories, the right information service is another vital element in the trinity which completes a fruitful academic or research environment.

MARKET-DRIVEN COLLABORATION

Academic and research libraries, especially in developing countries, are passing through a very challenging phase in their existence due to unfriendly trends in the emerging information market. On the one hand, these libraries are still left with many of the old problems such as poor budgetary support and weak infrastructure, as well as staff in fewer numbers and often with less expertise. But the new information marketing techniques, like the possibilities of delivering and accessing electronic information in diverse channels, force these libraries to be very vigilant and cautious in their approach towards information acquisition and services. Libraries and professionals in India were quick to understand the emerging information environment was forcing their users to depend largely on those resources, which are becoming more expensive day by day due to the rise in production costs, fall in subscriptions and inflationary trends of Indian currency.

When individual libraries found that alone they are not in a position to satisfy the information requirements of their clients, they formulated various collaborative arrangements with other libraries such as,

- *Interlibrary loan* (ILL) services,
- *Document delivery services* (DDS),
- Resource-sharing, and
- Consortia-based subscriptions.

PRESENT PRACTICES AND EMERGING GOALS

The special libraries attached to research and higher education were lucky enough to garner resources to automate their in-house routine operations and for hosting online public access catalogues (OPACs); some of them also set up facilities to search electronic databases. A few of them evolved the desired infrastructure for Internet surfing, for hosting of full-text database access, and for setting up digital libraries. The major advantage of the progress in computerization is a considerable increase in the amount of information available online. We have experienced that at the start of computer applications only the surrogates (metadata) existed online, but some full-text content has been made accessible online in recent years.

These libraries are experiencing the virtues of electronic information in different forms such as e-journals, e-books, bibliographic/full-text electronic databases on CD-ROMs and through Web access. Due to publishers' 'electronic plus' policies, libraries are able to access electronic versions of printed sources such as journals either for free or by paying an additional fee. However the goal these libraries in specialized research and academic centres should have set for themselves is to enhance their information facilities to fully functional digital libraries, comparable with similar facilities in the developed countries.

CULTURES AND CONFLICTS FACED BY LIBRARIES

The fixed roles suggested by Levy for researchers, publishers and libraries are either overlapping or changing in the electronic scene. There are cases where an author or a library is acting as electronic publisher, and there are publishers providing a wide variety of information packages beyond the contents of printed journals.

The real question is: has the library really lost ground in the emerging information scene? Even the critics will not say so. The concerns expressed are only to revitalize the professional skills of librarians, rejuvenate the style of working and reorient the library towards its rightful place in effective dissemination of information. Maybe the common feeling that the library is a central place in the institution visited everyday by large numbers of users, like any public utility, has lost some ground in the electronic scene. Nonetheless, apart the continuing provision of information services for print sources, the electronic revolution has reaffirmed the library more as an information service and access centre than as an information storehouse.

TECHNOLOGY SYSTEMS AND THE PROFESSIONALS

With the advent of the information age and the radical change in library materials, media and means of access to information, the nature of certain types of building systems have changed accordingly. The most dramatic of these changes was the evolution of building communications and its associated equipment into the broad category of technology systems.

Technology systems in a building now encompass any digital device, digital media, routing devices, operating systems, digital networks and servers, audio-visual systems, cabling systems and digital wireless devices, that are used to provide access to sources of digital information, modify that information, or even create information. The technology infrastructure is the name usually given to the equipment, the control and operating subsystems, the network connections, and the cabling of the total technology system as it resides in the building.

The building's technology infrastructure is connected to utility services outside the building, such as telephone or cable service; this incoming service is referred to as the technology utility.

The technology infrastructure in a building continues to evolve in complexity and in its features and characteristics, and a new type of design professional has emerged with the type of expertise required to analyze, plan and design the technology system and its infrastructure. The technology consultant must not only be an expert in state-of-the-art technology systems, but must also be capable of anticipating the directions of development of new technologies as well as understand the physical interaction of components of the system with users and with the building.

In the past, because of the simplicity of the communication system and its similarity with electric power systems, the consulting electrical engineer provided the basic design of this system for the building. Given the critical importance today of a well-designed technology infrastructure for the functioning of the library building for its primary use, the expertise of a technology consultant is now required as part of any library design team to bring both technical knowledge about advanced systems as well as planning and coordination to the total design process.

The technology consultant may be part of the electrical engineering team, or may be an independent consultant coordinating with the architect and the other engineering disciplines. The role of the technology consultant in library design is now as important as that of the electrical engineer or the HVAC engineer. The technology consultant's specific scope of work may include:

- Structured wiring system design (cabling) supporting the technology infrastructure.
- The design of distribution facilities housing the technology equipment (*e.g.*, telephony PBX, voicemail system, voice-over-IP equipment, data network switches, routers, servers, etc.) and cable conveyance infrastructure elements supporting network and device interconnectivity throughout the building.
- Audio/visual systems design for multimedia presentations and information display.
- Voice, data, and video network design and configuration.
- Telecommunications utility services connections (*e.g.*, high-speed Internet service, DSL, T1 lines, etc.).
- Universal control system design, interconnecting voice, data, and video network equipment with other technology system components such as audio/visual, security, information retrieval and systems, and even lighting controls.

The technology consultant can also provide valuable information to the architectural design team during both the development of the design programme and the initial space planning. Determining the appropriate characteristics and features of the technology system for library patrons and staff is an important element in the proper implementation of technology in a modern library building.

TECHNOLOGY SYSTEM PLANNING

A Building Programme is a document that outlines the expectations and design criteria for the building project. As such, the document provides a wealth of design information to be used and re-evaluated during the planning and design process. In addition to covering collections, services, and support requirements, the building programme will also typically address specific facility requirements, and should include a comprehensive plan for the technology systems and infrastructure, or a Technology Plan.

Just as a collection development policy identifies goals for the number of reference volumes, current periodicals or audio books, a technology plan is also a key component to the process.

The technology plan should address the library in the context of a larger technology plan, if one exists for the city or other jurisdiction. It should consider the library's relationship to any cooperative or consortium that may exist, as well as the general global context of how information will be managed and delivered in the digital world. The Technology Plan can address issues and state intentions in a number of ways:

- By stating certain assumptions, such as "an increasingly higher percentage of the population will own laptop portable computers or other Internet information appliances in the near future".

- By setting general conditions for the library project, such as requiring all areas of the library to have library network access.
- By stating specific criteria or objectives, such as the requirement that the library network be wireless to the fullest extent possible.
- By setting a specific number of public workstations.
- By allocating a specific percentage of the acquisitions budget to electronic resources.
- By setting goals for instruction and training programmes.
- By making determinations about delivering print from digital sources.

At the very least, the Technology Plan will set forth the technology goals in the delivery of library services, and will develop a schedule and budget for acquisition and replacement of hardware and software required to meet these goals.

THE TECHNOLOGY UTILITY

The options and requirements for incoming communications service, or the technology utility, have changed as technology has developed. The technology utility now includes telephone, data, video, modem and fax lines, CATV, alarm systems, and Internet service. Voice service is available through a connection from a local phone service provider. This includes the copper trunk lines for analog circuits, which support incoming and outgoing telephone calls. Besides being used for voice applications, analog circuits are also used for modems and faxes. When considering voice service, provision must be made for both local and long distance calls. If the anticipated volume of long distance calls is high, then separate circuits for long distance can be more cost effective.

Voice lines can also support data and Internet services, although as bandwidth requirements increase this source of service is rapidly becoming obsolete. Fortunately, there are now many choices for high-speed data and Internet services that use dedicated lines. High-speed connections include DS3 (or T3), T1, DSL, and ISDN services. Recently, coaxial cable (typically used for CATV service) and small satellite antennae (dishes) have been used to deliver high-speed data services. Television and closed-circuit video services (*e.g.*, distance-learning, video conferencing) can be provided to modern buildings over a variety of transmission systems, including high-speed dedicated lines such as T1, CATV-type coaxial cable, fibre-optic cabling, and satellite antenna systems.

TECHNOLOGY CABLE DISTRIBUTION METHODS

Vertical Backbone (Riser) Distribution

Intra-building pathways are used to interconnect the service entrance, main equipment room, MDF and any IDFs that may exist as part of the infrastructure design. The interconnecting cable media required is typically referred to as riser cable. Generally, this riser cabling is categorized as part of the "vertical" distribution system within a building. However, this vertical distribution system in many cases may actually run in horizontal pathways, depending upon the building architecture and cable plant topology. In situations where distribution rooms are stacked, the vertical pathways may be conduit sleeves in the floor decks. The installation of these sleeves should be such that a minimum of one spare sleeve is provided within each distribution room. Where distribution rooms are horizontally separated, conduit runs, cable trays, or hanger systems may be used as the pathway for cable conveyance. If conduit is used in a horizontal run, large-radius (36" minimum) sweep bends are required and no more than two 90-degree bends are to be allowed between pull boxes in a run.

HORIZONTAL DISTRIBUTION

The horizontal pathways connect the distribution rooms to the actual outlets. These are the most heavily used pathways in the system. Horizontal pathways may have multiple sections that are not truly "horizontal." In a small building, all outlets on all floors may be served from one closet on one floor. There are a significant number of methods available for horizontal cable conveyance, which vary substantially in price and serviceability. This is typically an area that is overlooked, insufficiently budgeted, and/or under-designed for future cabling upgrades.

Cable Tray

Cable tray is widely used within modern communications cabling infrastructure, and is the preferred method of conveyance both exterior and interior to the distribution room. The type of cable tray selected depends upon the area of application.

In-Room Cable Tray

Tray within the various equipment and distribution rooms must convey the various OSP and ISP building cabling to the patch bays and must facilitate cable management of temporary patch cords and cross-connect wiring. This product allows cables to be easily "hooked" over the tines, which facilitates the frequent changes associated with patching and cross-connects.

Cable Tray Outside the Distribution Room

The preferred method for main arterial distribution (*e.g.*, corridors, main cable runs) within accessible ceiling spaces is cable tray. Cable tray should be sized per NEC requirements for 50 per cent cable fill. Product used in this application should provide semi-continuous supports for the cable and have built-in sidewalls. Ventilated-bottom trays are best for this application because they combine low weight with the ability to have cable pulled through after the initial installation has been completed. Ladder-type trays are not recommended for in-ceiling use as cable can "snag" on the rungs during installation. Also, subsequent cable installation attempted by pulling through the tray is not facilitated by ladder tray.

"Hanger" Cable Support Systems

A less expensive alternative to cable tray is the use of "J"-shaped hangers known as J-hooks. To ensure that cable is properly supported without kinks or danger of cuts or snags, the J-hook should have wide bearing surfaces (1 inch or more) and rolled edges. There are also several types of cable slings or "saddles" manufactured for communications cable conveyance. The saddles are made with a large metal plate that has rolled edges in the direction of cable flow. These devices can be attached to the building structure using various hanger-wire or rod support devices. The slings are similar in design to the saddles, but are treated with fire retardant, plenum-rated cloth. Slings may also be opened and closed many times.

Floor Duct System

Floor duct systems are a network, or grid, of metal raceways with channels that can accommodate both electrical wiring and technology cable. The ducts are cast into and embedded in concrete floor, which allows horizontal distribution of the wiring and cables. The system allows a certain amount of flexibility for cable installation in open areas. Because of the construction technique, this distribution method can be considered only for new construction. The advantages of using floor ducts are the mechanical protection it provides for cables, a certain amount of power and data outlet layout flexibility and increased security. The major disadvantage of the floor duct system is its high initial cost of installation. The system is not supportive of furniture layouts that are subject to frequent changes, as an existing access point cannot be moved to a new location off of the original grid. Also, the limited volume of space within the ducts leads to packing of the raceways as cabling systems change and a large quantity of cable is left behind and abandoned in the floor system.

Raised Access Floor System

Distribution of cables can also be accomplished through various types of Raised Access Floor System. The low-profile type is usually 3" - 4" high and is used for cable and electrical wiring distribution. The relative cost of the low-profile system is high. In recent years, great success has been achieved at providing the high flexibility of raised access floor systems at low or no additional cost compared to other systems, by utilizing a high framing system, minimum 14" to 18", and supplying air through this plenum. The elimination of conventional overhead air ductwork, plus the high energy efficiency of this method of heating and cooling, combine to produce a total system that is often less expensive than typical building infrastructure systems.

The high flexibility comes about through the ease of changing cabling and wiring under the raised floor to service new or changed locations, and also because of the integral outlet boxes and air diffusers built into the 24" X 24" floor panels. To move either a data or power outlet location, the floor panel is simply moved to the desired location. Similarly, if air supply is required in a new location, a floor panel with a built-in air diffuser can be placed there and the pressurized plenum below causes air to be delivered at the design air conditions.

The architectural benefit of the raised floor plenum system is that the ceiling area above can be clear of wires, conduit and air ducts, eliminating the need for conventional ceilings and allowing the use of glare-free indirect lighting and higher spaces.

WIRELESS ALTERNATIVES FOR DATA APPLICATIONS

The increase in the use of laptop computers and the change in work and study practices have fuelled the demand for wireless networks. These wireless networks are a natural complement to fixed wired systems in most libraries, allowing "un-tethered" access to library and Internet resources. A wireless LAN (WLAN) is just like a wired LAN, with the cable replaced by a radio signal. It allows a patron to have access to networks and "real-time" information while roaming around the library. Wireless networks are evolving rapidly, as are the standards that govern transmission over these networks. These standards and the associated technology evolution have significant impact on the design and deployment of WLAN's within a library building.

Deployment TOpology

Wireless networks require the deployment of Wireless Access Points (WAPs) throughout the desired coverage area. The WAPs are connected to a local IDF via a standard data cable (CAT6) facilitating interconnection with the Ethernet switch electronics located within the IDF. All WAPs require power, provided either through the data cable or via an electrical receptacle installed at the WAP location. This power requirement places further demands on the infrastructure design supporting WLAN technology, since the exact locations of WAP's are very difficult to determine during the design phase of a project. Each WAP has a specific coverage pattern (or area of coverage) beyond which connection to the network is lost, much like a cell phone. This coverage area is a 150 foot radius from the WAP location. However, the actual coverage may be significantly less than this 150-foot maximum due to interference from physical building construction and/or other electronic devices that may be transmitting in the same frequency spectrum as that of the WLAN (2.4 GHz, typically). A good rule-of-thumb is to plan for access deployment using a practical 50-foot radius coverage range from the WAP location. However, final placement of WAP's should be determined in conjunction with a radio frequency spectrum study completed on site when the building construction has been substantially completed.

Whenever possible, it is desirable to deploy WAP technology that utilizes power over the data cable, in lieu of installing an electrical receptacle at the WAP location. When considering Power over Ethernet (POE) it is important to allocate additional power within the distribution facilities (MDF and IDFs) since the network equipment that provides power to the WAPs over the connecting data cable will contain much larger power supplies. It is not unusual for the POE-capable network equipment to require dual 30A, 208V, single-phase circuits.

Advantages

A wireless LAN within a building or campus allows rapid deployment and support for mobile personnel. The mobility that wireless networks allow also eases management requirements because stations can be deployed where the data is generated.

Wireless LANs can be cost effective when compared to fully wired networks, and can often reduce cost by eliminating the need for installed outlet hardware.

Disadvantages

The major disadvantage is restricted bandwidth when compared to traditional wired networks. Technology utilization that is dependent on wire speed network connectivity (*e.g.*, streaming video, high-end graphics applications, etc.) cannot be effectively supported over a WLAN at this time.

However, research and development activity is expected to produce wider bandwidth capability in the near future. The WLAN can also be difficult to integrate seamlessly with wired technologies and is not as scalable or as secure as the wired networks.

TECHNOLOGY-ENHANCED LIBRARY SERVICES

TECHNOLOGY ADVANCES

The major technology breakthroughs in the context of libraries include:

- Advent of printing press and mass production of printed documents enabled democratization of information. Libraries had a major role in the print era, as no one can own a large number of books on a particular subject whereas libraries by their very purpose concentrated on doing so.

- Microforms helped to preserve less used information in a compact space and as a smoother delivery option for voluminous sources. Libraries had their unchallenged role even in the microform era as the special purpose readers for microfilms and microfiche were costly and exclusively housed in the library.
- The economical and affordable copying technology revolutionized the concept of information use as it spearheaded the trend of owning copies of relevant portions of library resources. The copying technology freed the user from sitting in the library for long duration for reading, since one can simply get a copy quickly and leave.
- Computing is the biggest technology revolution so far, as it is a major enabler in the information dissemination chain; also it is not a stand-alone technology unlike earlier technologies and can be networked and integrated with a whole lot of other devices and technologies. It not only revolutionized the production of books and microforms but also brought the arrival of online and CD-ROM databases, electronic information resources, Internet and the digital revolution.

PRODUCTS AND SERVICES

Adapting IT for library applications is an ongoing process, right from procuring or developing IT enabled information products through computer aided processing and management to delivering IT-enriched services. Library professionals in India are already exposed to the different offshoots of IT for library organization and information services.

LIBRARY AUTOMATION PACKAGES

The availability of a wide variety of library automation software to suit the varied needs of libraries themselves is a reflection of the progress libraries have made in automating the operations of procuring, processing and providing information sources. Procurement is the end of the story for many other software/databases used in a library, whereas library automation systems will open a floodgate of issues.

What the vendor provides is a structure to build information concerning the collection and users, to conduct various aspects of organizing the collection and offering information services. Thus software needs to be evaluated for its suitability for the target library before purchase. This may include case studies from other libraries using the software, evaluation of hardware and operating system required, computer awareness among staff and users, network as well as computer infrastructure in the institution, and above all estimation of cost and charges for after-sales support. Using suitable software for library automation will significantly reduce manual operations and enable professionals to dedicate more time for professional jobs.

CD-ROM AND ELECTRONIC DATABASES

Due to the poor communication infrastructure prevalent in India and to the immense costs involved, online database services were used only by few institutions. The distribution of the same content of online data repositories subsequently in CD-ROMs made it affordable to a larger number of institutions. While the library automation package gave search-and access facility to information sources present in the local collection, CD-ROM databases attempted consolidated access irrespective of holdings to the bibliographic data of publications in a discipline.

CD-ROM databases have also freed library professionals from conducting searches and allowed the end user to conduct the searches. CD-ROM is so common nowadays that a library holds a good number of them not only for bibliographic, numeric and full-text databases, but also those received along with printed books and other reference sources. Managing and serving these high capacity discs was a problem earlier due to the stand-alone software required, whereas the onset of networking and hard-disk cached solutions provides an effective and functional way to enable access to them through the intranet.

WEB

Since the 1990s, the Internet has changed the dissemination of information, such as electronic copies of traditional paper-based journals and conference proceedings, free electronic-only refereed journals, haphazard copies of all kinds of material on home pages and a handful of electronic preprints archives. Most libraries in India now have a web site and they use the site to present the basic strengths of the library and to host services such as the OPAC and Web access to electronic information.

The 'size of the catalogue card' and the field lengths of primitive database technology are surpassed in the Web era. Types of information resources on the Web also vary from authentic primary information about the latest research results to ephemeral product catalogues. Issues worth consideration are often the content of the sites that are deleted, modified or changed to new machines without proper redirection and the extraction mechanism through search engines, when a flood of sources is retrieved against a query, of which few are relevant. The Internet and Web demonstrate that a large amount of electronic information can be hosted in a decentralized fashion in a cost-effective manner. The Web has also freed the user's dependence on library resources for finding information related to address and contact details of a person/institution, contents pages of books, journals, etc.

As far as possible, especially for reference and information services, looking at the Web has become an innovative trend in the reference service to complement dated print sources. Many publishers visibly feel the benefits and reach of the Web, and have considered it as an alternate medium for delivering information sources; some publishers even permit unrestricted access of tables of contents and abstracts of their primary journals. As a result of these initiatives, the 'print and distribute' paradigm is challenged by 'distribute and print' paradigm.

CONSORTIAL LICENCES

The term 'consortial licences' designates library groupings to negotiate access rights to electronic information with publishers and vendors aiming at enhanced access to more resources at better pricing. "Consortia can be a means to introduce products to a previously untapped market" for vendors and "consortia provide shared expertise, access to new electronic and print resources, professional development, new sources of funds, and safety in numbers" for libraries. In contrast to earlier library collaborative arrangements such as ILL and resource sharing, the publisher and trade community are parties in the consortial agreements.

In resource-sharing, libraries concentrate on collaborative subscriptions by avoiding duplication, where as in consortial licenses, the emphasis is to strike the 'best deals' even if the library suffers some duplication. The publisher community experience is that increased subscription costs lead to a reduction in the total number of subscriptions, further raising the subscription cost every year. Publishers also found it difficult to enforce ownership rights with electronic sources, even after adopting the latest technology tools and forcing libraries to sign the toughest of the legal clauses.

The good marketing wisdom of the publisher and trade community prevailed to open up information access rights through consortial licenses for a large part of the product spectrum to at least those libraries or groups of libraries which procure products beyond a certain threshold value. The *Indian National Digital Library in Engineering Science and Technology* (INDEST) is the first and the major consortium in India. It is under the aegis of the *Ministry of Human Resource Development* (MHRD). Before the creation of the consortium, access to electronic journals in these institutions remained at 60 per cent of subscribed titles, but the number of online journals has increased 10 times after the establishment of the consortium.

The rates for access offered to the consortium are lower by 50 per cent to 90 per cent depending upon the category of institution and the consortium paid only 11 per cent of the list price to access these resources. Info net, another consortium, floated by the *University Grants Commission* (UGC) for Universities, is also gaining strength. Similar consortia are also operational for research institutions under the Council of Scientific and Industrial Research (CSIR) and the Department of Atomic Energy (DAE).

DIGITAL LIBRARIES

Libraries in India are engaged in the development of prototypes of digital information resources, as influenced by developments in other countries. There are certain types of content which lie inaccessible or less used in their present physical forms that can be put to more visible and enhanced use through digitization. Also heavily used content presently available in limited numbers of copies can be identified for conversion to electronic format. The linear text in many of the print sources presents difficulties for providing a hypertext approach or a multimedia feeling, for simulating learning by doing; sustaining attention and interest for long duration calls for using electronic technologies to enable content to be more functional.

The static content in printed sources fails to attract users who are increasingly exposed to the widely appealing features of broadcasting and IT-intensive presentation tools. Multimedia-enabled digital information will be useful to a large percentage of illiterate and older population also. There are cases such as papers in journals and conferences in print form that never get their deserved visibility and often end up with out reaching the target population. The digital dissemination of this content may lead to very effective teaching and more focused research in most areas.

To demonstrate the efficacy of digital libraries and collections, libraries must be able to identify materials in the public domain, sources generated in-house, and similar materials to overcome the constraints of copyright. Digital library (DL) development needs a two pronged strategy to digitize local content as well as to devise options for providing access to external resources obtained as free or as part of existing subscriptions or access licenses. The typical academic or research library in-house digital library on an Intranet must include the following components:

- Consortial access to electronic journals and electronic databases;
- Free/paid Web access to journals subscribed in print format;
- Subject gateways and virtual libraries;
- Free/paid e-books from publishers and portals;
- Intranet access to bibliographic and full-text databases, and CD-ROM publications;
- Local archiving of free and paid e-books;
- LAN serving of e-supplements of purchased books;
- In-house digitization of copyright-owned and copyright- free printed books in the collection;
- Born-digital in-house publications such as research reports, annual reports, convocation reports, teaching materials, theses and

dissertations, in-house journals, proceedings of conferences, seminars, workshops, etc., conducted by the institution;

- Preprints and post-prints of research papers sent for publication to journals, conferences, and books, especially with respect to the Open Archives Initiative gaining ground to provide further access to research published in toll journals and to make the results of publicly funded research available to those who need them;
- Publications in the public domain, such as government publications, publications from non-profit institutions, etc.

But many libraries are unable to provide these components due to lack of awareness or due to the hurdles invariably faced by libraries in India. The lack of interest on the part of parent institutions and the absence of action plans or priorities is the major hindrance. Though computer and communication infrastructure is improving, their availability for information work is not appreciated in many organizations. Paschoud commented how several of the speakers and many of the delegates at the International Conference on Digital Libraries (ICDL) 2004 conference in New Delhi focussed on addressing what most European libraries would consider very basic issues such as network/ Internet connectivity and management.

Even in places where infrastructure is available, there is an acute shortage of competent labour to take up the task of digitizing local content and evolving digital information repositories. The students, faculty, curriculum and training methodology at the disposal of library schools have to be improved visibly to meet this challenge. Coupled with this is the need for continuing education for retraining the working professionals. Institutions, individuals, or private publishers have rights over content, and motivating them to ease these rights when they are not inclined towards digitization is not a simple task. Levying charges for access is a distant proposition; instead sponsorships from institutions, government bodies and library suppliers can be explored.

Even when hosted as a free facility, enough security mechanisms must be evolved to prevent any trespassing by hackers. Selecting useful content requires careful review and evaluation by subject experts, as digitization will only help to preserve the record, and not its enhanced and continued access. Internet bandwidth in India has to be sufficiently augmented to allow faster access to Web content as more content is being hosted on the Web. The different funding agencies, research councils and institutions are not currently offering monetary support to the desired extent for digital library development.

TECHNOLOGY AND SUPPORTING FORMAT IN LIBRARY SCIENCE

The Dr A P J Abdul Kalam, President of India, International Conference on Digital Libraries: Knowledge creation, preservation, access, and management on 24-27 February 2004 keynote address conclusion, said that Digital Library is a national mission. We should see that all the schools, colleges, and universities digitize their libraries in their own native languages and connect to the outside world within 4 years. We have to ensure availability of fibre optic cables, satellite communication and wireless infrastructure especially in remote areas. It is also essential to realize high bandwidth technology like Multiple 10 Giga Bits connectivity across the country. The topic of " Digital Libraries" is currently the subject of world wide debate and research. To some simply suggests " Computerization of traditional libraries" to others, who have studied library science it calls for carrying out the function of libraries in a new way encompassing new types of information resources, new approaches to acquisition, new methods of storage and preservation, new approaches to classification and cataloguing, new modes of interaction with and for patrons more reliance on electronic system and networks and dramatic shifts in intellectual organizational and economic practices.

The handling and use of rare books, fragile books and non-book materials are not new problems to libraries. In recent years libraries are acquiring non-book materials and have been developing special collections at an accelerated rate. As a result of this many university libraries have established a separate unit of special collection. This collection covers rare-books, maps, manuscripts, pamphlets, posters, broadsides, newspapers, musics, non-musical recordings, micro facsimile, microfilms, university archives, slides and films, book plates, pictures, painting, graphic materials, coins and currency, stamps, little magazines, clipping files. Etc.

NEEDS FOR DIGITIZATION

Most of India's ancient manuscripts were written on bhurj patras. Ancient India was well developed in the subjects like Astronomy, Mathematics, Space Science, Medicine, Defiance, Political System, Economics, etc. Unfortunately many of these valuable manuscripts were lost due to improper care. Some of them were destroyed due to water, fungus, fire and som were purposely destroyed by foreign invaders. Book is one of the medium which deal with comprehensive knowledge and information. Preserving the books and other reading materials is a burning question which the librarians of past and present are facing. Therefore, it is urgently needed to find out some permanent solutions to preserve the library materials.

OBJECTIVES

The main objectives of the digital library are:

- To capture, store, manipulate and distribute information,
- To introduce and provide new services,
- To provide need-based and retrospective search services to the user,

- To have large number of database in CDs'
- To avoid routine and redundant activities,
- To provide facility for networking and resource sharing,
- To access national and international journals which are being published only in machinereadable form,
- To digitize the documents for preservation and for space saving,
- To support library functions such as circulation, serial control, acquisition control, stock maintenance and other routine office works and developing in house database, and
- To improve the cost effectiveness of library operations.

COMPONENTS

Digital libraries require well-tested and proven information technologies including the multimedia kit. Much of the work in digital libraries is achieved through E-mail service, by participating in Usernet, by accessing the database or servers through network, little Internet. Locally developed databases will contribute a lot to develop digital libraries. In other words, the components of digital libraries are:

- Data-Technical Data: This consist of books and journals stored in digital form in a computer disk store. These are two ways to storing this information. One way is to photograph a page and Scan the image with a scanner. This form of storage is called a bit mapped form. It is practical way of storing old manuscripts, texts and journals. The practical way of storing old manuscripts, texts and journals. The image of the page may be retrieved and displayed on the video screen of the computer. The other way of storing a text is to present each character by its ASCII Code.
- Numeric Data: Consist of tables of various types such as physical property data of various materials from experiments, astronomical table's, etc. Such numeric data stored digitally may be used by curve setting programmer spreadsheet programmes, etc.
- Graphic Data: May be photographs, maps, drawings, etc. The simple way of storing such data is to scan the image and store it as a bit patterns. Data should in this form eases retrieval.
- Photographs: Colour and Monochrome are stored in bit mapped form using compression algorithms to reduce storage space.
- Audio-Data: Autio-data is digitized compressed using a commonly accepted standard comprehension algorithms and stored. A musical scores may also be coded and stored with Audiodata.
- Video Data: Audio-data is digitized compressed using a commonly accepted standard comprehension algorithms and stored. A musical scores may also be coded and stored with Audio-data.

- Indexing: Indexing and inter-linking multimedia data is extremely import and for ease of retrieval. Keywords in textual documents are selected and linked to related words with logical links by appropriate software. This is called hypertext. For materials on other media also related elements are selected and linked in what is known as hypermedia.
- Linking: The information collection of the digital library will normally not be stored in one computer. It will be distributed in may computers known as servers. All these servers will be linked by highspeed communication links. The fact that the information in the digital library is distributed need not to be known to a user as it is not relevant from his/her point of view. A user gets easy access to the information based on his/her request regardless of its geographical location.
- User: Access the library from anywhere using a terminal or a computer connected to the network to which the information servers of the library are connected.

TECHNOLOGY

Until recently, not many people were happy to read from a computer screen. Quality of display was one of the factors behind it. Recent advances in the field of Information technology have improved not only the quality of computer display but also the font displayed on them. Besides, a variety of software are now available which are capable of manipulating and rendering information.

Personal computers are getting cheaper and cheaper not only in the developed countries, out are also available at an affordable cost in the developing countries. With the availability of computers, capable of computing at a very high speed and having large disc storage space, it is feasible to digitize and store information in the form of high quality graphics, colour images, voice signals and video clips at a low cost.

HARDWARE OF DIGITAZATION

In the early years of computing, computers were so expensive that it was difficult to purchase by libraries. Today, computers are cheap and middle-sized libraries in India are having computers. Apart from this, in the past, lack of hardware and absence of proper technology was also a hindrance in creating a digital library. In the present time, however, we have many hardware equipments available for digitization process. Some of these are mentioned below:

- Flatbed Scanner: Till today, the flatbed scanner is probably the most common piece of equipment available having compatibility with any personal computer. The scanner has a glass plate onto which the source document is laid face-down. The *charged coupled device* (CCD), which allows to convert analog to digital, moves beneath the surface of glass and records the reflected light as an array of pixels. Flatbed scanners are both quick and economical to use. In the past their speed is increased and only single pass is required under the document. These flatbed scanners are often bundled with their own scanning software and sometime with *Optical Character Recognition* (OCR) software. The cost of these flatbed scanners have come down dramatically and now available at the rate as low as five thousand rupees. However, the main disadvantage of the flatbed is that it relies on contact scanning, and is thus unsuitable for rare or fragile material. It also requires the document to be placed flat on the glass, so any curvature of the source material will distort the image.

- Sheet feeders – Sheet feeders are very useful in case a library is having loose leaf documents for processing. The benefit of this type of scanner is its remarkable speed and one can leave it churning through the documents unattended. However, one can not load more than 100 pages into the feeder at one time. Yet one more demerit of the sheet feeder is that it is unable to deal with fragile or brittle items. Furthermore, these are not suitable for oversized documents, though various models of these scanner are available in the market.
- Drum Scanners – These are called as drum-scanner because the source document is actually attached to a glass drum. Though these scanners offer the highest resolutions but rarely found outside a dedicated scanning agency because of their high cost. Several other kind of scanners are also available such as slide scanners and Microfilm scanners. Some of these are extremely cheap. Quality of scanning is normally in resolution, measured in dots per inch. For the textual material 300 dpi is a minimum quality of scanning, and 600 dpi is considered a good-quality resolution.
- Digital Camera – The digital camera is particularly useful in case of fragile or brittle items as these items can not bear the pressure of flatbed scanners. Many vendors have launched their products in the market over the past few years, for example, Kodak, DC215, Kontran Progress 3012, Minolta, etc. Some of these are in use in libraries in India and overseas. For instance, the central library of *University of Hyderabad* (UOH) is using a model of Minolta for digitization project of theses and dissertations. Large projects such as those running at the National Library of Scotland, the Arnamagnean Institute in Iceland, British Library, etc also uses high level cameras which are capable of giving an effective resolutions. However, there are some inherent problems with the digital camera in general. For example, the scan time can be quite long meaning there by lighting conditions have to be maintained throughout potentially damaging procedure particularly

when using warm lighting on documents. Also the are cumbersome pieces of equipments, which most of the time require some form of stand or cradle. Furthermore, these are not effective in the digitization of books that could not be opened beyond 45 degrees because of delicate binding.

DIGITIZATION SOFTWARE

Software for digital imaging covers three main area:

- Capturing the image
- Processing the image
- Delivering the image

Initially, as suggested, need a piece of software having interfaced with the peripheral device used for scanning such as the camera or scanner. Important point to take into consideration when choosing the capturing software is the type of output file formats. This can be extremely significant particularly when it comes to create master image. TIFF is perhaps the most important image format available at the moment. It is widely used as the cross-platform and archiving format in most digitization projects, particularly as it allows for high-quality images to be saved without any loss in the original capture. Moreover, it is not tied to any particular scanner or display. Conversion from TIFF to other formats is relatively straight forward.

Furthermore, images in TIFF are the best suited for universal accessibility and high resolution archival storage. However, the software should also be capable to produce *Joint Photographic Experts Group* (JPEG) derivatives for display on the World Wide Web. The JPEG and the *Graphical Interchange Format* (GIF) are the most popular image files delivered via the web and are ideally suited for displaying in all browsers. Many digitization projects create JPEG or GIF files format from their TIFF masters for subsequent delivery via the web. This is what know as processing the image and making it suitable for the end-purpose.

Once the actual conversion process over, the most important issue is the eventual delivery of the digital collection. In this step, primary emphasis should be given on what does the user want to see? The catalogues should be searchable and browsable. Facility for simple and complex searches should made available. Navigation aids should be both intuitive and apparent, and consistency maintained throughout. Additionally, there should be online help. On the one hand, the interface should be aesthetically pleasing while on the other hand, it should be open to accommodate the latest developments in technology.

FUNCTIONS

The primary function of digital libraries is to enable searching of electronic collections distributed across networks, rather than merely electronic repositories from digitized physical materials.

A digital library should have the following five integrated functions:

- Creation and capture of content process of turning: Integrating and importing multimedia objects into digital information – digital library content from many diverse sources different type to format.
- Storage and Management: Process of organizing and managing digital content to ensure that it is available to users whenever they want access to it. Providing stable, reliable storage and management of data in an open environment across a broad spectrum of platform.
- Search and Access: To be able what the user need quickly.
- Distribution: To enable information owners to distribute their material in numerous ways: through existing networks, clients/server business solutions or the Internet.
- Right Management: Providing extensive access control capabilities enabling content owners to capitalize on their protected assets.

NEW INFORMATION TECHNOLOGY IN SPECIAL LIBRARIES

Planning for library automation has been defined as planning for "integrated Library management systems" that computerize an array of traditional library functions using a common database. As physical, spatial and temporal barriers to acquiring information continue to crumble, libraries must plan for a broader and more comprehensive approach to providing automated services. Currently, libraries find themselves confronted with a second computerization wave. The first wave took place during the seventies and turned manual back-room activities, such as acquiring, distribution and cataloguing, into computer-controlled activities. Essential in the computerization wave of the 90s is the deployment of computer networks: campus-wide networks at universities as well as national and international networks.

These networks provide access to remote electronic information by means of library information systems. Furthermore, available electronic information is no longer limited to socalled secondary information. Also primary information has now become electronically available. Presently, we can refer to the electronic full-text versions of scientific journals. Electronic textbooks and readers enable us to consult information outside the library, *i.e.*, at the professional and private work site of the library's traditional customer. We must realize that all traditional library activities are being affected by this innovation: the character of all library tasks is about to change as a consequence of technological developments. Within this context, we can observe a number of trends. One very important trend is the fact that the physical collection is becoming less important.

Of course, in the humanities books will keep playing an important role in the next decades, but the number of electronic sources will gradually increase. The library is shifting its focus from concentrating on supply towards centering on what is asked for by its customers. In correspondence with this trend, information reference is becoming more and more significant. The library acquires a gateway function, referring to information, irrespective of the location where it has been physically stored. Growing emphasis will be put on navigation. By and large, users will prefer to find their own way across the large amount of available information. To an increasing extent, service will be provided from a distance: the users will choose to consult their sources sitting at their own desk, at their own computer. This, in turn, implies that the library needs to increase the accessible electronic collection, which is accomplished by disclosing sources elsewhere, but also by electronically providing material that has already been available on paper. Of course, this development entails new problems related to the storage of electronic information.

IMPORTANCE OF LIBRARY FOR ORGANIZATION/R AND D CENTERS IN IT ERA

Special library have been in existence from the beginning of this centuries, whereas information centre engaged from the fifties and have now developed into major group of information institutions. Although special libraries and information centers has over lapping functional characteristics. Special libraries disseminate information and matter acquired by them answers, research questions, and direct users needs details on research information to appropriate some and handle towards periodicals to keep their user informed current development in this field. Parent organization special libraries after serves a widely distributed group of users who only link being the common subject interest. The concepts of special libraries have been change in all aspects and librarians are known as cyberians.

NEED OF LIBRARY AUTOMATION IN SPECIAL LIBRARIES

In the changing scenario of information storage and retrieval, we have no option but to automate our information and library systems due to various reasons. Consequently, there is urgent need to reply following questions before/ and after automation planning. Questions you might ask are basic but important:

- What are the information needs of the organization ?
- Who will access the database?
- What will the content be?
- What is our computing environment or can it be changed?
- Who will maintain the data?
- Who will determine the process and procedural controls and standards?

We have to discuss the said questions with library staff, library committee and with users for better planning for library automation and use of new information technology in library.

STEPS FOR PERFECT LIBRARY AUTOMATION

Redefining and Planning for Library Automation

Library automation is a very complete process and needs exhaustive planning looking to the present and future needs of the users. This includes hardware, software, *moony manpower, materials and mechanics* (4M's), obsoleteness, updating, adoptability and very fast changing IT environment.

Selection of hardware and others required equipment

- System Purchase: Purchase of the System if not available latest configuration of hardware and software, as well as the cost of preparing a site for the computer system. As having following latest configuration as follow:
  - Processor: Intel Pentium 4 processors up to 530J with Hyper threading
  - Operating system: Windows XP Professional
  - Memory speed: DDR2 PC2-4200 SDRAM
  - Memory expansion: Four DIMM slots for expansion to 3GB memory
  - Graphics: Integrated Intel Graphics Media Accelerator 900

Hard Disk Drive: Up to 200GB 7200rpm Serial ATA]

- Networking of Computers (LAN) in library: Think and complete the library networking if not already available, etc., as Telecommunications dedicate at least one standard phone line that the vendor can use to dial up to your system. Internet accessibility is become more common for vendor troubleshooting, but you may still need that extra phone line.
- Retrospective data conversion costs are those associated with the creation of machine-readable bibliographic and, for circulation systems, patron records.
- Site Preparation—updating power supply, updating electrical wiring, cable for networking, furniture, remodeling that may need to be done, adequate HVAC system
- Conversion Costs—This includes the costs of converting the catalogue and patron records. However, also consider the cost of staff time dedicated to the project. Bar-coding costs also fall into this category.

Operating Costs—This category is often forgotten in automating a library. Typical costs in this category include on-going utility and telecommunications costs, software license renewals, software updates, system maintenance fees, and miscellaneous supplies

Selection of Library Software and others Required Software

Following criteria might help the librarians to select the right software for other housekeeping operations:

- Who are the developers, whether an institution, or reputed company or few individuals. The preference is for institution and second preference is for the reputed company. One has to be skeptical about the software developed by individuals as there will be no continuity
- How many times the software has been revised since the time of its first launch.
- How many parameters are available for each module? More the parameters better will be the flexibility and needs no or minimum customization.
- Whether the software has facility to import bibliographic data available in MARC 21 format and similarly export of data in this format
- Training and guidance after installation
- Whether available on major operating systems.
- Whether it is web interfaceble
- Whether it can be interfaced with the e-mail system of the campus network.
- How many installations it has got in the country, since when and major clients.
- Whether it can offer OPAC and different rights to different logins
- Database architecture, Database migration, maintenance, database security, etc,

The Following are LatestTrends to be Considered Library Automation Software

- Integrated library Management system: An automation system in which the various applications share one bibliographic database. Each system comes with a set of core modules as well as additional modules, which can be added on, if necessary. The system should not only
- Core modules as: Circulation, cataloguing and online public access catalogue are necessary minimums. Additional modules often cost extra and are therefore not always used by as many of the system's clients which can lead to less responsive development. Additional modules include acquisitions, community information, course reserves, imaging, *inter-library loan* (ILL), materials booking and serials. Acquisitions and serials are sometimes part of the same module and are often part of the core package, content management, e-learning, etc.
- Client-server architecture: Turnkey systems are quickly becoming a thing of the past. A client/server system is identified by a more powerful server machine that handles database manipulation and retrieval while leaving the user interface to the desktop client software. This shares the computational load between the client and

server machines and gives the user a better experience through a faster interface.

- Z39.50: This is a protocol for computer-to-computer information retrieval. It allows users to access dissimilar library catalogues from the host institution's catalogue while using a familiar interface. Both a Z39.50 client and server are needed if you want to visit others and have others visit your catalogue. A Z39.50 client allows access to others' catalogues. A Z39.50 server allows others to access your catalogue. Ideally access works both ways.
- GUI interface for all modules: Graphical and menu-driven interfaces have or are replacing commanddriven interfaces in systems.
- MARC 21 and non-MARC compliance: First, library systems developed to use MARC records. Now systems must allow for cataloguing formats, such as Internet resources, for which no MARC formats yet exist alongside MARC records.
- Web-based patron catalogue: Patron access is greatly increased when catalogues can be accessed remotely via the World Wide Web. Better systems contain password-protection to allow patrons to access portions of their own records remotely.
- UNICODE: This protocol expands the character set allowed and is essential for collections with materials in non-Roman languages. UNICODE encodes 65,000 different characters compared to the extended ASCII character set of 256 characters. Not all vendors have fully implemented this yet, but most are working on it.
- RFID (Radio Frequency Identification Technology): RFID is the latest technology to be used in library theft detection systems. Unlike *Electro-Mechanical* (EM) and *Radio Frequency* (RF) systems, which have been used in libraries for decades, RFID-based systems move beyond security to become tracking systems that combine security with more efficient tracking of materials throughout the library, including easier and faster charge and discharge, inventorying, and materials handling? Following are the advantages of RFID systems, *i.e.*, Rapid charging/discharging, Simplified patron self-charging/ discharging, high reliability, High-speed inventorying, automated materials handling, long tag life, etc.

Accordingly, today's integrated system must not only provide access to the traditional cataloging, circulation, public catalogue (OPAC) and acquisitions modules, but must be capable of connecting through the local system into the systems of other vendors, remote bibliographic databases, CD-ROM drives on a local area network (LAN), and the Internet.

Users are expecting that their library systems be capable of, among other things:

- Providing seamless integration between online gateway and OPAC modules;
- providing access for external users on the Internet to the library's OPAC;
- Monitoring the usage of remote databases that have been accessed through the gateway; and,
- accessing the Internet using a variety of online database

Essentially, what this means is that libraries must plan to use a library automation management system as a gateway for achieving access to resources outside campus. Stimulated by the Internet, which has created universal connectivity to information resources heretofore public/society/respected community and by Z39.50 interoperability standards and "gateways," users of individual are expecting to access the resources of other systems— anywhere and anytime. Moreover, the traditional definition of "publishing" has been stretched by the creation and CDROMS, E-books, online databases, informational home pages and Web sites worldwide.

Finance Matter

Finance is an important aspect of any planning and automation is no exception to it, these are: Hardware, Software, Training, Staff, Networking (LAN, WAN, MAN and Internet). Speaking of funding, planners need to be aware that there are certain cost elements involved in the installation and operation of any automated system. These may be summarized as follows: Planning and consulting costs include direct, out-of pocket costs and indirect costs associated with getting started, etc.

Developing a Library "Profile"

One of the most important planning tools involves collecting basic statistical information on the library collection, library in-house activities, user services, users' education, etc. The following are examples of commonly needed data of:

- Number of titles and volumes in the collection, current and projected;
- Number of borrowers, current and projected;
- Number of materials circulated current and projected;
- Number of new materials acquired current and projected;
- Interlibrary loans lent to and borrowed from other libraries;
- Description of any cooperative arrangements involving the library; and,
- Library in-house activities and hours of operation.

In addition, it is important to take stock of any existing automation in the library by compiling the following data:

- Percentage of collection that has catalogue records in machine-readable form;

- Description of collection without machine-readable records, by category;
- Description of currently-automated library functions;
- Estimates of the location and number of workstations; and,
- Specifications for any existing equipment to be re-used with any future system.

At the same time that this data is being assembled, it is important to assess user needs and set service priorities. This can be accomplished by undertaking a focused, strategic planning process designed to involve the library's "stakeholders."

Developing a Strategic Plan

A library planning to automate should undertake a process by which representative staff and users can identify service needs and objectives. The purpose of such an effort is to allow participants to articulate their interests and concerns share perspectives and learn about possibilities in a collaborative setting. Group interaction is an important contributing factor in the success of the goal, which is to develop and sustain library automation in the years ahead. Here are the basic steps involved in this process:

- Ask participants to identify strengths, weaknesses, opportunities and threats in the library's environment
- Group these factors into critical issue areas that are likely to have an impact on the libraries' future in developing and sustaining automation.
- Ask participants to explore their ideas and perceptions in relation to the question: "How do you see the library providing user-friendly, cost-effective automated services as *Current Awareness Services* (CAS), *Selective Dissemination of Information* (SDI), online database, online journals, etc.
- Through a method of your own devising, ask participants to prioritize all of the ideas that come out of the above two "brainstorming" exercises.
- Ask participants to shape these priorities into the draft of a strategic "vision" for automation development consisting of a statement of purpose, goals and objectives for the library.

Setting Service Priorities

Your strategic vision must now provide the framework or context for the next step in the automation process, which is to determine which library functions should be automated and in what order of priority. For example, processes that are repetitive, occupy large amounts of staff time, require retrieving information from large, unwieldy files, or are high-profile functions of the library are prime candidates for automation.

Developing a Formal Specifications Document

It is very difficult to compare systems sensibly and pragmatically solely by randomly looking at systems, talking to sales representatives, reading literature or comparing broad cost quotations. For this reason, libraries use a formal document — often known as a "Request for Proposal," or RFP — that organizes and standardizes the information provided to and requested from the various system vendors. Utilizing an RFP to solicit written responses from vendors makes it possible for you to systematically compare functionality, cost, maintenance, support, and all the other issues that are involved in system procurements. The process can save you money and will result in a wiser decision.

An "Request For Proposal" Document

The following points should include these essential elements, among others:

- Library Background Information
- Libraries Service Plan, Mission Statement, Technology Plan, other supporting information
- Technical Inventory-Inventory of your existing hardware/software, and infrastructure:
- Size of your collection
- Number of terminals
- Number of patrons
- Network operating system
- Number of servers
- Type of wiring
- Existing database that may need to be migrated into the new system—People soft, access database, etc.
- Specifications-Detailed listing of requirements the system should provide.
- Module Requirements: Circulation, Bibliographic Maintenance, Acquisitions, Serials, General System, and Report Generator, etc.
- System Technical Requirements
- Network, System Design, Database Management System, Data conversion requirements, Hardware requirements
- System Performance and Testing Requirements

Be ready for the Following Upon the Receipt of Vender Proposals against our Floated RFP

- A description of how the proposals should be arranged and submitted;
- Instructions on receiving vendor business and financial information;
- Criteria the library will use to evaluate vendor proposals;
- Questions regarding vendor training and documentation;

- Your functional and technical specifications;
- Also, vendors should be asked to describe:
- How they will create bibliographic, item and borrower databases;
- Their system maintenance programmes and services;
- Their site preparation requirements;
- Their delivery and installation methodologies;
- Their system performance guarantees; and
- Their pricing and cost strategies.

Criteria for Vendor (for Hardware and Software) Selection

Upon the receipt of vendor proposals, it will be time to begin the process of system evaluation and selection. This process involves a number of key steps:

- If possible, form a project team of persons to assist with the evaluations and the selection who have some knowledge of automation or who work in the area(s) being automated. People involved in the strategic planning process would be a good choice.
- Try to weed out proposals that are "fatally flawed," *e.g.*, where the vendor fails to reply to any of the functional specifications or the system is missing a module for a high-priority function.
- Begin in-depth reading of the "surviving" proposals, carefully noting both deviations from the requirements as defined by the RFP and any aspect that is handled unusually well. Make a list of any parts of the response that are not clear and require further clarification.
- Schedule system demonstrations. They are an important component of the evaluation process. Allow the vendors to show off the vendor's system in the most attractive light; however, be prepared with a list of what you want to see along with questions you would like answered. Use the same list with each vendor. This permits more effective cross-comparisons.
- Consider using computerized spreadsheet software in order to compare and evaluate vendor cost proposals. Costs may not be what they seem at first glance.
- Contact some of each vendor's current clients— sites of the same library type, and of similar size, where the hardware and software modules that have been proposed to you are currently in use.
- Assign point values to the criteria listed in the RFP and assign scores to the different proposals. The system with the highest score becomes the number one finalist, the system with the second highest score number two and so on. To maintain a negotiating edge, it is better to cut to two vendors rather than one. If that is impossible, maintain the illusion anyway. Remember: The selection process is not over until the contract is signed. Until that point, never let any vendors

know that they have been eliminated, including those with fatal flaws.

- Compare studies: Do compare study of all received proposal from venders with theirs features, etc.

Putting your System into Place

After the system selection process is complete, there are several important steps which must occur. You and your vendor will have to negotiate and sign a contract. You will want to test the system and make sure it suits your needs. You will want to make provisions for system maintenance. Finally, you will want to train both your staff and your users as much as possible to prepare them for when the system is up and running. With regard to training, the following must be considered: In thinking of automation planning, there is often a tendency to focus on the hardware and software aspects of planning, and to ignore the human aspects of automation— training and public relations. Without these, however, even the most carefully designed system may not be accepted by library staff or library users.

To assure the success of your hard planning work, training and public relations plan should be part of any automation project. Fortunately, training can begin long before the system is installed. By involving staff at all levels in the analysis of operations, the identification of needs, the setting of priorities, the development of specifications, and the evaluation of systems, staff will gain much of the knowledge they need as the planning progresses. User acceptance and enthusiasm for your new automated system is certainly an important ingredient in a successful planning effort. If you are implementing a public access catalogue, it is probably the most important measure of success. Public relations can allow you to accomplish three things:

- Make users aware of your new system and services;
- Motivate them to use the system; and,
- Train them in using the new system and services effectively.

About the Database

In the rush to acquire hardware and software, librarians often forget that their most valuable product is the library's database. The creation of a high-quality machine-readable database provides the cornerstone upon which all present and future automation efforts rest. Vendors will come and go, hardware will become obsolete, software will be replaced, but a well-constructed, well-maintained database, with its accompanying local holdings, will be the library's transportable and viable link from system to system. Moreover, as library users begin to access not only their local system but systems in other libraries as well, the quality of respective databases will influence both the outcome of search strategies and the availability of materials. Database readiness has several important facets:

- Catalogue records must be carefully converted from manual to machine-readable formats;
- Collections must be prepared for conversion through effective and ongoing weeding and inventory programmes;
- Once converted, collections must be properly maintained as titles are added, withdrawn, transferred and re cataloged; and,
- Standards — for bibliographic, item and patron records as well — must be adhered to. In particular, adherence to well-established and accepted standards of description for bibliographic information in a machine-readable database is critical because
- Without standards, files cannot easily be transferred from one automated system to another, and,
- It is essential for libraries wishing to participate in resource sharing arrangements with other libraries, which will require such adherence as a condition of participation.

Results of your Good Planning

- Confidence that you have selected the best possible system available, give technological and financial constraints;
- Confidence that you have addressed the priority needs of your library;
- Confidence that you have established a firm basis of understanding and a methodology for future planning;
- Confidence that automation activities are being implemented as part of a clearly articulated, overall plan for the development of library services; and,
- Confidence that you have the ability to respond quickly and effectively to unexpected opportunities and challenges, with a clear understanding of how these unexpected developments may be used to support the library's long range goals.

Feasibility Study of your Plan

Immediately after the analysis and design for the system has been completed, a feasibility study must be conducted. The aim of a feasibility study is to determine if the project is achievable, if the benefits outweigh the disadvantages and to examine alternative solutions. It is designed to answer these questions: Is the proposed system realistic? Is it necessary? What other options is available? Is it affordable? The final output of a feasibility study is a report to be presented to the management.

6

Electronic Resources in Library Science

Electronic resources can be defined as resources in electronic format or computerprocessible format that provide information or an indicator to the information and are generally accessible over the Internet or stored on media like CD ROM/ DVD ROM or other storage devices.

The emergence of Internet and the World Wide Web (WWW) in early 1990s, as a new media of information storage and delivery, came as a real boon for evolution of electronic resources. While searching bibliographic databases became popular, it created demand for actual content in full-text that became difficult for libraries to obtain.

Coincided with evolution of World Wide Web (WWW), display technology evolved, cost of storage came down drastically and networks became faster. It became possible for publishers to deliver content, either as a bitmap page images or other structured formats such as HTML, PDF or RTF. Increasingly larger number of publishers started using the Internet as a global way to offer their publications to the international community of scientists and technologists given the fact that technology is in a position to deliver more content to more users at a significantly lower cost per user.

Electronic resources on the Internet manifest themselves in numerous flavours and categories, although most of them emulate the traditional publishing while others are revolutionary in their design and approach. While the present trend to imitate and emulate the traditional models of scholarly communication may continue for some time, eventually the capabilities added by the new media would be used in more innovative ways. Some of the important types of e-resources are described here.

RESEARCH IN ELECTRONIC DATABASES

An electronic database consists of electronic resources integrated in highly organised fashion so as to provide controlled access to it by their commercial providers. The first databases were bibliographic in nature and were online version of existing indexing and abstracting services such as Biological Abstracts, Index Medicus, Chemical Abstracts,,etc.

By the year 1988, only half of all databases were bibliographic in nature. With introduction of a number of online databases containing textual information, news, statistics, commodity prices,,etc.,, a third type of databases holding text of full-length documents started appearing. Several full-text of encyclopaedia, directories and articles from journals are now available online.

Most of the publishers now provide access to their full-text journals through their web site or through other electronic publishing platforms.

While there are a number of public-domain databases, most online databases require annual subscription for accessing them. Thousands of databases are now available on compact discs (CD-ROM) as well as on the Web.

ELECTRONIC JOURNALS

Electronic journals, or 'e-journals', are used for those journals and newsletters that are prepared and distributed electronically. Electronic journals may be defined very broadly as any journal, magazine, e-zine, webzine, newsletter or type of electronic serial publication which is available over the Internet and can be accessed using different technologies such as WWW, Gopher, ftp, telnet, e-mail or listserv. Several traditional journals are now being published both on the Web and in print.

Content lists for most of the journals are available on the Web or distributed to subscribers as an e-mail text messages or through technologies like RSS and Atom. Internet-based electronic journals started to appear in the beginning of 1990. These journals were mostly delivered as an attachment to e-mail while their back issues were mounted on anonymous ftp sites and users were required to download them from these ftp sites. The libraries and information centres made them accessible through their gopher site.

1995 witnessed peak of Gopher technology which then dropped suddenly and dramatically by 1997. With advent of WWW technology in 1993, electronic publishing became more than a novelty, the web as a means of delivery of electronic information has grown steadily Since, then. As publishers experiment with different publication modes and models, the very definition of a journal is undergoing change in the electronic environment. New journals have evolved based on the graphic capabilities of the Internet that are available only in electronic form. Like print journals, current and archival issues of electronic journals can be browsed through their content pages. Moreover, e-journals can also be searched not only on their metadata but also in full-text through sophisticated search interface. Currently, there are more than 50,000 peer-reviewed, scholarly electronic journals that are available on the Internet.

ELECTRONIC BOOKS

An electronic book is digital reading material that a user can view on a desktop or Personal Digital Assistant (PDA), laptop or on a dedicated, portable device with a large storage capacity and the ability to download new titles via a network connection.

More and more traditional book publishers, as well as those catering to the professional and business communities, are launching their e-book collections. The electronic books market consists of two distinct components, *i.e.*, i) electronic books consisting of digital material or contents; and ii) electronic book hardware including ebook reading appliance, PCs, laptop or PDA.

The digital material or content that make an electronic book are simply textual and graphical files consisting of bits that can be transported any digital storage media or delivered over a network connection. It is designed to be viewed on some combination of hardware and software ranging from dumb terminals to web browsers, on personal computers to the new reading appliances. More and more books are now being released on the web through enhanced interfaces that offer features such as increased search capacity within a book or entire collection of books, ability to highlight and flag a page, ability to make notes on text without damaging the book, ability to e-mail quotes from the books to other colleagues, etc.

Most publishers like Springer, Wiley InterScience, Taylor and Francis, Cambridge University Press, Oxford University Press, etc., offer their e-book collections on subscription/ one-time purchase basis. Besides, there are a number of e-books aggregators that make thousands of books available online for libraries and individuals at relatively lower cost. Three major ebooks aggregators are Questia, Ebrary and NetLibrary. However, just like other e-resources, e-books come with restrictions such as limit on downloads, in terms of number of pages, *i.e.,* one page at a time or one chapter at a time or no download at all.

ELECTRONIC THESES AND DISSERTATIONS

Theses submitted to the universities as requirement for the award of Ph.D. degree constitute a useful source of information for the new and ongoing research. Doctoral dissertations submitted to universities and academic institutions are originally created in digital format using one of the word processing software packages like MSWord, LaTex, Word Perfect, Word Pro, etc.,

or one of the desktop publishing packages like Page Maker, Ventura, etc. These documents are undisputedly highly valuable collection especially in digital format that qualify to be an important component of a digital library. The documents composed on word processing packages/ desktop publishing packages can be easily converted into PDF, Post Script or XML using appropriate software tools so as to host them on the web.

Several universities and institutions have already implemented electronic submission of doctoral dissertations under the overall umbrella of an international digital library initiative called 'Networked Digital Library of Theses and Dissertations' (NDLTD).

AUDIO, VIDEO AND STREAMING MEDIA

Streaming multimedia is sequential delivery of multimedia content, including video, audio or some other learning objects, over a computer network that is displayed (or played back) to the end-user as it is being delivered by the provider.

The advent of the MP3 players and the iPod resulted in a greater effort to deliver downloadable media. Moreover, web documents are now coming with greater integration of text with media. Encyclopaedia now have articles with audio files, video clips and animation to illustrate a given topic. Media can broadly be categorised into three category, namely.

- Commercial movies that have greater copyright restrictions,
- Educational media typically are lesser controlled and many a time are made available free-of-cost; and
- Media targeted for individual users, such as movies and songs, that comes with restrictions in terms of copying and distributions.

SUBJECT GATEWAYS OR LIBRARY PORTALS

The web, being a hypermedia-based system, allows linking amongst electronic resources stored on servers dispersed geographically on distant locations.

The portal sites or gateways redirect a user to the holders of the original digital material. The librarians, being the earliest users of the web, started to gather and organise link to important web-based resources on various subjects. A subject gateway can be defined as facilities that allow easier access to web-based resources in a defined subject area.

The simplest types of subject gateways are sets of web pages containing list of links to resources. Some gateways index their lists of links and provide a simple search facility. More advanced gateways offer a muchenhanced service via a system consisting of a resource database and various indexes, which can be searched and/ or browse throughout a web-based interface.

Subject gateways are also known as Subject-based Information Gateways (SBIGs), subject-based gateways, subject index gateways, virtual libraries, clearing houses, subject trees, pathfinders,,etc. Subject gateway is an important component of a library web site designed for the library users so as to help them discover high-quality information on the Internet in a quick and effective way. In the traditional information environment human intermediaries, such as publishers and librarians, filter and process information so that users can search catalogues and indexes of organised knowledge as opposed to raw data and information. Subject gateways work on the same principle,, *i.e.,* they employ subject experts and information professionals to select, classify and catalogue Internet resources to aid search and retrieval for the users. Users are offered access to a database of Internet resources descriptions which they can search by keywords or browse by subject area. A description of each resource is provided to help users assess very quickly its origin, content and nature, enabling them to decide if it is worth investigating further.

In the process users get benefited from the expertise of librarians and subject experts with subject gateways rather than having to locate, evaluate, filter and organise the resources themselves. Specialised software are available as freeware or as priced software to create and maintain professionally developed subject gateways.

SOME OF THE PROBLEMS RELATING TO ELECTRONIC RESOURCES

Online full text implies availability of articles rather that the entire content of a particular journal. The complete contents of a publication are seldom put into a full text database. This implies that an author one might have seen in a physical publication may not be traceable in electronic format. This predicament also applies to archiving where there is uncertainty about the percentage of a journals content that is archived in digital format.

Another concern is that the academic library in a sense has lost control over the resources it make available to its users. When academic libraries subscribe to aggregator databases, *e.g.* EbscoHost or ProQuest they subscribe to a service, a list of titles bundled together of which many are useful and many not so useful. One of the problems is that aggregators sometimes drop titles. Typically this would happen when publishers withdraw all their titles.

The Chronicle of Higher Education has reported in 2003 that Elsevier has been removing articles from aggregator files because of various reasons, *e.g.*, scientific misconduct, plagiarism and errors. On the Web there are masses of information available. With search engines, *e.g.* Google or Yahoo one may find useful information and record the URL or title. There is however no guarantee when one wants to revisit the site that it may still be available. Sites on the Web sometimes disappear overnight. An organisation may have merged with another one or the host server might have become dysfunctional.

The quality of information available on the Web is also sometimes questionable. Any individual with access to the Web and basic hardware and software can publish on the Web regardless of whether the person's views are factually correct. On the Web are more than an estimated billion Web pages and this create problems for users of the academic library to distinguish between what is useful or not. Another problem is that search engines cover only a small portion of what is what is available on the Web. There are lots of information behind firewalls and thus inaccessible. Many crawlers of search engines only focus on html and ignore graphics. Generally ASCII files will not be found. To assist users academic library services should try and inform users when sites have relocated or are no longer available.

CHANGES IN THE EDUCATIONAL ENVIRONMENT

ICT have changed every fibre of society including education. Lifelong learning has become essential. A very competitive working environment has influenced this. Even educational methodologies have changed. Greater interaction between learner, educator and material is becoming the norm. Learners have greater choices in terms of curricula. The 24 hour networked classroom became reality leading to the birth of the virtual library.

Network technologies and new educational methodologies have empowered learners, given them a greater measure of control and participation in the learning process and enabled network interaction with both fellow students and lecturers. Change in institutions of higher education will compel academic libraries to change accordingly. The most dramatic change according to visionaries will take place in distance education. This was a direct influence of the Internet. When the day dawns when distance education becomes the norm, universities the way we know them may vanish and virtual libraries may become a reality. Recently an author warned that the railroad managers overlooked the fact that they were in the transport business. He noted that universities must remember they are in the education business and not the campus business. If campuses disappear libraries will disappear.

There are already examples of cyberspace universities, *e.g.* Phoenix. If academics should fail to restructure their institutions' external forces will do it. Of cardinal importance is to focus on what education wants to achieve and how one can fulfill it. Survival of the academic library will depend on its ability to continuously reshape and reorganise.

Distance Education

New technologies driven by ICT innovation have enhanced the virtual delivery of academic programmes and stimulated unparalleled growth of distance education at institutions of higher learning. The phenomenal growth in distance education technologies has lead to an escalation in the availability of online academic programmes and a tremendous increase in remote users. In order to support these programmes academic librarians have developed excellent portfolios and programmes for remote students. One aspect that is neglected is evaluation of these programmes.

What is of critical importance is to establish how these programmes are used, which ones are used more frequently than others and why. Monash University library in Australia provides online curriculum content to their students all over the world. The university library provides online access to more than 440 online databases, 140,000 e-books and 20,000 e-journal subscriptions. Apart from full text databases and e-books the university library also provides digital audio recordings of lectures that become available minutes after conclusion of lectures.

According to Ho Monash University library has made a paradigm shift to a complete new service module that utilises e-commerce technologies. Moyo is of the opinion that the transformation in distance education has created a need for distance librarianship.

Changes in Scholarly Communication

The rising of the Internet and subsequent Web during the 1990's has resulted in the decline of the printed journal as the principal medium of scholarly publication. The costs of journals have increased dramatically driven by commercial publishers trying to control research content. This resulted in depriving many researchers of access to needed resources. The Web has also made fast and easy electronic publication possible and has increased direct communication between researchers.

Publishers immediately started making electronic versions of printed journals available on the Web. This was however seen as perpetuating the status quo in a new medium. Scholars started seeing in the new technology the potential to develop a new model for publishing research and an opportunity to return ownership of scholarly output to the rightful owners of the research.

These sentiments were driven by shortcomings in existing scholarly journal publishing which were:

- The time to publish an article was to too long.
- The existing model demanded transfer of copyright to the publishers.
- A too rigid peer review system that tends to favour publication of authors from the more prestigious institutions.
- Journal prices had become unaffordable.

One of the outcomes of this dissatisfaction was the birth of the e-print which is essentially an electronic version of a research paper. E-prints lead to the development of e-print repositories that are an archive of e-prints accessible to the public. Some of the advantages of e-print repositories are the reduction of publishing barriers, increased visibility of research and rapid dissemination of research results to a wide audience.

Consortia Collaboration

Initially libraries got involved in consortia in order to reduce costs particularly with regard to the acquisition of e-resources. Consortia development is thus an attempt to maximize limited resources through co-operation and resource sharing. In the consortia scenario the emphasis is on access to information rather than ownership. Consortia collaboration provides more power when it comes to negotiating contracts. It also provides a platform for libraries to co-operate in terms of services. Nowadays libraries also turn to consortia to provide advice and guidance in complex decision-making. The input of consortia is also valuable in terms of evaluating e-resources in terms of quality, different options, *e.g.*, whether to subscribe to journals or pay article-by-article.

The South African Scenario

In terms of network infrastructure South Africa is not on par with first world countries where consortia cooperation is very effective. For the establishment of an information society in South Africa proper connectivity infrastructure is an absolute prerequisite. There is an uneven distribution of telecommuni-cations infrastructure across South Africa stemming from the political ideologies of the apartheid government. This inequity is also prevalent in South African academic libraries. Institutions for the privileged white people were well financed and resourced under the apartheid regime. Institutions for blacks were under funded and thus under resourced; hence the distinction between advantaged and historically disadvantaged institutions. Because of this there are great differences in wealth and the collections of academic libraries. In South Africa there are five academic library consortia.:

1. CALICO (Cape Library Cooperative) based in Cape Town.
2. ESAL (Eastern Seaboard Association of Libraries based in Kwazulu-Natal.
3. FRELICO (Free State Libraries and Information Consortium) based in Free State.
4. Gaelic (Gauteng and Environs Library Consortium) based in Gauteng.
5. SEALS (South Eastern Academic Libraries System in the Eastern Cape.

Essential for the development of successful consortia is low cost tariffs coupled with high bandwith connectivity. Academic institutions constantly engaged with government agencies to achieve this ideal. Library consortia can also be invaluable in assisting member libraries with change management because "An organisation needs external coaches to catalyse, guide and facilitate a change process", the reason being that people within the academic library are sometimes to closely involved with daily activities to see things objectively. An outside view often helps to see things in the right perspective.

ICT MANAGEMENT ISSUES

Libraries are caught midstream between print versus a digital setup. To navigate the transition from print to digital remains enormously challenging. Rapid ICT development had resulted in lots of incompatible systems being used within libraries. To manage ICT is a complex and daunting task. To select the right ICT technologies is a major management issue. It is very difficult in a world where hardware and software changes at a phenomenal rate.

The shift in the academic library from printed resources to electronic resources that are accessible via campus networks or remotely and the fact that users can even request services via the network has lead to a decline in users visiting the library. The growing electronic nature of the academic library is resulting in it becoming less visible as a physical entity to its users.

What is also disturbing is the fact that users are often oblivious to the fact that they are using library resources because of the seamlessness of access. Users are not aware of the fact that to make those resources available are costly in terms of subscriptions, infrastructure and staff. Academic libraries need to find a way to reverse this scenario of the library loosing its visibility. Hooper suggests that the academic library should use ICT to stimulate interaction between user and the library. It should be done in such a way that the user could identify with the academic library providing the service and experience a sense of ownership.

As a starting point the academic library can interact with the user relating to loans, database searches and other services available. It is also important to create an environment where the user can provide feedback relating to service shortcomings and suggestions that could lead to improvement. Stakeholder relationships are also very important. It is of vital importance for the academic library to ensure that their operations dovetail with the strategic goals of the university it supports. In these days where accountability is becoming the norm it is essential to run operations in such a way that the academic library at any point is in a position to provide proof of the value of its services as a return on investment made by the university authority.

RESOURCE GUIDE IN ELECTRONIC PUBLISHING

For the purposes of this resource guide electronic publishing is defined as:

- Making the content of the journal available online.

This chapter will also address the use of electronic tools to facilitate the processes of, publication, for example online electronic editorial processing.

WHY DO ELECTRONIC PUBLISHING AT ALL

Many journals around the world struggle to attract authors and readers, and frequently suffer from a lack of resources—both human and financial. In addition, research habits are changing and researchers increasingly expect any information to be found online, which means that a journal which cannot be located on the web may be effectively invisible. Online publication can help to address some of these issues. At the same time, many readers still seem to prefer print so you may not feel you can stop producing a print edition as well. Publishing a journal electronically sounds very attractive. There are a number of good reasons for doing so, but it does have disadvantages too. Before committing yourself and your organisation to the effort and expense involved, it is sensible to look carefully at both the advantages and disadvantages.

In the end, the decision will depend on what your main objectives are, so it is important to be clear about why you are publishing, or planning to publish, in the first place: what information you want to disseminate, and to whom. Electronic publishing is often considered to have six advantages over print: international reach, speed, additional capabilities, lower cost, new publishing opportunities and sustainability.

INTERNATIONAL REACH

If a journal is available on the Internet, it is true that readers all over the world can obtain and read your journal; you do not have to arrange for printed copies to be mailed to different parts of the world, which can be both expensive and slow.

However, if readers are going to obtain and read your journal they need to know of its existence, and they must want to read the articles you publish. To enable readers to discover your articles/journal, you need to be visible on the main search engines and to encourage use, you really need to carry out some international promotion to raise awareness and trust in your publication.

SPEED OF PUBLICATION

An online journal has a great advantage over a print journal, as it is possible to publish an issue as soon as it is ready, and not wait for it to be printed and bound, then despatched. What is more, you do not need to wait until you have enough articles to make up a complete printed issue. You can, if you wish, publish articles individually as soon as they are ready.

These time savings can be very helpful to authors, particularly in fast-moving subjects such as some of the sciences where speed of publication is extremely important. Many of the important processes of publication, however, cannot be speeded up if you want to produce a quality journal. If it is a research journal, you will still need to arrange for peer review to be carried out—and peer review is often the most time-consuming step between submission of an article and its eventual publication.

The transmission of papers to referees, and of their reports to the editorial office, can be done instantly by electronic means, and make some time savings, but the reading, thinking and writing of reports will take exactly the same amount of time.

It is also important to recognise that even online publication is not instantaneous; preparing the files correctly, loading them online and maintaining the online service all take time—further time is inevitably introduced if you are working with a third party host.

ADDITIONAL CAPABILITIES

The online environment offers the potential to provide readers with more functionality. One key feature of online publications is the ability to search for articles—at a minimum within one journal, and frequently across multiple journals Another feature commonly added to online journals is that of linking. This refers to the ability to go from one place online to another, at a click of a button—the most common example being the link from a citation within the body of an article to the relevant reference at the end of the article, and from there to the actual article which is being referenced.

Reference linking in scholarly journals is now increasingly being undertaken using DOIs, which are unique identification codes assigned to online articles, and which provide permanent links for the user. This is one of the international standards being developed to assist different systems to communicate and link with each other, to help with visibility and discovery of online material. The methodology of using DOIs in scholarly journals is being managed by an organisation called CrossRef. Electronic publication also makes it possible to include material which you would not include in a print journal, either for space reasons or because the material is difficult, costly or even impossible to print.

Research articles online can be accompanied by the full data-sets from which the results were reached—ideally in a form which readers can manipulate for themselves. Colour illustrations may be prohibitively expensive in a printed journal, but present no such problems in an electronic journal.

Moving images, sound, or animations may also be included, although relatively few authors automatically think of providing such material at present and the technical comple-xities may outweigh the benefits. Before introducing any additional features within the online journal, you must consider whether your readers are likely to have the necessary software to make use of the additional material.

It is also worth noting that linking is generally rated very highly by readers, who find it an invaluable way of enhancing their research; however, other additional features are much less highly valued. It may, therefore, not be worth spending a great deal of time and money on these. One final consideration is that the additional capabilities which online publishing can offer may be of particular relevance to you, as the publisher, and not so much use to the user. These may involve the ease with which you can upload your content, and streamline your working practices.

One particularly important new facility which online publishing can provide you with, is a tool to measure and monitor online use. Most commercial hosts will automatically offer sophisticated usage statistics, and most of these will be COUNTER compliant, which is another increasingly important international standard which online publications should comply with.

REDUCED COSTS

It was originally assumed that publishing online introduced immediate cost savings. However, this is only true if the journal is no longer printed at all; continuing to print even a few copies removes most of the cost savings.

If you decide to cease printing altogether, you may save a significant percentage of your total direct costs, although many costs will be unchanged—however, most readers still seem to want print copies. The cost of administering an electronic version will also be considerably lower if you are able to make it available to everyone, free of charge.

Depending on the way the journal is funded, however, you may need to replace subscriptions income by raising author-side charges; this will require an administration system, which will reduce the savings.

The costs of publishing a journal can be split into direct costs and indirect costs. Direct costs are those where an invoice is received from an external supplier, and the journal needs to find the money to pay them. Indirect costs are those costs which are covered by the parent organisation, and the journal may be unaware of them. Introducing online publishing may provide an opportunity to reduce direct costs but is likely to increase indirect costs.

NEW PUBLISHING OPPORTUNITIES

It is perfectly possible for an online journal to work in all respects exactly like a print journal. However, the online medium does make possible new ways of doing things—new ways of publishing, new ways of covering costs, and new processes—which may help to address the problems of a struggling journal.

New Ways of Publishing

Publish Often, Print Infrequently

This approach may be particularly attractive if you have difficulty publishing issues on time, whether this is due to lack of funds to pay for printing and distribution, or to a shortage of articles.

Online issues would be published regularly and frequently, but you might only produce one, archival, print issue per year. This can help to improve regularity of publication, whilst at the same time saving some of the print and distribution costs.

Article-by-article Publication

This approach may be even more attractive if rapid publication is important to authors in your subject area. Articles would be published online individually, as soon as they are ready. In addition to offering fast publication for authors, this will bring readers back to the online journal frequently, thus increasing usage.

Separate Online and Print Content

Some journals have separated their print and online publications so that they are almost different journals—an example of this is 'electronic long, paper short' used in the British Medical Journal. This model publishes the full article online, but only publishes a shorter version of the article within its print journal. Some journals include additional sections within their online journal, and some exclude some materials from online version that appear in the print journal. However, if you decide to publish different content in the print and the online publication, this brings extra complexity into the way of dealing with your content, which is likely to increase your editorial costs overall.

New Publishing Processes

Open Peer Review

The Internet makes it easy for readers to comment on papers after they are published by the journal. This may be done once papers have gone through the normal peer review process, or it may precede or even replace it. Some journals then allow authors to modify their articles in the light of feedback. However, this makes for considerable extra complexity, and makes it essential that readers know which version of the article they are actually reading; this approach may not be welcomed in all disciplines, as scholars differ in their willingness to expose their unfinished work to their colleagues, so it is important that you know your reader/author community before making a decision.

Index

You may be able to do without an index if the web site allows searching of the full text of articles, particularly if it also allows searching by specific fields. However, human indexers add considerable value-electronic searching will only find the exact word you are looking for, whereas an indexer can think of synonyms, and will not index irrelevant occurrences of the word. If you can afford it, many publishers believe that a human-compiled index is still worth having.

ELECTRONIC RESOURCE MANAGEMENT INITIATIVES

As institutions realised that effective communication about their common problem of managing electronic resources could lead to satisfying solutions they began to seek discussion outside their own academic institutions. The "Web hub for developing administrative metadata for electronic resource management" was constructed to facilitate the sharing of information about institutions developing their own electronic resource management systems. The Web hub was a Web site managed by Adam Chandler and Tim Jewell, which listed the names of the universities that were building systems or creating initiatives to address their own electronic resource management needs. The site also listed descriptions of the systems and contact persons at each university.

The site was built so that universities could read how other institutions were developing their tools, and could communicate with those universities if they had similar needs. The Web hub was a successful facilitator for those institutions that were considering building their own electronic resource management systems but needed more information or support before beginning their projects.

The creators of the Web hub started the Digital Library Federation's Electronic Resource Management Initiative steering group in 2001. The purpose of the Electronic Resource Management Initiative (ERMI) was to define an essential list of data elements that would construct a full and complete electronic resource management system. In addition to defining the data elements, the group sought to develop workflows and promote standards for the management of the data.

The Web hub served as a fertile space from which the ERMI could pull information to begin their discussions. In the final report of the Digital Library Federation's ERMI seven functional areas required to construct a comprehensive management system are identified: 'listing and descriptive;' 'license related;' 'financial and purchasing;' 'process and status;' 'systems and technical;' 'contact and support;' and 'usage'. By identifying these functional areas the ERMI hopes to convey accurately to vendors or others wishing to build management systems what elements are needed. As the Digital Library Federation's ERMI outlined its own goals it also included conversations with library vendors. By communicating with the vendors the ERMI created a successful ongoing rapport about what was needed to develop a complete electronic resource management system. By including vendors in this discussion the ERMI could provide the data backbone of a system that could then be developed by the vendors; in this way libraries could depend on vendors for development support and collaboration rather than acting as independent system creators.

FEATURES OF SYSTEMS

Features of some ERM systems include:

- Supporting acquisition and management of licensed e-resources
- May be integrated into other library system modules or may be a standalone system
- May have a public interface, either separate or integrated into the OPAC
- Providing descriptions of resources at the package (database) level and relate package contents (*e.g.* e-journals) to the package record

- Encoding and perhaps publicly displaying licensed rights such as e-reserves, course packs, and interlibrary loan
- Tracking electronic resources from point of order through licensing and final access
- Providing information about the data providers, consortia arrangements, access platform
- Providing contact information for all content providers
- Logging problems with resources and providers
- Providing customisable e-mail alerting systems
- Linking license documents to resource records

ELECTRONIC ACCESS RESOURCE AND THEIR TYPES

Direct Access Resources

These are the resources which can be used at any time, *e.g.* Databases available in CD form.

Advantages:

- Can be used at any time and only computer is required.
- Searching and downloading is easy and quick.

Disadvantages:

- Database CD can be protected from scratches or other things which may spoil it.
- Information contained by these is getting out dated with minute span of time.

Remote Access Resources

These are the server and client based information resources. These are the online resources in which location of the server is somewhere else, may be in another country and clients are located in different geographical location (countries), *e.g.* Science Online, Chemical Abstract Services (CAS), etc. This type of access can be given on specific range of IP (Internet Protocol) within the campus, access through username password in which information can be downloaded from anywhere with the help of Internet. Access through IP range, as well as username password is also there (in combined).

Advantages:

- Update is regular feature of these types of resources.
- Can be used by any number of users at a same time.

Disadvantages:

- Required Internet to use the resources.
- Processing of quarry depends on Internet speed and processing speed of the remote server. Some problems at the server can hinder information access.

Type of e- Resources

To keep bibliographical control over the published information, with the help of computer and communication technology various methods have been developed and adopted by the libraries from time to time. Broadly three types of e-resources are available to cater scholarly information needs of the users.

- *Bibliographical resources:* These are the resources provide bibliographical information only like- title, author, name of the journal, volume and issue number, publication date, publisher and most importantly an abstract of the entry. Bibliographic eresources are mainly containing information on single subject. These resources are not providing full-text but facilitating the user by providing linking facility to the fulltexts in some of the cases, *e.g.* Biological Abstracts (database covering biological sciences), MathSciNet (bibliographical database deals with mathematics), Chemical Abstract Services (biggest bibliographical resource for chemical sciences), etc.
- *Full-text E-resources:* These e-resources provide full-text of the document apart from its bibliographical information. The approach in these databases is journal-wise or publisher-wise only, *e.g.* American Chemical Society is the database and containing titles published by the American Chemical Society. The same way there are, Institute of Physics, Cambridge University Press, Springer Journals, Elsevier Journals and Taylor and Francis, etc. are various publishers who are providing access to full text journals/databases through Internet.
- *Portals/Aggregator products:* It is just like a super market, where one can get everything from a single shop. Portals provide a single interface to search various databases, *e.g.* Under UGC-Infonet: E-Journals Consortium Indian universities are accessing more than 20+ different databases or products. User has to search individually (has to open all the web sites one by one to search within them) for a single term if s/he wants to search in all the provided products then this exercise needs much time to cover all 20+ products. Here portals can help a user; portals will search the needed term in all the products from single interface. There is no need to go for individual database. Portal does not have its own contents but all the contents have been taken from the member publishers and provide the linking facility to the full-text. Ingenta and J-Gate are the examples of these portals. So as the aggregator products, aggregator purchased the contents (on mutual or legal understanding) from the actual publishers and providing the access to users, *e.g.* EBSCO, JSTOR and ProQuest are the aggregators who are providing access to 1000+ publisher's journals from single window. Aggregators cannot provide latest issues of journals but they keep some embargo period for access. But even

smaller libraries can have important journals through aggregators due to various low price subscription models.

Some of the challenges that Electronic Resource Management systems and LIS Professionals claim:

- Acquisition processes for electronic resources typically are more complex than for printed materials. They may involve trials that require supporting technology, license terms that require negotiation, and systems configuration to ensure that users have access to the material for which a license has been agreed. A single information source, such as a journal, may be available individually or as part of different packages from several different sources using potentially several different interfaces. Access to an electronic version of a serial may depend on a print subscription so the two forms of material need to be linked for acquisitions purposes, and of course budgets for print and electronic materials must be consolidated for financial control.
- Libraries may participate in consortia for acquiring materials, further adding a layer of complication. Some titles or collections may be purchased for the entire consortium and others simply purchased for individual libraries through a consolidated order process. Costs must be allocated to different member libraries based on a variety of possible criteria.
- Different licensing restrictions for different publisher, suppliers or aggregators means that detailed information must be recorded and tracked in order to control access to electronic resources. Licensing information needs to be made available to users and to a wide variety of library staff. Ideally, licensing information should be actionable, that is to say, it should be driving the process of controlling access to the electronic resource itself.
- Users in many libraries rely more and more on electronic materials, yet resource discovery is not simple with electronic materials. Serial titles may have records in library catalogues, but catalogues may only include print titles, not all titles to which the library has electronic access. Libraries may supplement the catalogue with separate web pages of alphabetical or topic-based lists of serial titles. Holdings information may be difficult to keep up-to-date when new issues of electronic journals appear or when the titles or coverage periods available through different bundled services of aggregators change. In most libraries, electronic journal articles can only be directly searched through external electronic resources such as abstracting and indexing services, but they may also be located using local link resolver services. Keeping all these sources up-to-date and accurate and maintaining ease of use for the end user can be a considerable challenge.

- Getting access to electronic resources requires technology and technical support not required for print materials. Authentication and authorisation services need to be set-up and maintained, in many cases both for on-site and off-site use by legitimate users. This may need to be done even before titles are licensed during trial or test periods. When users cannot access an electronic resource, local trouble-shooting will be required, whether the fault is with the information vendor's system, whether it involves a local system problem or whether it involves miscommunication such as failing to renew on time or to update IP address information.
- Libraries already have complex automated systems, including integrated library systems, library portals, digital asset management systems or link resolver services. Libraries may be producing alphabetic or topic-organised lists of electronic journals from other sources. These systems need to be integrated in some measure with electronic resource management systems in order to provide users with a coherent, easy-to-understand environment and staff throughout the library with a consistent service for consulting and maintaining information.

Responsibilities of LIS professionals to manage ERM systems:

- Manage the lifecycle of electronic resources from selection, subscription, licensing, renewal, access and to user support;
- Manage a small print serials collection including subscription, issues receiving and preservation;
- Negotiate license agreements to obtain the best possible terms and conditions, and assess vendor performance;
- Contribute to the development of policies and procedures to support efficient operations of technical services
- Administer use and development of Serials and Electronic Resources Management modules and linking management tools;
- Maintain systematic record keeping, update MARC records, collect and analyse data, and prepare reports related to electronic resources and associated issues;
- Work with Research Librarians on subscription and administration of licensed electronic resources, monitor contracts and maintain information accuracy in electronic resources management systems;
- Work with technical services staff in Acquisitions and Cataloguing and Metadata Services on procurement and bibliographic control of serials and electronic resources;
- Work with Systems Librarian to resolve technical problems and troubleshoot access issues for electronic resources and participate in the enhancement of ILMS related modules;

- Maintain awareness and engagement of trends and developments in e-resource acquisitions and management and transfers knowledge to staff across the library;
- Supervise a team of para-professionals;
- Participate in training sessions for library users

The serials/electronic resources librarian is responsible for all library continuation material in both print and electronic formats and for binding of print material. Reporting to the Associate Director for Technical Services, the librarian performs the following duties:

- Manages the serials unit of the library, establishing and documenting all necessary policies and procedures; hires, supervises, trains, and evaluates 3 support staff responsible for serials check-in, serials claiming, serials check-in record maintenance, data entry related to e-resources, binding, and sorting library mail;
- Manages all required work activities for the library's growing electronic resources including creating and maintaining electronic resource records in EBSCO's ERM Essentials and updating of any related check-in and order records; maintains licensing details, preferably electronically in EBSCO's ERM Essentials, or in paper format when necessary; monitors the lifecycle of library subscriptions to all electronic resources, including individual journals, databases, e-resources packages and other electronic content;
- Works with other librarians to coordinate the set up of trials for electronic resources; notifies Associate Director for Technical Services when orders resulting from trials should be placed;
- Monitors vendor performance; works with Systems/Emerging Technologies Librarian to set up and monitor usage statistics gathered through the proxy server, Serials Solutions, and/or collected directly from publishers and vendors;
- Coordinates with Systems/Emerging Technologies Librarian and Associate Director for Technical Services to troubleshoot access problems;
- Takes lead role in promoting electronic resources, working with both reference librarians and the Systems/Emerging Technologies Librarian to develop a wide array of activities that will increase the students' and faculty's awareness and use of the library's electronic resources;
- Works closely with Systems/Serials Library Specialist on claiming and replacement of print and other serials-related matters;
- Serves as a backup for placement of rush, faculty requests using a University of Pennsylvania purchasing card;
- Participates in a variety of library-wide planning activities and committees; participates in collection development activities; serves

as serials liaison with other library and law school departments, library patrons, other libraries and organisations.

SELECTING AND EVALUATING PRINT AND ELECTRONIC INFORMATION

Selecting and evaluating print and electronic information for the library's collection can be as professionally rewarding as providing expert information service. Reference librarians' involvement in evaluating and selecting titles for the collection helps them develop rich knowledge of the sources at their disposal, increasing their effectiveness. The responsibility for selecting reference materials depends largely on the size and scope of the library. In large academic libraries, selecting reference materials may be assigned to subject bibliographers whose work may be limited to collection development responsibilities.

On the other side of the continuum, the evaluation and purchase of resources in very small libraries may be the work of a single reference librarian or coordinator of reference. A range of shared evaluation and selection possibilities between these points include reference materials selection committees or group assignments. The question, "What makes a book a reference book?" has long been debated in our profession. For the purpose of this discussion, reference books are those texts set aside to be consulted for specific information rather than to be read as a whole. In other words, reference books contain content meant to be "looked up".

Typically, one turns to a reference source in search of something in particular rather than to the text as a whole. Another common characteristic of reference books is that they do not leave the library premises. This ensures that all works in the reference collection are always on hand, making for a consistently available body of knowledge. Note that labeling narrative or non-reference books as "reference" to deter theft or ensure that a popular volume is always available may lead to bloated reference collections, and it is not generally recommended.

Finally, with the addition of electronic reference sources, which are increasingly available to remote library users from their homes, dorm rooms, offices, and elsewhere, reference collections encompass much more than print books and serials and may be available twenty-four hours a day.

As the present trend towards shrinking budgets for reference collections, lean reference collections, and the elimination of duplication among print and electronic collections continues, the careful evaluation and selection of reference materials is essential. Libraries should determine the criteria that will be used in selecting sources for its reference collection. The following criteria may help determine whether an item is a worthy addition to a library's collection: scope, quality of content, appropriateness for audience, format, arrangement, authority, currency, accuracy, ease of use, unique coverage and cost.

Criteria for selecting electronic resources may vary, though all of the criteria used to evaluate print resources should be considered, especially in libraries that aim to avoid redundancy in their print and electronic reference collections. Some libraries select reference materials by reading reviews in the library professional literature such as *Library Journal* and *Choice* and *Booklist*'s "Reference Books Bulletin." Other institutions insist on physically reviewing reference sources at trade shows or through special arrangements with publishers of reference materials. Most libraries employ a combination of these two.

CREATING FINDING TOOLS AND WEB SITES

Another strategy employed by many reference depart-ments is the creation of finding tools and pathfinders for library users. Here, librarians act as cartographers, mapping out the best routes through familiar territory and pointing out interesting sites along the way.

Pathfinders are often prepared for commonly requested subjects such as high school and college assignments about capital punishment, drug abuse, and the history of Native American tribes. Similarly, public libraries may prepare pathfinders that address frequently asked questions of a quotidian nature such as: finding job information, checking the credentials of a health care provider, or researching a family tree.

Depending on the topic, audience, and needs, the path-finder may guide the user to a selection of appropriate reference books, relevant databases and search terms, a selection of current and authoritative Web sites, and tips for searching the library's *Online Public Access Catalog* (OPAC) for additional materials. Librarians also create Web sites of carefully evaluated links organized by topic, sometimes known as "webliographies" that serve as finding tools. Who better than librarians to organize the World Wide Web of information, pointing the users to "the best" sources and helping them steer clear of the dubious? Web-based finding tools offer several advantages to print pathfinders.

They are available to users 24/7, they can be updated as often as needed, and they can include direct links to Web sites and electronic reference tools. Depending on the circumstance and the nature of a library's Web presence such webliographies can be either general, providing direction to broadly targeted reference resources, or subject specific.

General all-purpose lists of librarian-selected Web resources include the *Internet Public Library* and the *Librarians' Internet Index*. Examples of library subject-specific webliographies include The New York Public Library's *Best of the Web* and the University of Washington's *Information Gateway*. Larger libraries, whether academic or public, often produce indexes of both types. Smaller libraries may be better served by developing webliographies for specific areas in which they have subject specialists and linking to a general reference site like the *Internet Public Library* or the *Librarians' Internet Index*.

PROMOTING AND MARKETING LIBRARIES AND REFERENCE SERVICE

Paying attention to promotion and marketing of libraries and reference service is becoming more important than ever. Without support from the community, the library will not stay viable. Promoting reference services among individual library users can go a long way towards achieving this goal, especially insofar as it demonstrates how the library can serve them. In large communities—urban public libraries, for example-promoting the library through individual users is not enough to attract new users and major marketing or publicity campaigns become important. In academic libraries, school libraries, and special libraries, promotion and marketing are equally essential. Use of print and online newsletters, Web sites, and opportunities to meet with faculty and staff can provide opportunities to promote the library's resources.

EVALUATING STAFF AND SERVICES

Libraries may seek to routinely evaluate their reference collections or reference service. In her book *Evaluating Reference Services: A Practical Guide*, Jo Bell Whitlatch wisely emphasizes the importance of defining the purpose of the evaluation before setting a strategy.

"The most important questions you must ask," according to Whitlatch, are these: "Why am I evaluating reference services" and "What do I plan to do with the study results?" The quality of the reference interaction, from either the user's or the librarian's perspective, may be assessed to help determine how effective the reference service is. Evaluating reference staff is one way to help determine how effective the reference service is, and is one way to help assure quality reference service.

The American Library Association's Reference and User Services Association has developed "Guidelines for Behavioural Performance of Reference and Information Service Professionals," which are intended to be used in the training, development, or evaluation of library professionals and staff. The performance of reference librarians is typically evaluated on both the information conveyed to users and the satisfaction of the interaction on the library user. The following factors are covered by the ALA Guidelines:

- *Approachability:* Are users able to identify that a reference librarian is available to help?
- *Interest:* Does the librarian demonstrate a high degree of interest in the reference transaction?
- *Listening/Enquiring:* Does the librarian identify the user's information need in a manner that puts the user at ease? Are good communication skills used throughout the transaction?
- *Searching:* Is the librarian skilled at creating search strategies that yield accurate and relevant results?

- *Follow-up:* Does the librarian determine if the user is satisfied with the results of the search/inter-action?

These performance guidelines may form the backbone of a library's staff evaluation instruments, whether the instrument is a simple self-evaluation checklist, a peer-evaluation tool, or a formal evaluation system influencing earning potential. In addition to evaluating staff, the library may measure its productivity or efficiency with quantitative measures that include the number of questions answered and the frequency with which print and/or electronic sources are consulted. Smaller libraries may continuously count the number and type of in-person questions answered by the reference staff.

In larger libraries, quarterly one-week periods are frequently used to estimate the number of questions answered over the course of a year. Depending on the available resources, data may be recorded using hand-held computers, by making hash marks on a form, or by any means in between. Avariety of other evaluation strategies are also available to libraries: Assessing the quality of the resources available may, for example, be another useful measurement. Issues of resource allocation may also be incorporated into departmental evaluations, if one includes how the library's budget allocates for library staff, print and electronic resources, computers and networks, and buildings.

Evaluation methods frequently used to gauge users' satisfaction with reference services and sources include questionnaires, surveys, focus groups, observation and interviews. It is crucial that library administrators determine what is to be measured and against what standards before choosing the preferred method of evaluation. Many sources are available for detailed information on designing evaluation instruments for libraries. Selecting the best method, developing and field testing the instrument, administering the survey, questionnaire, or interview, planning the observation, avoiding interviewer bias and scores of ethical issues should be carefully considered. Analysing data and developing conclusions and recommendations may require advanced training and in some cases evaluation experts are hired.

THE CHANGING NATURE OF REFERENCE

As the form of the library has evolved in the years since Samuel Green's seminal pronouncements in 1876, so too has the nature of reference services. Today it stretches far beyond the walls of the library and strives to far loftier ends than welcoming users to the library with a "cultivated female staff." Academic libraries in particular have already seen a slowing of traffic to the physical library and the increasing use of the library's online resources. Users can ask questions 24/7 through virtual reference and expect an immediate response. Likewise, they can access electronic resources that the library provides through its Web site.

Virtual reference is growing quickly; the appeal of instant messaging and like services point to a generational paradigm shift ahead. These online reference services have the advantage of being convenient and necessary in our fast-paced world. In numerous forms and fashions, technology continues to change reference services. Libraries must be ready to learn new technology and adapt to the needs of users unable to imagine a world without technology. Like few other professionals, librarians must be willing to ride the waves of such change, adapting to meet the needs of their users. Whether it is the cell phone, the Palm Pilot, the MP3 player, or the iPod, users will want to receive and read their information on this new technology.

New models of reference are also developing to meet different user needs. Libraries are adding more points of service. For example, an information desk near the front of the library, a reference service point combined with other library services or an in-depth reference center where a user can sit down with a librarian and work out a plan for researching a paper have all been instituted to positive effect at libraries around the world.

In other situations, librarians rove the reference area to help users who do not approach the reference desk. These and other new strategies are changing the way information services are offered. As we look ahead, we must be aware that reference work will no doubt be based increasingly on electronic means of communication. It will at the same time continue to be a personal service although not necessarily face to face. There will be more emphasis on electronic materials while some older materials will still need to be consulted in print format. Even so, the way we find information and convey it is as fundamental today as it ever was.

INDEXING AND ABSTRACTING SERVICE

An abstracting service is a service that provides abstracts of publications, often on a subject or group of related subjects, usually on a subscription basis. An indexing service is a service that assign descriptors and other kinds of access points to documents. The word indexing service is today mostly used about computer programmes, but may also cover services providing back-of-the-book indexes, journal indexes and related kinds of indexes. An indexing and abstracting service is a service, that provides shortening or summarizing of documents and assigning of descriptors for referencing documents.

The product is often an abstract journal or a bibliographic index, which may be a subject bibliography or a bibliographic database. Guidelines for indexing and abstracting, including the evaluation of such services, are given in the literature of Library and information science.

CENTRAL AUTHENTICATION SERVICE

The *Central Authentication Service* (CAS) is a single sign-on protocol for the web. Its purpose is to permit a user to access multiple applications while providing their credentials only once. It also allows web applications to authenticate users without gaining access to a user's security credentials, such as a password. The name *CAS* also refers to a software package that implements this protocol. The CAS protocol involves at least three parties: a *client* web browser, the web *application* requesting authentication, and the *CAS server*.

It may also involve a *back-end service,* such as a database server, that does not have its own HTTP interface but communicates with a web application. When the client visits an application desiring to authenticate to it, the application redirects it to CAS.

CAS validates the client's authenticity, usually by checking a username and password against a database. If the authentication succeeds, CAS returns the client to the application, passing along a security ticket. The application then validates the ticket by contacting CAS over a secure connection and providing its own service identifier and the ticket.

CAS then gives the application trusted information about whether a particular user has successfully authenticated. CAS allows multi-tier authentication via proxy address. A cooperating *back-end* service, like a database or mail server, can participate in CAS, validating the authenticity of users via information it receives from web applications. Thus, a webmail client and a webmail server can all implement CAS.

SERIAL DIGITAL INTERFACE

Serial digital interface (SDI) is a family of video interfaces standardized by SMPTE. For example, ITU-R BT.656 and SMPTE 259M define digital video interfaces used for broadcast-grade video. A related standard, known as *high-definition serial digital interface* (HD-SDI), is standardized in SMPTE 292M; this provides a nominal data rate of 1.485 Gbit/s. An emerging interface, commonly known in the industry as dual link HD-SDI and consisting essentially of a pair of SMPTE 292M links, is standardized in SMPTE 372M; this provides a nominal 2.970 Gbit/s interface used in applications that require greater fidelity and resolution than standard HDTV can provide.

A more recent interface, 3G-SDI, consisting of a single 2.970 Gbit/s serial link, is standardized in SMPTE 424M that will replace the dual link HD-SDI. These standards are used for transmission of uncompressed, unencrypted digital video signals within television facilities; they can also be used for packetized data.

Coaxial variants of the specification range in length but are typically less than 300 meters. Fibre optic variants of the specification such as 297M allow for long-distance transmission limited only by maximum fibre length and/or repeaters.

SDI and HD-SDI are currently only available in professional video equipment; various licensing agreements, restricting the use of unencrypted digital interfaces to professional equipment, prohibit their use in consumer equipment.

There are various mod kits for existing DVD players and other devices, which allow a user to add a serial digital interface to these devices.

DIGITAL SERVICES

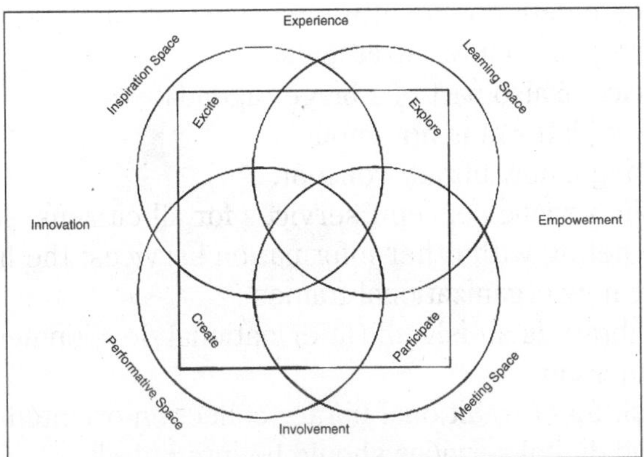

Fig. A New Library Concept.

Do we agree on the vision:

- To establish a coherent digital library covering all fields of media and library services from baby-to researcher level.
- Corresponding with the library space.
- Aiming at all citizens with segmented services and building on partnerships of all kind.

How do we get there:

- Establish a convincing strategy.
- Demonstrating capability by good working examples on new services.
- Lobbying and marketing for a new political under-standing of a library concept meeting the needs in the knowledge-and innovation society.

Digital means 'change' and 'divide':

- The gap between analogue and digital media is growing.
- The 'traditional' library still works well but we loose more and more users if we do not move faster building digital libraries.

The digital media landscape is part of a bigger agenda:

- The knowledge and innovation society.
- The changed economic balance between Europe and the new economies.
- The fragmentation of social life and growing tension
- Needs for better skills.

A European agenda:

- Knowledge societies imply globalization and a new competition pattern–jobs are moving east.
- The answer to the challenge is 'innovation' based.

- On more research, better education, lifelong learning, a strong identity and cohesion in society.
- We are in badly need of all these elements facing illiteracy, social tension in a more and more multi-cultural society.
- The fragmentation and cultural changes in the 'late modern society' are roaring for counter strategies.

E-book service is also part of a bigger agenda:

- An e-book platform is not enough.
- Developing a new library concept.
  - Public service concept: services for all citizens, segmentation.
  - Competing with other information services: the library niche.
- Creating new organizational frames
  - No library is an island: (inter)national development
  - Partnerships.
  - Break up of traditional library collection oriented organization.

Analogue and digital services should be integrated:

- The library space is for public libraries still the hub.
- The activities in the four spaces of the new library concept are virtual and real.
- The programmes support the agenda of society, from innovation to democratic inclusion and participation.
- Partnerships basic for organization.

7

Resarch Information Sources in the Library and Internet

The Internet has become a big library for all kinds of information. Some information sources are available online free of charge while others are fee-based. Examples include online books, databases, journals and reference resources. Some of these are free on the Internet while others are based on subscription or purchase. MEDLINE/PubMed is a good example of a free online database while EMBASE is based on subscription. The various categories of information sources that could be accessed through the Web:

- Reference;
- Monographs;
- Periodicals;
- Indexes and abstracts;
- Drug information; and
- Databases.

SAVING LIBRARIES WITH TECHNOLOGY

There has never been a harder time for libraries: unprecedented public funding cuts, required to cope with a deep economic downturn; the challenge of keeping abreast of rapid change in the technologies of content and search and discovery; and the quiet but insistent questioning of what role there is for public libraries in the modern world.

Responses have been varied but predictable. In one camp are those people who cling to the values which led to the development of the modern library service – books, education, self-advancement and personal development – and in the other those bureaucrats who argue that if money has to be saved libraries must be sacrificed in order to divert funds to more pressing social problems. Of course not everyone takes such extreme views, and many feel there is a middle way to be found which protects the best of the library tradition, exploits the existing network of buildings, and doesn't put pressure on rapidly dwindling funds.

Book Industry Communication (BIC) is firmly of this view. BIC is partially a creature of the library sector, having been set up in 1991 by the British Library, the – then – Library Association, the Booksellers Association and the Publishers Association to develop and promote standards for electronic communication in what we now call the supply chain. Its first chairman was Tony Hall, managing director of what is now Capita Software Services but was then BLCMP and subsequently Talis. Its original focus was to bring EDI (electronic data interchange) to the wider book world, but it quickly broadened its outlook to include bar code technology, product metadata, identification standards and subject classification. Much of the book trade – and a significant part of the library supply chain – runs on standards that BIC has developed over the past twenty years.

We believe that, unlike the book trade, the library sector has never been able to leverage available technology sufficiently to gain real cost savings from its deployment. The savings are there to be had, but only a comparatively small number of libraries have taken advantage of the opportunities. There are various reasons for this. One is the lack of the commercial drivers which galvanise interest from the book trade. Another is the lack of technical expertise in libraries themselves. Another is the huge diversity that comes from multiple library authorities making independent investment decisions on the basis of their own needs.

Perhaps the most telling, though, is the fact that the companies which exist to serve the library sector – LMS providers, RFID suppliers, stock suppliers and others – have made too good a living from the non-standard environment which these other factors have allowed to develop. Stock suppliers have made their money from servicing books to the specific needs of their customers rather than from the books themselves; LMS and RFID suppliers have been only too glad to tailor systems to individual needs rather than sell a standard product. These are the costs which BIC believes can be saved; and we are encouraged in this by the growing realisation by the companies involved that better delivery of standard products is in the end a more realistic and appropriate policy to adopt.

BIC's remit is about standards, collaboration and consensus. We believe there are huge wins to be made from eliminating waste in the library supply chain, by using technology and standards in a judicious way to cut away at the cost structures that have been allowed to exist in the public library sector because of its fragmented structure.

WHAT ARE THE KEY COMPONENTS OF THIS STRATEGY

EDI is one. Though the BIC standards are widely adopted by libraries and their suppliers, only a minority of libraries has implemented the full cycle of EDI messages – quotes, orders, delivery notes, invoices – and reaped the benefits of error avoidance, once-only keying and paperless transactions. Fewer still have been able or willing to create electronic links between library and corporate finance offices, so that invoices can flow electronically between approval and payment. EDI may be a little complicated to set up, but all the major library suppliers have invested heavily in standards-based electronic communication, and transaction costs are a fraction of any alternative and repay the investment many times over when it is in place.

RFID is another. This technology is hardly new, having been widely adopted by libraries, primarily as a more sophisticated alternative to bar codes for self-service applications, and where it has been implemented it has been universally acclaimed as a way to enable the more productive deployment of staff, facilitate longer opening hours, and provide a more welcoming environment for users. Now, with the help of the BIC/CILIP RFID in Libraries Group and its support for the new ISO 28560 standard, RFID is expanding its potential beyond self-service to stock management and other functions in the library, reducing workloads and providing ongoing cost reductions.

What is more, the standard enables libraries to invest in the technology, confident that they are not locked in to any specific vendor's software or hardware. BIC has published a UK profile for the standard, which has the acceptance and support of all the major RFID suppliers.

The work BIC has done on RFID has spawned other things too. For many years the required communication between self-service devices and LMSs has been handled by 3M's SIP2 protocol. In response to growing dissatisfaction from LMS providers, BIC has commissioned an entirely new communication framework which both extends the functionality of SIP2 but also defines web services as a mechanism for the transfer of information.

TYPES OF INFORMATION SOURCES

Information can come from virtually anywhere: personal experiences, books, articles, expert opinions, encyclopaedias, the Web. The type of information needed will change depending on its application. Individuals generate information on a daily basis as they go about their work. In academic institutions, staff and students consult various sources of information. The choice of the source to consulted is usually determined by the type of information sought. The three types of information sources are:

- Primary;
- Secondary; and
- Tertiary.

PRIMARY SOURCES

Primary sources are original materials on which other research studies are based. Primary sources report a discovery or share new information; they present first-hand accounts and information relevant to an event. They present information in its original form, not interpreted or condensed or evaluated by other writers. They are usually evidence or accounts of the events, practices, or conditions being researched and created by a person who directly experienced that event. Primary sources are the first formal appearance of results in print or electronic formats. Examples of primary sources are: eyewitness accounts, journalistic reports, financial reports, government documents, archeological and biological evidence, court records, ephemerals, literary manuscript and minutes of meetings etc. The definition of a primary source may vary depending upon the discipline or context. A diary would be a primary source because it is written directly by the individual writing in the diary. Interviews are primary sources because the individual talks about the topic directly from what he/she knows about it. Other examples are:

- Video of the inauguration of the first female president in Brazil.
- A scientific publication reporting the development of a new medication to manage patients with sickle-cell anemia.

A newspaper article reporting the bomb blast in Abuja, Nigeria, during the celebration of the country's 50th Independent Anniversary.

Note: The types of information that can be considered a primary source may vary depending on the subject discipline, and how the material is being used. For example:

- A research article in a peer-reviewed journal that proved the effectiveness of a newly developed vaccine for the prevention of HIV virus would be a primary source.
- A magazine article that reports the development of a new vaccine for the prevention of HIV infection would be regarded as a primary source.
- Information in a magazine article that reports a study of how compact fluorescent light bulbs are presented in the popular media could be considered a primary source.

SECONDARY SOURCES

A secondary source of information is one that was created by someone who *did not* have firsthand experience or did not participate in the events or conditions being researched. They are generally accounts written after the fact with the benefit of hindsight. Secondary sources describe, analyse, interpret, evaluate, comment on and discuss the evidence provided by primary sources.

Secondary sources are works that are one step removed from the original event or experience that provide criticism, interpretation or evaluation of primary sources. Secondary sources are not evidence, but rather commentary on and discussion of evidence. A secondary data are one that has been collected by individuals or agencies for purposes other than those of a particular research study. However, what some define as a secondary source, others define as a tertiary source. For example, if a magazine writer wrote about the speech Nelson Mandela delivered when he was inaugurated President of South Africa in 1990, it will be a secondary source.

The information is not original, but an analysis of the speech. If a government department has conducted a survey of, say, family food expenditures, then, a food manufacturer might use this data in the organization's evaluations of the total potential market for a new product. Similarly, statistics prepared by a pharmaceutical company on the production of a particular drug will prove useful to a host of people and organizations, including those marketing the drug. For secondary sources, often the best are those that have been published most recently.

If you use a secondary source that was published decades ago, it is important to know what subsequent scholars have written on the topic and what criticism they have made about the earlier work or its approach to the topic. The definition of a secondary source may vary depending upon the discipline or context. Most often how a source is used determines whether it is a primary or secondary source. For the purposes of a historical research project, secondary sources are generally scholarly books and articles. Also included in this category would be reference sources such as encyclopaedias. Other examples of secondary sources are:

- Bibliographies
- Biographical works;
- Commentaries;
- Criticisms;
- Dictionaries;
- Histories;
- Journal articles;
- Magazine and newspaper articles;
- Monographs, other than fiction and autobiography;
- Textbooks; and
- Web sites.

TERTIARY SOURCES

Definition

Tertiary sources consist of information which is a distillation and collection of primary and secondary sources. Generally, tertiary sources are not considered to be acceptable material on which to base academic research. Tertiary sources are usually not credited to a particular author. They are intended only to provide an overview of what the topic includes, its basic terminology, and often references for further reading.

Some reference materials and textbooks are considered tertiary sources when their chief purpose is to list, summarize or simply repackage ideas or other information. Examples of tertiary sources include dictionaries and encyclopaedias, *Wikipedia* and similar user-contributed online 'encyclopaedias' and reference materials, as well as various digests and schoolbooks.

FORMATS OF INFORMATION SOURCES

Information is available and accessible in two main formats namely, print and non-print and these include published and unpublished sources.

PRINT MATERIALS (PUBLISHED SOURCES)

Information could be in print format and these include: all printed books, periodicals, maps, bibliographies, indexes and abstracts, photographs, government documents, technical reports, etc. Books are the most common type of printed materials. *The Oxford Advanced Learner's Dictionary* defines a book as 'a set of printed pages that are fastened inside a cover so that you can turn them and read them.

A book is described by some people as a written work or composition that has been published, printed on pages bound together while others say it's just the content, separate from its container.

Books are categorized into two, namely: fiction and non-fiction. Fiction contains information that are not true and all the scenes and characters are made up by the author. Non-fiction books deals with information that is true, about real things, people, events and places.

NON-PRINT MATERIALS

In addition to printed materials, information is also produced in other formats (non-print) including audio, audiovisual, multimedia, microform and electronic books, journals, images, texts/records from the Internet.

AUDIO-VISUAL AND MULTIMEDIA

In the past decades, much of the information created by members of a given society is produced in audio, audio-visual and multimedia formats. Example of audio information is music recorded on CDs and books on audio or video tapes. Video information includes VCR tapes of TV shows, movies and documentaries. Other examples are information on CD-ROMs, DVDs, Flash drives and Web documents etc.

MICROFORM

The American Heritage Dictionary defines microform as an arrangement of images reduced in size, as on microfilm or microfiche. Microforms are any form, either films or paper, containing micro reproductions of documents for transmission, storage, reading, and printing. Microform images are commonly reduced about 25 times from the original document size, (miniaturized or compressed images) which cannot be read without special display devices (the reader). Archival materials are frequently placed in microform format because this medium is very stable and economical for storage of information for extended periods of time. There are two major types, namely: Microfilm and Microfiche.

MICROFILM

Microfilm is a roll of transparent film used to store micro-scopic images of documents. A microfilm reader is required to read the images in the microfilm. Documents are recorded in microfilm because of the risk of damage to a fragile original or to save storage space. Microfilm when properly processed and stored within special envelopes and placed in a climate-controlled room, has a life expectancy of approximately 500 years. Most libraries have a collection of microfilm stored in their archives.

MICROFICHE

Microfiche Is a small sheet of transparent photographic film usually 4 inches by 6 inches containing printed information in a size too small to be seen by the naked eye and needs a special device to read the images. The major advantages of microfiche include storage in a small space, stability of the format, and not needing knowledge to read it. As long as a microfiche machine is available to magnify the print to a readable size, anyone who can read the language can read the information on microfiche. When kept in a temperature-controlled environment, it can last for approximately 500 years; it is a good medium for saving and preserving cultural documents.

UNPUBLISHED SOURCES — INDIGENOUS KNOWLEDGE (IK)

In local communities in Africa, there is a rich body of information or knowledge which has been handed down by word of mouth from generation to generation. This is known as indigenous knowledge. It is neither written nor published but provides people in the community with strategies for survival. Indigenous knowledge is the sum total of knowledge and skills which people in a particular geographical area possess that enables them to get the most out of their natural environment. This information/knowledge is not systematically documented. It is oral in nature, usually transmitted through personal communication; it is culture-specific and often generated within communities for local level decision-making in agriculture, health care, food preparation, education, natural resources management and other activities. Examples of areas where indigenous knowledge has been very useful include, among others, African traditional medicine, conflict resolution and culture-dance steps and traditional attire.

WHERE TO FIND INFORMATION SOURCES

Places to begin looking for information are:

- Human sources;
- Archives;
- Libraries; and
- Internet.

HUMAN SOURCES (COLLEAGUES/PEERS)

Communication with peers and colleagues are a good way of obtaining vital information. For example, doctors have been found to rely on their colleagues for information in order to solve a patient's problems. The value of informal sources of information especially colleagues and peers cannot be overstressed. The good side of it is that human sources (colleagues/peers) are readily available to provide needed information at the right time. If the right person is contacted, quality and up-to-date information will be obtained. The downside of using human sources is that there may be some element of bias in the information provided, or some people will say things from their own point of view or exaggerate it.

ARCHIVES

Archives are places where records of all types and formats are kept and made accessible for research and other purposes. They are a good place to find primary sources, both unpublished materials and those that have been published for their parent institution's members or constituencies. Personal and institutional records of all types can be found in archives, as well as media, ephemera, oral histories, and even artifacts. The term *archives*can also refer to the records themselves. The materials housed in the archives are unique, usually one of a kind items. Archives store, preserve and make accessible records of enduring value that have not been produced in great quantities for the general public for research and understanding. Archival materials are rare and irreplaceable and therefore they are not loaned out to users.

LIBRARY

When you think about libraries, the first things that come to mind are probably printed materials such as books, journals and magazines. Libraries also provide access to resources such as fulltext journal and magazine articles, periodical indexes, and online encyclopaedias. Libraries collect quality information in a wide variety of formats. Academic libraries purchase these sources for their "community" of students, faculty, and staff. Unlike archives, libraries have mass produced items such as books, government reports, CDs, DVDs, magazines and journals. The exceptions are rare books, manuscripts, map and other special collections. These resources are different from most of the information that is freely available to you over the Web because they have been reviewed and recommended by the library with input from the faculty members.

Like archives, libraries have primary source materials in many forms: historical newspapers, published letters, diaries, and government reports are just a few of the types of primary sources that can be found in libraries. In addition, some libraries are similar to archives in that they specialize in information materials such as rare books and unpublished manuscripts.

WHY GO TO A LIBRARY FOR INFORMATION

The main purpose of libraries, particularly those situated in University campuses, is to collect a large quantity of scholarly materials from different time periods and on diverse topics to make research easier for members of the community they serve (staff and students in the case of a university.) Library resources are free for use by members of the community. Libraries purchase materials that are normally too expensive for library patrons. Library materials, unlike those found on the Internet, go through a review process. Librarians select books, magazines, journals databases and even Web sites for use by their patrons. This selection process enables the library to collect resources considered to be reliable, relevant and valuable. In addition, library resources are organized by subjects thus making them easy to find.

For easy access, each item of library material has a call number that indicates where it is located on the stack/shelf. Libraries have collections with in-depth information that has been published over time. Both current and out of print books and magazines are stocked in libraries most of which are in print formats. With the advent of the electronic age, some of these are now accessible through digital libraries collections on the Web. Libraries have trained staff called librarians who serve as a bridge between users and information sources. They assist users in sorting through the maze of information in their library collections. Librarians answer reference questions and also help patrons to learn how to use new information tools. If you need help with accessing information, contact your librarian.

SEARCHING THE LIBRARY CATALOG

Table. Sample Catalog Searches.

Primary	Diaries Nigerian Civil War
Secondary	Biography Nigerian Civil War
Tertiary	Encyclopaedia Nigerian Civil War

For example, you can search the library catalog of a University such as the University of Maryland or University of Zimbabwe to find primary, secondary and tertiary sources of information. When seeking information for academic purposes, it is advisable to start your search from the library and save yourself time and effort, as well as obtain relevant and quality information. You can then search the Internet if you need more information. Also, if you do not have the skills to search the Internet for relevant information, the librarians are there to assist you.

THE INTERNET

Definition of the Internet and the World Wide Web

The Internet is a global system of networked computers that allow user-to-user communication and transfer of data files from one computer to another on the network. It is a worldwide system of computer networks – a network of networks in which users at any one computer can, if they have permission, get information from any other computer (and sometimes talk directly to users at other computers) on the network. On the other hand, the World Wide Web (WWW) provides the technology needed to navigate the Internet is vast sea of resources. The WWW is a path-way of accessing information over the Internet via Uniform Resource Locator (URL) or web address.

Types of Information on the Internet

In the distant past humans sought to record information for future reference using clay tablets, papyrus, parchment and paper. However; the development of the printing press in the 16th Century forever changed the communication process. Currently the introduction of computers and the Internet has sky rocketed the amount of information now available to students, researchers, scientist, health care workers, policy makers, and faculty among others. Unlike the libraries, some of the information available on the Web is not peer-reviewed or referred as no one individual or group dictates what information should be published or how it should be presented. This freedom to post items allows individuals to publish their opinions, ideas and creative works on the Internet. As a result, the Internet has some information that may be interesting but cannot be referenced and used for academic purposes because no authority takes responsibility for it. Unlike libraries where librarians help users in accessing information, the Web is primarily a do-it-yourself endeavor.

The Internet contains all kinds of information sources including, among others:

- Bibliographic information such as library catalogs.
- Multimedia-Audio, video and graphical sources of information.
- Reference sources such as Encyclopaedias, Dictio-naries, Handbooks, and others.
- Journals, Newspapers, Magazines and Databases.

- Subject related gateways.
- Reports/Grey literature.
- Movies and videos.

REFERENCE SOURCES

These are authoritative works that provide specific answers or information. As you go through school, you will need to use reference sources to find information about topics, locate facts, and answer questions. There are many types of reference sources, including atlases, dictionaries, encyclopaedias, thesauri, directories, almanacs, manuals, biographies, and handbooks, among others. Each type is available either in print, on CD-ROMs and the Internet. Reference information sources can be general or subject specific. For example, The Encyclopaedia *Britannica* is general while *The Encyclopaedia of Stem-Cell* Research, *The Encyclopaedia of Pain*, and *The Gale Encyclopaedia of Medicine* are subject encyclopaedias. Other reference sources such as dictionaries, atlases, directories also have both general and subject categories.

MONOGRAPHS

A monograph is a scholarly piece of writing in form of an essay or book on a specific, often limited subject. It is a book that stands on its own rather than being part of a series. National Research Council (NRC), a monograph is a specialized scientific book. Monographs are written by specialists for the benefit of other specialists and demand the highest standards of scholarship. Most monographic manuscripts are critically reviewed and edited resulting in books that are expected to have a reasonably long shelf life. Monographs serve as an important means for conveying basic background information, such as a narrative description of a disease, path-physiology, diagnostic techniques and common therapeutic regimes etc. This trend remains true today, whether the monograph is in the print or electronic format.

Monographs can be located using bibliographies that list references of books with detailed bibliographic information (author, title, year of publication, publisher and date of publication). Bibliographies serve as tools for verification, location and selection of monographs. Today, many print sources for monographs are now in electronic formats. To locate monographs in a library collection requires using the library catalog and most libraries now have Online Public Access Catalog (OPAC). A good example is the National Library of Medicine LOCATOR plus.

PERIODICALS

Periodicals are publications such as journals, newspapers, or magazines published on a regular basis-daily, weekly, bi-weekly, monthly, bimonthly, quarterly, yearly, etc. The information in periodicals covers a wide variety of topics and is very uptodate. Periodicals are available in both print and electronic formats. Common examples of periodicals include popular magazines (or general interest magazines), professional and trade magazines, scholarly journals, newsletters, and newspapers. The two basic types of periodicals are: popular (or general interest magazines), and scholarly.

POPULAR

Popular magazines are periodicals of non-specialist nature. The published articles are usually written by staff writers, and chosen by the editor of the publication. Magazine articles are usually shorter, written in non-technical language, and designed for the general population. Articles in popular magazines are reviewed by one or two members of staff of the organization where they are published. Popular magazines have a glossy appearance, contains many photographs and advertisements. Examples of popular magazines are:

- O, The Oprah Magazine.
- Readers Digest.
- People.
- Time Magazine.

TRADE MAGAZINES

These are magazines that present information about a profession or a particular trade. They are written for members of a specific business, industry or organization. Trade magazines cover industry trends, new products or techniques, and organizational news written by staff or contributing authors. Good examples of trade magazines are: *The Economist, APA Monitor* and *Computer World.*

SCHOLARLY JOURNALS

Journals are written by experts or specialists in a particular field/discipline and geared towards other scholars. The purpose of scholarly publications is to report research or advance knowledge. The articles are usually longer and may contain charts, graphs, statistics, etc., as well as extensive bibliographies. The articles usually involve extensive research and in-depth studies. The writing style is more complex and the language may be technical. Examples of this type of periodical are academic journals and professional journals. Academic journals are written by members of an academic community and are reviewed by their peers while professional journals are written by member of a professional body including librarians, lawyers, doctors and nurses. Examples of academic journals are:

- British Medical Journal.
- New England Journal of Medicine.
- African Journal of Medicine and Medical Sciences.
- East African Medical Journal.
- African Health Sciences.

Examples of professional/academic journals include:

- Journal of the American Medical Association.
- Journal of the Medical Library Association.
- African Journal of Library, Archival and Information Science.

Access to journals either in print or electronic formats is based on subscription, however; fulltext articles of some electronic journals can be accessed free on the Internet. Also, more than 7000 electronic journals are available to students, researchers, scientists, health care workers, and policy makers in Africa through the Health Internetwork Access to Research Initiative (HINARI). Using this resource requires institutional registration and login with the User Identification and Password.

NEWSPAPERS

Newspaper articles are short and written in non-technical language. They provide first-hand account of an event and so are primary sources. Newspapers come in different forms and are designed for the general public and are business in nature. Newspaper articles are usually short and written in an easy to understand language by staff reporters and reviewed by staff within the organization. Newspapers are also good sources for secondary information. However, not all information in newspapers is reliable. Newspapers are published daily, weekly or monthly. Example of newspapers include: *The New York Times, The Guardian*, and *Nigerian Tribune* etc.

INDEXES AND ABSTRACTS

Abstracts and indexes provide citations to papers dealing with specific topics in a field of knowledge. Indexes provide the essential bibliographic information needed to identify an article or other publications and usually include information about the author of the work, the source journal or other publication, volume, issue, and pagination.

Abstracting tools include the same key elements but also a summary of the work usually written by the author or sometimes generated by the reviewer where an author did not submit one. Most indexing and abstracting services allow access to their content through subject and author indexes. However, each tool differs on how data is presented and the nature by which access is organized. Examples of abstracts and indexes include:

- Index Medicus.
- International Pharmaceutical Abstracts.
- Index to Dental Literature.
- Science Citation Index.
- Current Contents: Clinical Practice.
- Psychological Abstracts.
- Cumulative Index to Nursing and Allied Health Literature (CINAHL).

Most of the popular databases searched by librarians and library users originated from printbased abstracting and indexing services. For example, the Index Medicus resulted in MEDLINE now accessible online through PubMed.

DRUG INFORMATION SOURCES

Butros and McGuinness, drug information sources cover the fields of pharmacology, pharmacy and toxicology. There are as many drug information sources as there are various specialties.

DATABASES

These are systematically organized collections of information covering different subject matters or specializing in one given subject or topic. They may be arranged in a table of contents, alphabetically, in numerical order, in an index or in subject categories. A database is made up of records. Each item in the database has one record. Records consist of smaller units of information called fields.

Common bibliographic database fields are: author, publication title, article title, subject or keywords, publication date, volume, issue and page number. For example, in the MEDLINE/PubMed database, each journal citation has one record. The record consists of the following fields: author, article title, journal title, date of publication, volume, issue, page number, PubMed ID, and abstract. A digital database (8.3) is a computer programme that organizes, describes, and indexes information. It permits the user to search for specific types of information, depending upon the selected search parameters.

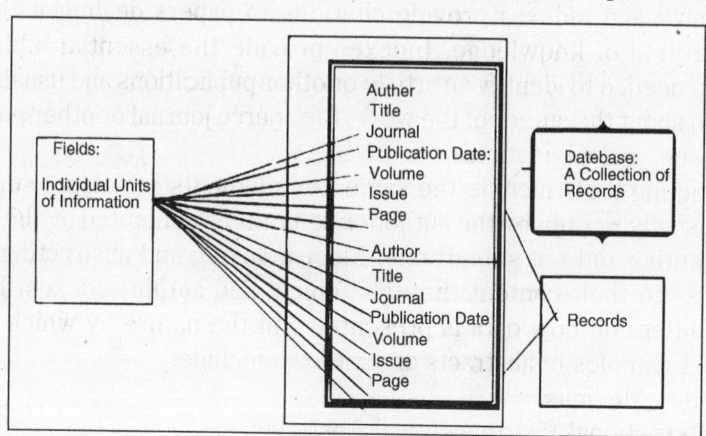

Fig. Components of a Biblographic Database.

INVISIBLE OR DEEP WEB

The "invisible Web" is what you cannot find using search engines and what you see in almost all subject directories. They are gold mines of information you need to search directly. These includes all of the licensed article, magazine, reference, news archives, and other research resources that libraries and some industries buy for those authorized to use them. There is lots of helpful information locked away in databases that can never be indexed by search engines. The services that let you search this "invisible Web" or "deep Web include: Invisi-bleweb.com, Lycos Invisible Catalog, Direct search and WebData.

Examples of searchable databases containing invisible web pages valuable in academic research are:

- Ipl2.
- Infomine.
- Online Bibliographic Databases:
  - African Index Medicus (AIM);
  - MEDLINE/PubMed;
  - Cumulative Index to Nursing and Allied Health Literature (CINAHL);
  - Web of Knowledge;
  - Scopus; and
  - EMBASE.

African Index Medicus (AIM)

African Index Medicus (AIM) is a collaborative effort between the World Health Organization (WHO) and the Association for Health Information and Libraries in Africa (AHILA). AIM gives access to information published or related to Africa and also encourages local publishing. A total of 140 journals published in Africa are indexed in AIM as of October 1, 2010. This database provides access to mainly abstracts and a few full-text articles published in African journals.

MEDLINE/PubMed

MEDLINE is the premier bibliographic database of the National Library of Medicine, Bethesda, Maryland, USA. It covers the field of medicine, nursing dentistry, veterinary medicine, the health care systems, the preclinical sciences and other areas related to the life sciences and is updated daily. MEDLINE records contain bibliographic citations from over 5,000 print and electronic biomedical journals published across the globe. It has over 12 million citations of which approximately 76 per cent include abstracts.

Cumulative Index to Nursing and Allied Health Literature (CINAHL)

Cumulative Index to Nursing and Allied Health Literature (CINAHL) CINAHL gives access to citations and abstracts for nursing and allied health information. It includes citations from over 2000 journals and abstracts are available for over 1200 titles with full text of over 7,000 records available in the database. This database also provides some coverage of biomedicine, alternative/ complementary medicine and consumer health information. CINAHL is based on subscription. However, it could be accessed free of charge through HINARI by institutions in Africa.

Web of Science

Web or science Provides access to the Science Citation Index Expanded and Social Science Citation Index. It covers science and provides technical journals in biochemistry, biology, genetics, biomedicine, genetics, microbiology, nuclear science with abstracts. It covers more than 8,000 journals. It offers current and retrospective bibliographic information, author abstracts and cited references and allows users to conduct broad-based comprehensive searches that uncover all the relevant information they need. It provides cited reference searching, the unique ISI search and retrieval feature that lets users track the literature forward, backward and through the database. It is updated weekly. Web of Knowledge (PubMed) is accessible free of charge via HINARI.

Scopus

Scopus is an interdisciplinary bibliographic database that indexes the content of more than 15,000 peer-reviewed journals from more than 4000 international publishers. It covers subjects such as the physical sciences, engineering, earth and environmental sciences, life and health sciences, social sciences, psychology, business, and management. Scopus content includes MEDLINE and EMBASE citations. Also, Scopus covers 1,000 Open Access Journals, 500 Conference Proceedings, Over 600 Trade Publications and over 125 Book titles. In addition, Scopus covers 386 million quality Web sources including 21 million patents.

Embase

Provides content to biomedical (clinical and experimental) information with extensive coverage of drug research, pharmacology, pharmacy, and toxicology, public health and mental health topics with abstracts back to 1974 and it is updated daily with pharmacological information. The database indexes more than 7000 journals, has over 18 million records. It has more than the 11 million EMBASE records from 1974 to date and seven million for unique MEDLINE records from 1966 to the present.

EVIDENCE-BASED MEDICINE (EBM) RESOURCES/DATABASES

Evidence-Based Medicine is about using information from the medical literature in making informed decision about patient care. Many EBM databases are now accessible online including, among others:

- Clinical Queries.
- Cochrane Library.

- Clinical Evidence.
- DynaMed.
- Best Evidence.

In this module, Clinical Queries and the Cochrane Library will be discussed

Clinical Queries

This is accessible through PubMed and covers three main areas namely:

- *Clinical Study Category Query*: This filters citations to a specific clinical study category and scope.
- *Systematic Reviews:* These filter citations for systematic reviews, meta-analyses, reviews of clinical trials, evidence-based medicine, consensus development conferences, and guidelines..
- *Medical Genetics:* Filter citations to topics in medical genetics.

The Cochrane Library

The Cochrane Library is a collection of databases, published on CD-ROM and the Internet and updated quarterly, containing the Cochrane Database of Systematic Reviews, the Cochrane Central Register of Controlled Trials, the Database of Abstracts of Reviews of Effects, the Cochrane Methodology Register, the HTA Database, NHSEED, and information about The Cochrane Collaboration. The Cochrane Library has about 4,000 reviews meant for use by health care workers to enable them to make informed decisions with respect to patient care. Reviews are unique because they are both produced by, and are relevant to everyone interested in the effects of health care. Based on the best available evidence, health care providers can decide if they should fund production of a particular drug. Practitioners can find out if an intervention is effective in a specific clinical context. Patients and other health care consumers can assess the potential risks and benefits of their treatment:

- Systematic reviews seek to collate all evidence that fits pre-specified eligibility criteria in order to address a specific research question.
- They aim to minimize bias by using explicit, syste-matic methods.
- The Cochrane Collaboration prepares, maintains and promotes systematic reviews to inform health care decisions (Cochrane reviews).
- Cochrane reviews are published in the *Cochrane Database of Systematic Reviews* in *The Cochrane Library.*

CONSUMER HEALTH INFORMATION RESOURCES/DATABASES

- MEDLINEPlus.
- National Institute of Health (NIH) Senior Health.
- New York Online Access to Health (NOAH).
- HealthyRoadsMedia.
- Toxtown.

- Toxnet.
- Household products database.

Medline Plus

Medline Plus is a product of the National Library of Medicine (NLM). Medline Plus offers information on selected, organized links to online consumer health information on hundreds of topics about diseases, conditions, and wellness issues in language you can understand. Medline Plus offers reliable, up-to-date health information, anytime, anywhere for free. You can use Medline Plus to learn about the latest treatments, look up information on a drug or supplement, find out the meanings of words, or view medical videos or illustrations. You can also get links to the latest medical research on your topic or learn about clinical trials on a disease or condition. It also includes tutorials.

Also featured are an online encyclopaedia, medical dictio-nary, audio-visual resources, and extensive links to Spanish-language health information. Medline Plus is the premier consumer health site. It should be any consumer health information seeker's first stop, and can fill the vast majority of information needs. The homepage is very well-organized; everything is accessible from there. When searching, multiple search terms automatically combined with "And". Search engine will detect misspelled words and suggest alternatives.

NIH Senior Health

This is a web site for the elderly, developed by the National Institute on Aging and the National Library of Medicine. Senior-friendly features include the ability to adjust font size and contrast, an audio option that reads text on the page aloud, and videos. Seniors with low vision, and anyone with low literacy needs, although most topics are senior-specific (*i.e.* Exercise for Older Adults). A short list of topics is easy to browse. No search option is included. Audio text reading function is very literal and function is spotty: may repeat phrases several times and/or skip words or sentences.

NOAH: New York Online Access to Health

A collaborative effort of New York librarians, NOAH provides access to selected, organized links to online consumer health information. It has a wide range of topics and extensive Spanish-language content. Non-Spanish-speaking users can navigate organized topic pages in English, and then click on "en espanol" link at bottom of page to access available Spanish language links for that topic. It is well-organized and easy to browse; browsing is often more efficient than using the search engine.

Healthy Roads Media

A collaborative effort of many different public health agencies, social services organizations, and librarians, HealthyRoadsMedia collects, creates and provides free online access to multilingual health information overviews on various topics in a variety of formats: audio, audiovisual, and written.

Health topics provided in English and eight other languages: Arabic, Bosnian, Hmong, Khmer, Russian, Somali, Spanish, and Vietnamese. It is best for patients with lower literacy English and/or need for information in a language other than English. Focus is on prevention and wellness, and safety. Not all topics are available in all languages.

Household Products Database

This database links over 10,000 consumer brands to health effects from Material Safety Data Sheets (MSDS) provided by manufacturers and allows scientists and consumers to research products based on chemical ingredients. Household product database was developed by the Specialized Information Services Division at the National Library of Medicine, National Institutes of Health, Bethesda, Maryland, USA.

The database is designed to help answer the following typical questions:

- What are the chemical ingredients and their percentage in specific brands?
- Which products contain specific chemical ingredients?
- Who manufactures a specific brand? How do I contact this manufacturer?
- What are the acute and chronic effects of chemical ingredients in a specific brand?
- What other information is available about chemicals in the toxicology-related databases of the National Library of Medicine?

Tox Town

Tox Town: is designed to give you information on:

- Everyday locations where you might find toxic chemicals.
- Non-technical descriptions of chemicals.
- Links to selected, authoritative chemical information on the Internet.
- How the environment can impact human health.
- Internet resources on environmental health topics.

Tox Town uses colour, graphics, sounds and animation to add interest to learning about connections between chemicals, the environment, and the public's health. Tox Town's target audience is students above elementary-school level, educators, and the general public. It is a companion to the extensive information in the TOXNET collection of databases that are typically used by toxicologists and health professionals.

Toxnet

Toxnet is a database on toxicology, hazardous chemicals, environmental health, toxic releases and other information resources from the Toxicology and

Environmental Health Information Programme. Developed by the U.S National Library of Medicine.

INTERNET PORTALS, DIGITAL ARCHIVES AND INSTITUTIONAL REPOSITORIES

- Health Internetwork Access to Research Initiative (HINARI) African Journals Online (AJOL).
- PubMed Central (PMC).
- *Bioline International (BI):* Through this site you can search through free and open access medical journals.
- *Biomed Central*: Open Access (OA) journal publisher that allow readers free access to published full text journal articles while authors pay fees to get published.
- *Scientific Online Library (SciELO):* An AO publisher that gives access to full text articles.
- *Directory of Open Access Journals (DOAJ):* Gives you free access to online journals related to your subject area.
- Loughborough University's Institutional Repository.
- *Google Scholar:* While regular Google can be a helpful tool, sometimes you just need scholarly results, and that's just what this tool does, paring down results to the most reliable and academic sources.

INFORMATION SOURCES ON SOCIAL NETWORKING APPLICATIONS

In recent years social networking applications popularly known as Web 2.0 are now being used as a means of communication, especially in sharing and dissemination of information. Libraries are also using this media to reach out to their clients. Common Web 2.0 applications that have become sources of information include:

- Facebook;
- Blogs;
- Twitter;
- MySpace;
- YouTube; and
- RSS.

RESEARCH IN LIBRARY AND INFORMATION SERVICES

Librarians often take great pride in the personalised information services they offer to their constituencies and the classes they teach to incorporate information literacy into the academic curriculum. While many of today's Net Gen students have grown up with technology, they do not necessarily have the requisite knowledge or skills to use technology and digital information in ways appropriate to the academy. Librarians should persist in their efforts to find ways to help students learn about digital information, including important policy issues in this arena, such as privacy and intellectual property. They should consider updating some of their methods for teaching students, incorporating gaming technology, or developing more visually oriented instruction aids, for example. One-on-one services offered electronically should be tailored to students' characteristics, such as their propensity to work late hours and use a variety of technologies, including laptops and cell phones.

FLUENCY WITH TECHNOLOGY AND INFORMATION LITERACY

Are Net Gen students already so technology literate and information savvy that they have no need for instruction or personal assistance in using technology and library and information resources? We know that Net Gen students come to campus having played hours of video games, having spent much of their spare time surfing the Net and instant messaging their friends, and having used multiple electronic devices simultaneously. On the other hand, we hear complaints from faculty that students use inappropriate sources from the Web to support their ideas in term papers instead of peer-reviewed academic resources; that they submit multimedia projects that are superficial and full of glitz, not substance —and that they no longer read, period.

When students graduate, their faculty in graduate degree programmes and their employers expect that they will have a facility with technology and with digital information that the older generations do not have. New office recruits are often hired because of their Internet skill and are given projects that exploit their technology and information skills, developed during their college years.

In addition, today's college graduates live in a world where it is important to understand key information policy issues. Intellectual property, privacy, and First Amendment issues are fundamental to operating as an informed citisen in today's information society and directly affect the work of individuals who create, as well as use, networked information. While Net Gen students generally can multitask, learn systems without consulting manuals, and surf the Web, they lack technology and information skills appropriate for academic work. Higher education institutions do not integrate or package technology and digital information skills instruction into the mainstream curriculum.

A National Academies report described a model set of skills for "fluency in information technology," which incorporates both information technology and literacy skills.

The report's authors divided skills into three categories: foundational concepts, contemporary skills, and intellectual capabilities. They recommended that each university's subject area curriculum develop ways to incorporate instruction in these topics; however, they lamented that this is not currently the case. The Association of College and Research Libraries (ACRL), a division of the American Library Association, has also developed guidelines for information literacy, but they have not been widely implemented by universities. Technology and information literacy are generally perceived to be "library" or "IT" problems, not overall curricular issues.

At Southwestern University, a team of IT professionals, librarians, and faculty developed a student survey based on both the National Academies' fluency with information technology principles and the ACRL Information Literacy Competency Standards. Their findings revealed that while students rated themselves highly in their ability to find information on the Internet, they recognised that they floundered when they attempted to find materials appropriate for their research and wasted much time in the process.

The students also expressed a desire for more technology applications to be integrated into their courses. This model is being explored through a Mellon Foundation–sponsored project at the University of California, Berkeley, where selected faculty and librarians are working in partnership to incorporate information literacy skills and undergraduate research into large-enrollment courses with the goal of assisting students in developing skills that will serve them throughout their coursework at the institution.

DELIVERING SERVICE WITH STYLE

Information and technology literacy represents a content area in Net Gen students' education that has not been fully addressed. Separate but related is the "style" issue of how best to deliver this educational content and provide information and technology services to Net Gen students. Net Gen students work in information environments, and a very important one in college is the course management system. Libraries should develop tutorials, exercises, and guides that can readily be embedded in course materials within course management systems, and some are already doing this. They can develop games to teach these skills; TILT, the Texas Information Literacy Tutorial developed by The University of Texas at Austin libraries, is an early example. Simulations such as Environmental Detectives can incorporate information-seeking skills into the game, reinforcing Net Gen students' interest in figuring things out and working in groups. Libraries should explore blogs as a mechanism for students to exchange information on valuable information resources they find for particular course assignments.

Blogs sponsored by the library might be particularly effective for graduate students beginning their dissertations and needing advice from peers and information professionals on locating materials for their literature reviews. An emerging area of literacy is the need for students to increase their fluency with representing their knowledge in the digital, multimedia world. George Lucas stated that students need to learn a "language of screens" in order to be effective communicators today. The Visible Knowledge Project, in which university faculty are working with multimedia content and developing assessment mechanisms to measure the effectiveness of their instruction, is also working on guidelines to assist faculty in evaluating student multimedia projects. While Net Gen students often prefer creating a multimedia project rather than a term paper that is entirely text, they need assistance in understanding how to represent their knowledge in a form that is appropriate for academic work, just as they need to learn to write in a way that meets the standards of the academy.

REFERENCE SERVICES

Although libraries have offered e-mail reference services for a number of years, they were slow to adopt chat and sometimes developed sophisticated but complex chat software rather than the simpler systems typically used by Net Gen students. Librarians might need to change their mindset of employing the most sophisticated software that enables features they believe could provide improved service, such as permitting the librarian to demonstrate a search or review an information resource in one window while chatting with the student in another, in preference for software that students are more likely to use. In one study where a library did use standard AOL Instant Messenger software, other roadblocks to student adoption were put into place.

The librarians noted in their report on the service that they did not staff it during late-night hours when students were most likely to use the service and that they did not market the service in information literacy class sessions for fear that the response might overwhelm their capabilities.

Instead, the service was not heavily used. They did collect some responses as to why students took advantage of the service, and convenience was the main reason. One student reinforced why this type of service has appeal to the multitasking Net Gen students by replying that he had used the service instead of phoning the library so that he could continue working and browsing while waiting for an answer from the librarian.

VISUAL, INTERACTIVE SERVICES

Students also like self-service, interactive Web sites, and it is surprising that libraries haven't developed visual representations of their services that students could explore. A survey by OCLC found that one of students' top suggestions for libraries was to offer interactive maps, study tips, and guides. An example of that type of environment is a Web site developed by the British Museum as a "student's room" for an exhibit of Mughal, India, an ancient civilization. Students see an office-style room that they can explore by clicking on components such as a globe, file cabinets, book shelves, and so forth. They are then led to museum resources including an atlas and primary resources from the museum's collections on the Mughal period. This type of model could be used for a library reference room and its resources.

Libraries could add value to key pages of their Web sites by including interactive tutorials on how to find information or how to judge quality information resources. Libraries could use part of their home page to highlight a "resource of the week," to better publicise information content that could likely assist students in their assignments. They could use customised mouse pads to advertise URLs for selected information resources. Libraries also need to think about new services using mobile technology such as cell phones.

They might allow students to reserve group study rooms and be alerted to availability via their cell phones, send simple text-message queries to library catalogs or databases, or check library hours via text messaging. Such services might be particularly valuable for students who live off campus. How will we conceive and design these new services? Librarians should consult with students in the design phase of services and incorporate students on teams that make decisions about the implementation of those services.

Making use of the imagination, creativity, technical skills, and perspectives of Net Gen students is the best way to ensure that new services will be responsive to both their needs and their style. To summarise, Net Gen information services will:

- Use students on teams that design new services and environments
- Integrate services into course management systems
- Explore services for mobile devices
- Represent services and instruction visually and in multimedia modes
- Focus on partnership models
- Emphasise how to evaluate information resources
- Emphasise information policy issues

ENVIRONMENTS

Although technology has transformed many campuses, physical spaces remain important in most higher education institutions. The library offers a venue where academic work can be carried out in a social context. As libraries renovate facilities to incorporate technology, they are also making them more suitable for student group work, informal socialising, and ubiquitous computing.

Information Commons often provide space, workstations, and software that encourage both access to information and the capability to create new information products. Some Infor-mation Commons offer joint support to users from both the library and IT units. It is less common for libraries to rethink their virtual services to provide a better complement to their physically based services. Libraries have opportunities to alter their marketing strategies and their use of visual representations of information to encourage more and new creative uses of digital information resources.

LIBRARY PHYSICAL SPACES

As the Leavey Library at USC demonstrates, students will flock to library facilities that offer environments conducive to Net Gen learners. What Leavey offers are hundreds of workstations in configurations that support both individuals and small groups, group study rooms where students can work together on projects, workstations equipped with a wide array of software that can be used for creation of new information products, and staff with both library and information technology expertise who can address subject-information requests and technology hardware or software issues. Many academic libraries are following the Leavey Library model and are transforming part of their physical space into information commons, multimedia production areas, classrooms, or all three. For example, the University of Arizona's Learning Center has components that include a library information commons where students can work on workstations configured for individual or group work, develop multimedia projects, and get advice from reference librarians. Adjacent to the information commons are multimedia classrooms and a computer lab with support by Information Technology staff. The Indiana University information commons, developed jointly by the library and IT and situated on the first floor of the library, incorporates single and multiuser workstation areas, group study rooms, and classrooms and offers a wide range of services supported from a circular central desk staffed by library and IT staff.

While there is no one widely accepted definition of an information commons, generally it is a physical space, not always in the library, that incorporates many workstations equipped with software supporting a variety of uses, offers work-space for individuals and groups, provides comfortable furniture, and has staff that can support activities related to access to information and use of technology to develop new products. While information commons are usually developed for student use, some incorporate centers for teaching excellence or instructional technology support services for faculty.These new types of library spaces communicate a welcoming attitude to Net Gen students. They are the opposite of old-style formal reference rooms where students were expected to sit on straight wooden chairs and work individually and silently, without access to technology. Instead, these spaces project a comfortable, relaxed environment, a celebration of technology, and an invitation to communicate.

Library physical spaces continue to be valued places for building community in colleges and universities. Importantly, they also provide an atmosphere in which social and academic interests can easily intersect.

When students were asked what they desired in an upcoming renovation of Teachers College at Columbia University Library, they replied that they wanted "a social academic experience." Libraries can promote community by providing comfortable spaces for informal gatherings of students. Many libraries are adding coffee bars to their lobby areas or a building adjacent to the library;

such spaces encourage students to continue conversations on topics of academic interest. Libraries might develop new ways of promoting community among students, related to course activity. For example, they may develop a message board or online mechanism for students to identify who else in the library building might be working on an assignment for a particular course if they need help from a peer or wish to study as a group.

INTEGRATING PHYSICAL AND VIRTUAL ENVIRONMENTS

Most libraries have not yet learned how to effectively integrate physical spaces with virtual spaces and services. For example, the introductory screen on work-stations in an information commons may have no description of the services or digital information products offered there.

Vassar College has remedied this in their Media Cloisters, where entering visitors are confronted with a brightly coloured set of screens introducing student members of the multimedia team and advertising their areas of expertise.

How might libraries market services to Net Gen students, who are often visual learners? One possibility is to literally project information onto the walls of the information commons.

In a changing display, libraries could develop programmes to project pages of electronic journals, guides to subject fields or topics that many students are working on during a specific week, quality Web sites with good visual displays (for example, museum Web sites), and student or faculty multimedia information products. Such displays would alert students to the broad array of electronic information resources accessible through the library and could prompt student interaction with a reference librarian to pursue similar sources for their projects.

AS INFORMATION RESOURCE MANAGER

The term Information Resource Manager refers to:

- "Individuals who are responsible for the provision of information resources—be they print or electronic or technical infrastructure—and the power of digital technology, which grows everyday. To provide the leadership to conceptualise and manage the broad array of information resources that are necessary to support its mission".

As an Information Resource Manager, the librarian would continually go through a ten-step process:

- *Step 1. Define the Customers:* Who are the library's primary customers?
- *Step 2. Understand the Customers Needs:* One of the best ways to help you analyse the needs of the workforce and effectiveness of your current information strategy, is to arrange an information audit examples:

— Implementation of custom survey designed to take an inventory of products, services and personnel related to information activities
— Interviews with key personnel
— Understand the users needs
— Analysis of surveys and interviews
— Creation of 'information strategy' designed to help maximize investment in users and services
— Recommendations

- *Step 3. Map Needs against Decisions and Sources:* This will list information originators and users; sources required and decision supported. It will also identify high pay-off opportunities, for example where certain information has multiple uses.
- *Step 4. Implement a Sourcing Strategy:* The source/needs map from step 3 will point to clusters of information needs that can give economies in purchasing. For example, purchasing a networked CD-ROM may be more cost-effective than doing multiple ad-hoc online searches.
- *Step 5. Define Information Policies and Standards:* Steps 1-4 will reveal, often to many people for the first time, the sheer wealth of information that is available. This step therefore involves:
  — Classification standards,
  — Ownership,
  — Life-cycle management standards
  — Agreed 'protocols and procedures' between owners and users.
- *Step 6. Select a Pilot Project:* Select a key decision process that involves people across several departments as a pilot.
- *Step 7. Select and Adapt Appropriate Technology:* With the selected pilot project acting as a focal point, now is the time to start detailed consideration example of the computer solution. The choices are bewildering, and are proliferating daily.
- Step 8. *Nurture the Intelligence Processes:* This requires encouraging interaction across departmental boundaries and subcultures. Therefore, the creation of events and forums to encourage this interchange is often a useful starting point.
- *Step 9. Focus Dissemination:* Issue weekly or monthly bulletins of key developments; it should be short and focused. They give organisation relevant and specific information that no external newsletter, with its generic coverage, can provide.
- *Step 10. Market the Capability:* Create two way interactions with library clients. Use all the techniques of marketing to reach the library's

internal audience and consider carefully the incentives the library can offer to encourage the regular inflow of useful information.

AS TRAINER

Ben regard managing technological change is somewhat akin to the Queen's concept of progress in Through the Looking Glass. He claimed *"It takes all the running you can do, to keep in the same place. If you want to get somewhere else, you must run at least twice as that."* Thus to 'manage' this frenetic running pace, training is critically important. Trainers have to be very philosophical people, very adaptable, too. MacKellar claimed that two million anecdotes of unhappy and unavoidable crisis situations, however, do not replace the necessity of thorough preparation and competent training coverage, especially with basic tools such as Internet, CD-ROMs and other electronic sources. He added, in the documentation manual for Folio VIEWS, the following four statements are listed, emphasising the fact that trainers have to train users to do more than simply be able to push the right buttons:

- *Information* does not equal knowledge.
- Use of *information* can lead to knowledge.
- If you can't find the *information* you need, gaining knowledge can be difficult.
- If you can't use the *information* once you find it, gaining knowledge can be impossible.

So, what can trainers do to move users from button pushing to knowledge gathering? They can be patient, teach some underlying technology, and explain some basic search rules. Erlendsdottir consider training in libraries as in other organisations, is divided into two main categories:

1. *Maintenance training*—that enables the library to maintain its existing procedures and include induction training for new entrants to the library system or particular parts.
2. *Basic updating and improvement training in identified areas*—whereby training should be concerned with the whole person, concepts, skills and behaviour patterns.

As suggested, the technological training needs of the librarians in libraries depend on the IT level of the particular level.

Thus, the librarian must:

- Know the Art of the Search.
- Know what the systems contain example how the shopping streets of information are laid out.
- Know the back alleys as well as the main routes to the information example on the CD-ROMs.
- Bargain with the system to get the 'best answers' in the cheapest, quickest way.

- Consider using a greater range of visual and auditory challenges in the presentation.
- Keep abreast of the ongoing and latest technological advancements.
- Able to identify the body of core knowledge and skills required by them to run information and communication technology applications.
- Improve and promote the existing and new library services to reach their clients.

Training library users to use these technological resources, and to understand the cultural rules and the new environment such as functional setup, linking, split screens, exporting, cutting and pasting) are the challenges. Trainers are similar in a way to personal shoppers for Westerners who land in Hong Kong and don't know the environment or culture. Thus the trainer's end goal is to see these clients finally doing their own shopping in the information marketplace, hopefully with enough expertise to be able to pick up a few bargains.

Why the Need for Training

The three major benefits are:

1. Appreciate the gaps that may exist between what is currently being done and what needs to be done.
2. Opportunity to make corrections in their systems within a safe environment.
3. Develop 'ownership' and reduce or eliminate staff and users resistance to change, thereby adding longevity to the system.

Training for trainers is regard a necessity in academic libraries and it is the library's responsibility to structure training so as to help librarians clarify both their own expectations and the expectations of their clients and the organisation itself.

AS RESEARCHER

In a complex and rapidly changing environment, higher education must help students to become information literate. Information literacy enables students to recognise the value of information and use it to make informed choices in their personal, professional and academic lives. An information literate student effectively accesses, evaluates, organises, synthesises and applies information from a variety of sources and formats in a variety of contexts. Information literacy requires an ongoing involvement in learning and in evaluating information so that life long learning is possible."

As research and teaching increasingly rely on global networks for the creation, storage and dissemination of knowledge, the need to educate information-literate students has become more widely recognised. Students often lack the skills necessary to succeed in this rapidly changing environment, and faculty need training and support to make use of new technologies for effective teaching and learning. The current environment provides an opportunity for librarians to playa key role in the evolution of an integrated information literacy curriculum, in contrast to past efforts which were sporadic and rarely programmatically based. Librarians have always played a key role in research activities in the academic environment.

They have conducted library instructional orientations sessions to assist students doing research. Thus, to assist clients in their research activities, the librarian must acquire the information skills to manage the overload of information available in many formats propelled by technological advancements.

The Search Strategy

The best strategy involves identifying "what type of information need and which library resources will best provide that information." The time spent developing a well-organised search strategy will reduce the overall time and effort required to assist and conduct research. Following the steps in the *flowchart* below will lead to a well organised research report:

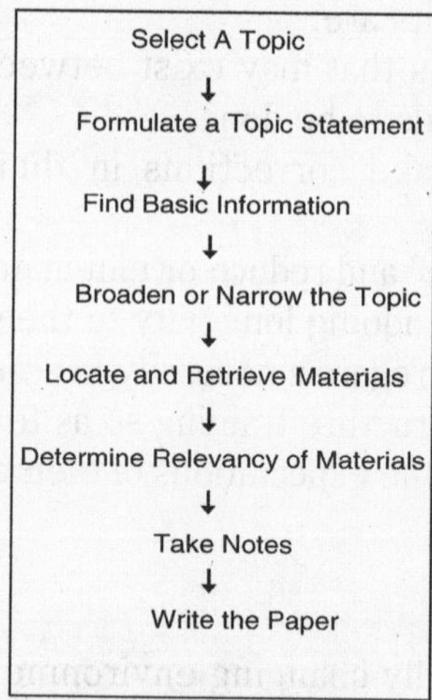

Fig. Follow chart

Information Literacy Competencies

The impact on student who is information literate is able to:

- Identify and articulate needs which require information solutions:
  - — Recognise a specific information need.
  - — Focus and articulate the information need into a researchable question.
  - — Understand that the type and amount of infor-mation selected is determined in part by the parameters of the need, as well as by the information available.

- Identify and select appropriate information sources:
  - — Recognise the availability of a variety of sources and of assistance with using them.
  - — Identify types of information resources in a variety of formats and understand their characteristics.
  - — Select types of information resources appropriate to a specific information need.
- Formulate and efficiently execute search queries appropriate for the information resource:
  - — Understand that different information sources and formats require different searching techniques, including browsing.
  - — Select the search strategies appropriate to the topic and resource.
  - — Understand that various resources may use different controlled vocabularies to refer to the same topic.
  - — Use search language appropriate to the source, such as a controlled vocabulary, key words, natural language, author and title searches to locate relevant items in print and electronic resources.
  - — Use online search techniques and tools to locate relevant citations and to further refine the search.
- Interpret and analyse search results and select relevant sources:
  - — Understand that search results may be presented according to various ordering principles.
  - — Assess the number and relevance of sources cited to determine whether the search strategy must be refined.
  - — Recognise the components of a citation and differentiate between types of resources cited, such as a book, periodical, or government document, as well as the format.
  - — Use the components of a citation to choose those most suitable for the information need.
  - — Perceive gaps in information retrieved and determine whether the search should be refined.
- Locate and retrieve relevant sources in a variety of formats from the global information environment:
  - — Understand the organisation of materials in libraries and use locally produced location guides.
  - — Understand how to use classification systems and their rationale.
  - — Use location information in the bibliographic record to retrieve locally owned resources.
  - — Use local resources to locate information sources in the global information environment.
  - — Understand that libraries have developed methods for locating and sharing resources not owned locally and use the appropriate

resource sharing system, such as interlibrary loan or document delivery, to retrieve information.

— Understand that the Internet may be a useful resource for locating, retrieving and transferring information electronically.

- Critically evaluate the information retrieved:

— Use a variety of criteria, such as author's credentials, peer review, and reputation of the publisher, to assess the authority of the source.

— Assess the relevancy of a source to an information need by examining publication date, purpose, and intended audience.

— Recognise omission in the coverage of a topic.

— Recognise and evaluate documentation for the information source, such as research methodology, bibliography or footnotes.

— Distinguish between primary and secondary sources in different disciplines and evaluate their appropriateness to the information need.

— Apply evaluation criteria to all information formats.

- Organise, synthesise, integrate and apply the information:

— Use appropriate documentation style to cite sources used.

— Summarise the information retrieved.

— Recognise and accept the ambiguity of multiple points of view.

— Organise the information in a logical and useful manner.

— Synthesise the ideas and concepts from the information sources collected.

— Determine the extent to which the information can be applied to the information need.

— Integrate the new information into existing body of knowledge.

— Create a logical argument based on information retrieved.

- Self-assess the information-seeking processes used:

— Understand that information-seeking consists of evolving, non-linear processes that include making multiple decisions and choices.

— Describe the criteria used to make decisions and choices at each step of the particular process used.

— Assess effectiveness of each step of the process and refine the search process in order to make it more effective.

— Understand that many of the components of an information seeking process are transferable and, therefore, are applicable to a variety of information needs.

- Understand the structure of the information environment and the process by which both scholarly and popular information is produced, organised and disseminated:

- — Understand that information structure, *e.g.*, how information is produced, organised, and disseminated, can vary from discipline to discipline.
- — Understand that the value of a particular type of information resource may vary from discipline to discipline.
- — Understand that the information structure in a particular discipline can change and modify search strategies to accommodate these changes.

- Understand public policy and the ethical issues affecting the access and use of information:
  - — Understand the ethics of information use, such as knowing how and when to give credit to information and ideas gleaned from others by appropriately citing sources in order to avoid plagiarism.
  - — Respect intellectual property rights by respecting copyright.
  - — Understand concepts and issues relating to censorship, intellectual freedom, and respect for differing points of view.
  - — Understand the social/political issues affecting information, such as:
  - — Privacy.
  - — Privatisation and access to government information.
  - — Electronic access to information.
  - — The exponential growth of information.
  - — Equal access to information.

CYBRARIANS

The word 'Cybrarian' was coined by Michel Bauwens, Information Officer at BP Nutrition in Antwerp, Belgium, to describe the staff in a virtual library.

We may expand this definition to an Information Professional/Librarian who utilises digital and networked communications technologies to the fullest to retrieve, evaluate and disseminate information.

While it is not currently possible to obtain a degree in 'cybrarianship', there are possibilities for advancing your knowledge of these technologies.

Characteristics of Cybrarians

So, what then are the characteristics of cybrarians. Keller commented:

- They remember the fundamental functions librarians perform: selection, description and intellectual access, interpretation, distribution, and preservation.
- They remember that they are present to serve the current, local population of readers first, but also perhaps remote readers as well, thanks to the networks.
- They remember also that they perform a vital role as custodians of culture, assuring that the records of man's investigations and creative works survive for those not yet born.

- Many of them are subject specialists, expert and educated in a discipline as well as prepared to 'teach' in structured and unstructured settings.
- Many of them are technical specialists, catalogers, circulation librarians, conservationists.
- Some of them were either subject specialists or technical specialists or both and then became managers or leaders.
- All of them are comfortable with the constant on-rush of LT. and realise their fundamental functions must be performed regardless of the media or format of the information carrier.
- All of them are acutely aware of the need to be as responsive as possible to individuals even while translating a cacophony of individual needs and requests to systems and services intended to serve whole populations, whole communities.
- All of them will be ready to work with their colleagues in the next building, the next city or town, the next country or continent by using the communications potential of the networks.
- None of them will need a lot of sleep, for there will be more and more for them to do.
- Many of them will have strong entrepreneurial spirit.

MULTILINGUAL ACCESS TO INFORMATION IN A NETWORKED

One of the great benefits of digital libraries is the ability to make information available to a wide audience without geographic constraints. As large-scale digital libraries contribute to the dismantling of the geographic barriers to information access, however, the barrier raised by language considerations becomes apparent. In order to make information available to the widest possible audience, this language barrier must also be tackled. Ideally, a global digital library would provide access to information in all the languages of the world, to all people, all the time. Anyone anywhere could create information in their native language, yet others, wherever they are, could discover that information and have it translated into their favoured languages and formats. Such an ideal situation may well be beyond our reach at the present moment, but it raises issues worthy of investigation.

No single collection, user interface, or set of system capabilities will serve young and old, novice and expert, artist and physicist, in New Delhi and New York. Nor will any single system provide adequate access to books, music, movies, and numeric data, much less serve applications as diverse as ecommerce, weather modelling, census tracking, library catalogues, and virtual classrooms. Yet people with varying backgrounds and skills, speaking in different tongues, have similar information needs. Content of interest may exist in a wide variety of forms and languages, and the same content and collections may be of interest to a wide range of people, for many different reasons. The prospect of a global digital library presents several opportunities like,

- Making information resources accessible to particular user communities while at the same time making those same resources accessible to a broader, improperly-defined, and perhaps unknown audience, and
- Enabling users to bridge the many formats, representations, and languages of individual digital libraries in their quest for information resources.

The issue of multilingual access to information is an example of the tradeoffs between tailoring to local communities and generalising to a global audience. This particular issue is

- Urgent in view of the rate at which new text is being created,
- Long-term — in view of the relative stability of languages compared to the ephemeral nature of new media formats, and
- Broad-reaching — in view of the fact that some form of textual content is involved in most forms of electronic communication, whether alone or as descriptions of other media.

FROM MONOLINGUAL TO MULTILINGUAL DIGITAL LIBRARIES

Language is one of the most critical factors in access to information. Information is usable and useful only if it is in a language that can be read or otherwise understood. Communication between people speaking a common language, whether English, French, Mandarin, or Hindi, is influenced by factors such as subtleties of phrasing, vocabulary, regional accents, and knowledge of the subject matter being discussed. In monolingual information retrieval, some of these difficulties are ameliorated through

- Standardising forms,
- Controlled vocabulary, and
- Algorithms that employ knowledge of grammatical structure and word frequency in the language.

People often need information that exists in languages other than those they read or speak, however. Human translators can bridge language in oral and written communication. They can translate between spoken languages in real time, and they can translate texts. Translation is a challenging intellectual task, as no two languages map precisely onto one another. A word in one language may have several meanings in the other, and the interpreter must determine which is most appropriate. Conversely, one word may incorporate multiple meanings in another language and the appropriate subset must be identified. Often, a narrative explanation is needed in place of a single word.

Meaning depends on context as well as on choice of words. Metaphors and idioms are particularly difficult to convey in other languages. Translators are really interpreters of meaning; that is why automatic translation is so limited. Computers can provide approximate translations, particularly of scientific texts, but are far from a reliable substitute for expert human language interpreters. Providing access to information in multiple languages is a challenge inherent in constructing a global information infrastructure. It is also fundamental to tailoring and interoperability trade-offs. Given a choice, people generally prefer to communicate in their native language, both online and offline. Communication in international environments frequently involves multiple languages, however, and people often need information written in unfamiliar languages. The problem of multilingual access to information affects not only users in countries in which several languages are spoken but also all those who search material in information sources or databases containing material in more than one language.

This is the case in the majority of scientific or research databases. In addition, the growth of networks means that we can easily access information/ databases outside our own immediate circle — in another country, another continent. In doing so, we encounter problems concerning not only search interfaces, but also concerning search keys like, subject or even author in another language. Multilingual information access is a pervasive problem in automation, and it is of great concern for anyone exchanging information over computer networks. Multilingual access issues affect e-commerce, information institutions such as libraries, archives, museums, academic institutions at all levels, and those who produce hardware and software for network applications.

However, it is important to understand the connotation of the term 'multilingual access.' Multilingual access is frequently used to cover a variety of topics, and it is necessary to define the use of the term 'multilingual' in the context of this paper.

We frequently hear talk of multilingual systems in reference to search environments, whereas the actual access points themselves are in fact monolingual. Multilingual user environments are now standard in the majority of systems.

MULTILINGUAL ACCESS TO INFORMATION

Multilingual digital libraries are being created by countries with more than one national language, by the European Union, and by international research consortia and international businesses. Major scientific, technical and medical databases, such as INSPEC and Medline, long have contained metadata in English to represent materials in other languages. Monolingual digital libraries also are being created in many different languages. Many of these digital libraries are of interest well beyond the borders of the countries creating them, and to users who are native speakers of other languages. A fundamental challenge of constructing a global information infrastructure and a global digital library is to provide access to these collections, regardless of the language of the content and the language of the information seeker. The World Wide Web offers access to information resources in many languages. Certain developments facilitate multilingual exploitation of these resources.

Some search engines, for example, allow the user to restrict retrieved sites to those in particular languages; some also provide the searcher with an interface in a chosen language. Many Web sites also offer their information in several languages, one of which typically is English. Systran, a machine translation system available from the AltaVista search engine, can even translate a search statement or a retrieved page from one language to another. Despite these features, however, language also creates obstacles to full exploitation of Web resources. Not all languages are catered for by these multilingual tools. Machine translation output typically is but a rough and ready version of a human translation. The varieties of scripts in which the written forms of the world's languages appear also create major problems in searching, inputting, displaying and printing text in non-Roman scripts. Multilingual access to information is a complex problem. Peters and Picchi have divided it into two basic parts:

- Multiple-language recognition, manipulation, and display — involving matters such as encoding character sets and symbols so that they can be manipulated, and
- Multilingual or cross-lingual search and retrieval — referring to search for content in other languages, otherwise known as "cross-language information retrieval."

The first point addresses the problem of allowing digital library users to access the system, no matter where they are located, and no matter in what language the information is stored; it is a question of providing the enabling technology. The second point implies permitting the users of a digital library containing documents in different languages to specify their information needs in their preferred language while retrieving documents matching their query in whatever language the document is stored; this is an area in which much research is now under way. Let us first have an outline of this second point

Cross-Language Information Retrieval

The interface of a multilingual digital library must include features to support all the languages that will be maintained by the system and to permit easy access to all the documents contained. However, it must also include functionalities for multilingual or cross-language search and retrieval. This implies the development of tools that allow users to interact with the system, formulating the queries in one language and retrieving documents in others. The problem is to find methods which successfully match queries against documents over languages. This involves a relatively new discipline, generally known as *Cross-Language Information Retrieval* (CLIR), in which methodologies and tools developed for *Natural Language Processing* (NLP) are being integrated with techniques and results coming from the *Information Retrieval* (IR) field. Peters and Picchi have identified three approaches that are being studied for solution of the CLIR problem:

- Text translation by machine,
- Knowledge-based techniques, and
- Corpus-based techniques.

Text translation can be divided further:

- Translating the full content of the digital library into another language, or
- Translating only the query.

Translating the full content is rarely feasible except in very small and specific applications. For example, in the area of meteorological reports automatic translation is reasonably successful. For most applications, translating queries appears to be more promising. Queries in English, say for example, can be translated into Japanese and searched in Japanese databases, and vice versa. Knowledge-based approaches involve multilingual dictionaries, thesauri, or ontologies. In these approaches, searchers can construct a query using terms in their own language. The multilingual thesaurus is then used to translate the terms into the target language; they are then submitted to databases in that language. Thesauri can be translated pair wise or among a larger number of languages. In the latter case, a common core of terms would be established, and then the linguistic equivalents in each language would be determined.

Corpus-based techniques involve linguistic characteristics of a language and the distribution of terms in a collection of documents. Information retrieval techniques developed for monolingual retrieval, such as vector-space models and probabilistic methods can be employed for multiple languages. Usually some test databases in each language are required to "train" the algorithms about the relationships between corpora in each language. Each of these methods is both promising and problematic. None are complete solutions, and all are under active study. For any of the cross-language techniques to be effective, however, underlying technical issues in managing multilingual text must be resolved.

Multilingual Recognition and Representation

Despite its name, until recently the World Wide Web had not addressed one of the basic challenges to global communication: the multiplicity of languages. Standards for protocols and document formats originally paid little attention to issues such as character encoding, multilingual documents, or the specific requirements of particular languages and scripts.

Consequently, the vast majority of WWW browsers still do not support multilingual data representation and recognition. Ad-hoc local solutions currently abound which, if left unchecked, could lead to groups of users working in incompatible isolation. The main requirements of a multilingual application are to:

- Support the character sets and encodings used to represent the information being manipulated;
- Present the data meaningfully;
- Manipulate multilingual data internally.

CHARACTER ENCODING

Character encoding is at the heart of the data-recognition, data-manipulation, and display components of multilingual information access. The creation of characters in electronic form involves hardware and software to support input, storage, processing, sorting, displaying, and printing. Each character – or ideograph in languages such as Chinese, Japanese, and Korean – needs a unique code to ensure that it sorts, displays, prints, and is matched properly upon searching. Additional codes are required for punctuation, direction of text, carriage returns, and line feeds. The internal representation of each character determines how it is treated by the hardware and the application software. To the dismay of those whose languages have far larger character sets, typewriter keyboards were initially designed for the English language; thus, they contain only 26 letters, 10 numbers, basic punctuation, and a few special symbols.

Only a few more symbols and function keys were added when the typewriter keyboard was adapted to become a computer keyboard. Many versions of the QWERTY keyboard are now in use worldwide, varying the location of letters. Special characters, such as letters with diacritics, can be generated by programming individual keys or by programming key sequences, often using escape key. The same key sequences on two different keyboards may produce two different characters, depending on the encoding system employed. Conversely, key sequences required to generate a character vary by keyboard and encoding system. Effective data exchange is heavily dependent on character encoding.

Characters produced from different applications may appear the same on a screen or a printout but have different internal representations. Merging or transferring data between applications requires a common character-encoding standard or software to map variant encoding formats. Searchers need to have the appropriate keyboards and software to generate characters in the encoding standard in which the contents of a digital library are stored, whether locally resident or available through mapping software located at the digital library site or elsewhere. Local printers and displays must have the appropriate software to interpret and produce characters accurately. These factors are not specific to digital libraries; rather, they are issues for all distributed applications on a global information infrastructure.

MONOLINGUAL, MULTILINGUAL, AND UNIVERSAL CHARACTER SETS

For character encoding many standards and practices exist, viz.

- Those that are language specific,
- Those that are script specific, and
- The remaining are universal standards that support most of the world's written languages.

Digital libraries employ many different character-encoding formats, and this often leads to problems in exchanging data. After many years of international discussion on the topic, it became evident that adopting a universal character set offered the greatest hope for exchanging text in digital form. If data in all written languages were encoded in a common format, then data could be exchanged between monolingual and multilingual applications, whether e-mail, e-commerce, or digital libraries. Which common format to accept was a matter of long debate, however. In 1991, the Unicode Consortium and the *International Organization for Standardization* (ISO) finally reached an agreement to merge the 16-bit Unicode Standard and the 32-bit ISO standard into a common 16-bit Unicode Standard. Version 1.1 was first published in 1993; version 4.0 is currently the accepted Unicode Standard and the latest revision is numbered as 4.1.0. Unicode can support more than 96,000 distinct characters. Version 4.0 of the standard provides about 96,382 characters from the world's alphabets, ideograph sets, and symbol collections. Version 4.1.0 of the standard has included a further 1273 new characters. A growing number of world's major hardware and software vendors are supporting it and it is being incorporated into popular operating systems and programming languages. A list of such Unicode enabled products can be found from the Unicode Consortium's homepage. As software for e-commerce, digital libraries, automated library management systems, and other applications begin to support Unicode, it will become more widely adopted. Unicode Standard represents a tremendous advance for multilingual computing, but more work is needed in order to achieve a truly multilingual Web.

The impact will be manifold: it will help in the publication and preservation of materials in ancient and historic scripts, facilitate the online teaching of languages using such scripts, and provide universal access to our cultural and literary heritage. As storage costs continue to decline, the storage requirements of Unicode will be an insignificant issue, particularly for new applications. In the meantime, substantial amount of text continue to be produced not only in language-specific and script-specific encoding standards but also in local and proprietary formats. Any of this text maintained in digital libraries may become legacy data that has to be mapped to Unicode or some other universal standard in the future. For the present, digital library designers face difficult trade-offs between the character-set standards in use by current exchange partners and the standard likely to be in worldwide use in the future for a broader range of applications.

TRANSLITERATION AND OTHER FORMS OF DATA LOSS

A long-established intermediate approach to character encoding for languages that cannot be typed on a standard computer keyboard is transliteration, which matches characters or sounds from one language to another but does not translate meaning. Languages written in non-Roman scripts, such as Japanese, Arabic, Chinese, Korean, Persian, Hebrew, and Yiddish, Russian, and Devanagari, are transliterated into Roman characters in many applications. Transliteration is necessary when mechanical devices such as typewriters and computers do not support the necessary scripts. It also is helpful for people without full proficiency in the scripts of the language. The transliteration process may be irreversible, and thus some data loss takes place. Despite the existence of an international standardization body, multiple transliteration systems exist for Cyrillic, Asian, and other character sets. Thus transliteration can be inconsistent, which is why the same Russian name may appear as "Tchaikovsky" or as "Chaikovoskii" depending on which system is used to transliterate Cyrillic characters. Data also are lost when languages written in extensions of the Roman character set, such as French, Spanish, German, Hungarian, Czech, and Polish, are stored without the diacritics that for additional characters, all of which are collapsed into o if the diacritics are omitted).

Data loss is not exclusive to text, however; it is widespread in visual and aural media. Image compression is essential for efficient transmission of either still or moving pictures, and application-specific image compression standards exist for such applications as facsimile transmission, pictures, moving images, and high-definition television. Compression algorithms are made more efficient by discarding some of the data to reduce the granularity of the image. Images subjected to "lossy" compression are legible and suitable for many applications, but the original image cannot be reconstructed. "Lossless" compression retains the full content but requires more storage and more transmission time. Similarly, for music, a popular compression algorithm known as MP3 is used to squeeze digital audio by a ratio of 12:1. MP3 compresses music sufficiently that audio files can be sent via the Internet or stored on a hard disk. Music compressed in MP3 can be expanded and played by an MP3 player with a near-CD-quality sound, yet the files are small enough to be attached to an e-mail message. The music industry is promoting another standard, and Microsoft is promoting yet a third standard named Windows Media Audio for music compression and distribution.

The acceptance of technical standards for music and other audio may be determined as much by the availability of playback devices as by the quality of reproduction. The amount of data loss that is tolerable varies by application. Far more data loss is tolerable in e-mail and in teleconferencing than in financial, legal, or bibliographic records. Textual data that have been transliterated or stripped of diacritics are likely to contain variant forms of words that will not match and sort properly, incomplete words that will not exchange properly with digital libraries using complete forms, and incomplete forms that are not adequate for authoritative or archival purposes.. In digital libraries, any kind of data loss can result in information retrieval errors.

INTERNET-BASED COMMUNICATION SERVICES

Libraries use Internet-based communication system while attending their day-to-day routine works. An Internet-based communication system allows communication between computer users hooked into a network.

Internet-based communication system is used for communication between person-to-person, person-to-group and group-to-group. A document or message sent through electronic system may contain text, graphics, image, speech as well as other types of information.

Electronic Mail (E-mail)

Electronic Mail, or e-mail, is a fast, easy and inexpensive way to communicate with other Internet users around the world. It is the most popular and widely used services of the Internet. E-mail is the term given to an electronic message, usually a form of simple text message that a user types at a computer system and is transmitted over some form of computer network to another user, who can read it.

E-mail offers speedy and economical transfer of messages anywhere in the world. Sending e-mail messages are virtually free even to long-distance destinations. Most integrated library system support e-mail-based communication to library users (for circulation and acquisitionrelated activities) and to the vendors/ publishers (for placing orders, reminders, cancellation, etc).

Listserv

Listservs are electronic groups that typically centre around broad topics such as Digital Libraries or Reference Service,,etc. Listservers of IFLA with the name IFLA-l, Digilib-l LIBJOBS-l are good example of this. Every e-mail message sent to the listserv is distributed to all members of that listserv, which is potentially hundreds or thousands of people.

It does not cost anything to subscribe to a listserv, but simply requires that the user sends an e-mail message to the appropriate address with the message: subscribe (listserv) Firstname Lastname. Each Listserver has one address where a user sends requests to subscribe, un-subscribe, search the archives, etc., and another address to send actual questions or responses to the readers of the list. Apart from organising discussions, job announcements and conference announcements are popular usage of Listservs.

Chat or Instant Messengers

Chat refers to any live discussions conducted using the Internet, usually between more than two persons using their keyboard to communicate. Chat Programmes allow users on the Internet to communicate with each other by typing in real time. It is a feature offered by many online services or Web sites that allows users to 'chat' by typing messages which are displayed almost instantly on the screens of other users who are using the chat room at a given time.

After entering a chat room, any user can type a message that will appear on the monitors of all the other users. Chatting is one of the most popular uses of the Internet. Generally the users remain anonymous by using nicknames or pseudonyms to identify themselves online. A variation of chat is the phenomenon of the instant messenger. Instant messaging can be used to communicate privately with friends, relatives or co-workers.

To send and receive instant messages, a user needs a connection to the Internet and instant messaging software such as Gmail Messenger, Yahoo Messenger and MSN Messenger.

The instant messaging software enables a user to set up a list of contacts who also use the same Programme. Once this list is set up, one can see each contact as they come online. A chat session can be started with them quickly and easily. Most conversations are typed text messages that are sent back and forth, though more advanced users can exchange voice, video, files and more.

Conferencing

One of the most exciting features of Internet is to communicate, talk, and see groups of people in different locations around the world, without the expense of travel. Conferencing can take many forms, such as web chat, audio conferencing, video conferencing, multimedia conferencing, screen-sharing, etc.

The conferencing Programmes, such as the popular CU-SeeMe, allow workgroups to use the Internet to see each others' faces in small windows on the computer screen and to hear their voices through computer speakers.

One can use desktop video and audio simultaneously or audio can be used alone, or just use the screen-sharing capability without either audio or video.

Audio Conferencing or Internet Telephony

Internet telephony also called IP telephony is a combination of hardware and software that allows the Internet to be used as a telephone carrier. Internet telephony is the conversion of analogue speech signals used on current telephone systems into digital data, allowing calls to be sent over the Internet, bypassing long distance charges.

While the Internet was first devised as a way of transmitting data, it is now being used to make voice calls. Internet telephony is projected to explode as the costs plummet. After the costs of initial set-up and access to an Internet Service Provider, long-distance voice calls can be made via the Internet free of charge, but current quality of voice transmission over the Internet is not always as good as direct telephone service.

There are also PSTN/ Internet gateways that allow regular telephone callers to make Phoneto- Internet-to-Phone connections. There are PC-to-Phone connections and Phone-to- PC connections.

Video Conferencing

Video conferencing is one of the most exciting areas of development in telecommunications, with applications ranging from business to government to education to home and family. Video conferencing involves sending video signals as well as audio and computer data signals. Conferencing can be done one-to-one, one-to-many (called multicast), and many-to-many (called multipoint). While video conferencing, one can talk as well as see the people sitting miles away as if all are discussing in one room facing each other.

One of the most popular applications is transmission on news from various locations by the TV news channels. It also has enormous potential for enhancing communications for small and mid-sized companies, as well as distance learning. However, video conferencing requires sufficient bandwidth to transfer video files of acceptable quality. Desktop conferencing, therefore, is not yet widely implemented for business and educational use. As bandwidth increases, desktop video conferencing is expected to blossom. The PictureTel and Vtel are two of the largest companies that sell video conferencing equipment.

NetMeeting

Microsoft NetMeeting facilitates a new way of talking, meeting, working and sharing over the Internet. It uses Internet phone voice communications and conferencing standards to provide multi-user applications and data sharing over Intranets or the Internet.

Two or more users can work together and collaborate in reach time using application sharing, whiteboard, and chat functionality. NetMeeting can be used for common collaborative activities such as virtual meetings. It can also be used for customer service applications, telecommuting, distance learning, and technical support. The product is based on ITU (International Telecommunication Union) standards, so it is compatible with other products based on the same standards.

NetMeeting supports text chat, video shared whiteboard, transferring of files, directory of connected users. Files, such as documents or pictures, can be exchanged. One of the problems with net meeting is the break-up in audio that sometimes becomes inaudible when using it on the Internet, though it works fine over a high-speed company network.

News Groups

Another Internet service similar to listservs is a newsgroup. News Groups are like an International bulletin board. Each group is a forum for a different subject, where a subscriber can post his/her questions or answers.

There are thousands of groups covering just about every area of interest. The difference between listserv and news group is that when a user joins a group, the mail is no longer automatically deposited into his mailbox. Instead a user is expected to go to the newsgroup himself to read it. Some listservs can also be accessed as a newsgroup. A good analogy to a newsgroup is a bulletin board, *i.e.,* one can go to it, as opposed to having mail delivered to his/ her desk. The mails from newsgroup does not get cluttered and it can be easily regulate how often messages are read.

A drawback of a newsgroup lies in the fact that a user must remember to go out to the newsgroup to look for the information. There are hundreds of newsgroup communities. They centre around topics such as computing, news, recreation, social, and 'alternative' topics. There are newsgroups dealing with virtually every topic under the sun and new newsgroups appear every day.

INTERNET-BASED CONTENT PUBLISHING AND DELIVERY SERVICES

The World Wide Web- know as WWW, W3 or simply, the Web help people to publish, organise and provide access to information on the Internet. The WWW can be defined as a hypertext, multimedia, distributed information system that provides links to hypertext documents, as well as to many other Internet tools and databases.

The Web serves as a platform for several specialised content publishing and delivery services. Some of the important tools for content publishing and delivery services applicable to libraries and information centres are described here.

Blogs

A blog (an abridged form of term web log) is a Web site, usually maintained by an individual, with regular entries of commentary, descriptions of events, or other material such as graphics or video. Entries are commonly displayed in reverse chronological order. Blogs are considered as lightweight publishing tools.

Blogs provide control to an individual or group of individuals for publishing contents or making commentary on it. Technologically, blogs are easier to use, platform-independent, and accessible online over the Internet. Broadly, blogs can be said to be online dairies, however, thousands of blogs are maintained by experts in different subject areas who are willing to share their knowledge, understanding and opinions with other people. Michael Casey, who coined the term 'Library 2.0', for example maintains a blog on Library 2.0 called LibraryCrunch.

The most obvious application of blogs for libraries is to use it as a tool for promotion, publicity and for outreach services. Libraries can disseminate information to their users, make announcements for its new resources and events through its blogs. Blogs can be used to initiate debates and interaction amongst users and staff. Moreover, library staff and user can be encouraged to use Library blogs to get to know each other and interact at personal level.

Wikis

A wiki is a collection of web pages designed to enable anyone who accesses it to contribute or modify content, using a simplified markup language. Wikis are often used to create collaborative Web sites and to power community Web sites. For example, the collaborative encyclopaedia, Wikipedia is one of the best-known wikis, that has broken down one the golden rules of librarianship, *i.e.,* content validation and authenticity of information. Wikis are also used in businesses to provide affordable and effective Intranets and for knowledge management.

Ward Cunningham, developer of the first wiki software, WikiWikiWeb, originally described it as "the simplest online database that could possibly work". Wikis can essentially be equated to open web-pages, where anyone registered with it can publish on to it, add to it, amend it and change it. As in case of blogs, Wikis do not have reliability as traditional resources.

Inspite of this, their value as information resource cannot be undermined. Wikis are not only popular but de-facto source of information for people inspite of the fact that it is not validated or authenticated. The lack of peer review and editorship in case of Wikis is a challenge to librarians. Wikis as items in a collection, and the associated instruction of users in their evaluation, is certainly an important task for libraries. Libraries can use wiki as a communication tool to enable social interaction among librarians and patrons.

Users can share information, ask and answer questions, and librarians can do the same within a wiki. Moreover, a record of these transactions can be archived for perpetuity. Transcripts of such question-answer sessions would serve as a resource for the library to provide as reference. Furthermore, wikis will ultimately evolve into a multi-media environment, where both synchronous and asynchronous audio and video collaborations will take place.

Podcasting

The word 'podcasting' is derived from two words, namely 'broadcasting' and 'iPod' (popular MP3 player from Apple Computer). Podcasting is defined as "process of capturing audio digital-media files that can be distributed over the Internet using RSS feeds for playing-back on portable media players as well as computers.

Users can subscribe to such feeds and automatically download these files directly into an audio management Programme (such as iTunes, Windows Media Player or MusicMatch) on their PCs. When a user synchronises their portable audio device with their personal computer the podcasts are automatically transferred to that device to be listened to at the time and location most convenient for the user. Podcasts can be used with a variety of digital audio formats and play on almost any MP3 player or portable digital audio device - as well as any brand of desktop computer or laptop.

Though podcasters' web sites may also offer direct download or streaming of their content, a podcast is distinguished from other digital media formats by its ability to be syndicated, subscribed to, and downloaded automatically when new content is added, using an aggregator or feed reader capable of reading feed formats such as RSS or Atom. Several libraries use podcasts to support library orientations programmes. Taking advantage of podcasting and other consumer technologies (*e.g.*, PDAs, iPods and other MP3 players) as a deliver media of Library's content and services is a great leap forward for library profession.

Vodcasting

The 'VOD' in Vodcasting stands for 'video-on-demand'. It is identical to podcasting. While podcasting is used for delivering audio files, vodcasting is used for delivering video content. Like podcast content, vodcasts content can be played either on a laptop or on personal media assistant (PMA).

RSS Feeds

RSS stands for Real Simple Syndication or Rich Site Summary. The technology, on one hand allows a web site (or e-publisher) to list the newest published updates (like table of contents of journals, new articles) through a technology called XML, on the other hand, it facilitates a web user to keep track new updates on chosen Web site (s). Like a personal search assistant, RSS feed readers visit pre-defined web sites, look for updated information and fetch it automatically on to the user's desktop.

It provides users a way to syndicate and republish content on the Web. Users republish content from other sites or blogs on their sites or blogs, aggregate content on other sites in a single place, and ostensibly distil the Web for their personal use. Libraries are already creating RSS feeds for users to subscribe to, including updates on new items in a collection, new services, and new content in subscription databases. They can also republishing content from other scholarly web sites on their sites.

AUTOMATIC REFERENCE LIBRARIANS FOR THE WORLD WIDE WEB

The Automatic Reference Librarians for the World Wide Web, a DLI-2 funded project at the University of Washington. The central objective of this project, according to them, "is to create software agents that posses reference intelligence I a limited understanding of complex technical topics, but a very sophisticated understanding of how and where to find high-quality information on theWorld Wide Web". Etioni and Weld reported the basic working principles of the proposed system, which works on a wrapper technology. The basic steps involved are:

- The user asks a question;
- The Query Router assigns a topic to the query;
- The topic maps to a number of relevant wrappers;
- The parallel Web search module sends requests via wrappers to the sites;
- Responses from the sites are obtained and sent to the fusion engine for collation;
- User gets the response.

SIFTER is an interdisciplinary research collaboration among faculty and students in the Computer and Information Science Department and the School of Library and Information Science at Indiana University. The broad aim of the project is to develop information agents that would perform a number of functions such as culling information from complex resources residing in diverse locations, and conducting analysis, synthesis and customisation according to the requirements of the user. The specific objectives are:

- Dealing with heterogeneous information sources that may change over time;
- Handling shifting requirements and interest of users with minimal human involvement;
- Creating a robust agent architecture for reactive, proactive and collaborative filtering;
- Supporting agent collaboration based on natural or artificial economic frameworks for multi-agent tasks.

LEVERAGING THE DOCUMENT SELECTIONS OF EXPERT PROBLEM SOLVERS

This is a DLI-2 project at the Oregon Health Sciences University and Oregon Graduate Institute. The goals of this project are "to understand how experts select information in a large and complex information space and to develop tools that assist them in this process", The project aims to capture the trace of information used by experts in the health field, for example medical doctors. The basic idea is that as medical experts traverse the large and diverse collection of documents, they make explicit choices about which information resources to examine more carefully and which ones to ignore.

These choices create a subset of documents relevant to a given problem and this subset of documents may be of interest to other users concerned with the same or similar problem.

Thus, by capturing this information that is inherent in the selection of appropriate information resources for problem solving, this project aims to come up with models that may be useful for other users. The project proposed to develop:

- A trace that describes the path taken by an expert in solving his/her problem by using the available information resources;
- A precis of information about each document, its content, and the history of its use by experts; and
- Navigation tools that would assist subsequent problem solvers using the collection by exploiting the knowledge inherent in the existing traces.

Though the project specifically deals with medical experts and looks into their problem-solving processes, the project team expects that the resulting technology will be scalable, because the value of a set of precis and bundles within a collection should increase as the document collection grows and as more experts use the collection.

VIRTUAL REFERENCE DESK

The Virtual Reference Desk (VRD) is a project sponsored by the US Department of Education, and its objective is "the advancement of digital reference and the successful creation and operation of human-mediated, Internet-based information services".

VRD defines a digital reference service as Internet-based question-and-answer services that connect users with experts. The basic idea of VRD is that when a given user asks a question that cannot be answered by a participating centre, it is forwarded to the VRD network for assistance.

VRD services include the following:

- *Collaborative AskA Service*: A network of AskA services and volunteer information professionals.
- *The Learning Center*: A Web site for the K-12 community with curriculum-related Web sites, frequently asked questions, and other previously asked questions.
- *AskA+ Locator*: A searchable database of high-quality K-12 AskA services.

VRD also supports research on interoperability standards, metadata and other aspects of digital reference services.

WEB BASED LIBRARY SERVICE

A digital Library service manages and develops electronic services, the library Web sites and library staff. According to White, it can be defined broadly as 'an information access service in which users ask questions via electronic means, *e.g.,* e-mail or web forms'.

Library service on the internet requires many of the same qualities as traditional references: accuracy, promptness, courtesy, an understanding of the information need. It provides users with the convenience of accessing information in their own time, saving them traveling cost and time and new options for answering reference questions. The provision of these services is not constrained by the traditional opening hours but can be offered on a 24-hour, seven-days-a-week basis known as 24/7. And while there may be a disadvantage in not having a face-to face encounter, there are many advantages to this new medium and the greatest advantage is that many more users can be helped by using electronic library services. Advantages and disadvantages of electronic access over printed form access are showed in table. Web based services are established due to the following reasons.

- Ensuring the needs of users and the accessible information sources are suitable matched at all times.
- Delivering those information sources to the user in a timely and appropriate fashion.
- Ensuring the information provided is high quality, accurate and appropriate.
- Assisting the user in interpreting the materials, if necessary.
- Promoting user awareness of new services and information sources as they develop.
- Providing users with individualised guidance and support as they build their information search and application skills.

DIFFERENT RESOURCES FOR WEB BASED LIBRARY SERVICES

Today, users may have access a variety of textual information resources. There are different kinds of webbased reference resources and services for accessing information from libraries such as OPAC, Gateways, Portals, Subject Portals, Electronic Journals, Online Databases, Subject Directories and Search Engines. These resources overlap considerably in the type of information they cover, and sometimes it is difficult to distinguish between some of them. A library should have a good collection of these resources like selected Web links, subscription resources, and library materials in well-organised pages for serving better services to their users. Many libraries and organisations are providing digital reference service through collaborative services. Existing library consortia are adding digital reference to current shared services, and networks of libraries. Some regional library consortia are offering member libraries the opportunity to share reference questions with each other using the Internet and other technologies.

OPAC

OPAS's - On Line Public Access Catalogues, form an important part of many digital library's collections. It allows users to search for the bibliographic records contained within a library's collections. Now days, some OPAC also provide access to electronic resources and databases, in addition to the traditional bibliographic records.

GATEWAYS

A gateway is defined as a facility that allows easier access to network based resources in a given subject area. Gateways provide a simple search facility and a much-enhanced service through a resource database and indexes, which can be searched through a web based interface. Information provided by gateways is catalogued by hand. Gateways cover a wide range of subjects, through some areas, such as music and religious studies, currently lack subject gateways. Some well-known gateways are as follows:

- Internet Public Library (IPL),
- Bulletin Board for Libraries (BUBL),
- National Information Services and Systems (NISS),

PORTALS

In the library community, portals may be defined as an amalgamation of services to the users where the amalgamation is achieved through seamless integration of existing services by using binding agents such as customisation and authentication services, search protocols such as Z39.50, loan protocols such as ISO10161, and e-commerce.

The result is a personalised service which allows the individual to access the rich content of both print-based and electronic systems. Portals are either commercial or free web facilities that offer information services to a specific audience. The facilities include web search to communication to e-mail to news,etc.There are three kinds of portals; Consumer (or horizontal), Vertical and Enterprise.

- Consumer portals are aimed at consumer audiences and offer free e-mail, games, chat,etc., Examples are Yahoo!, MSN and AOL.
- Vertical portals, target a specified audience, such as a particular industry, and offer many of the consumer portal features. Example includes VerticalNet.
- Enterprise portals on the other hand are similar to consumer portals, but they are offered only to corporations or similar organisations.

Examples include Epicentric and Corporate Yahoo! These portals can be best understood as electronic pathfinders for users, pulling together in one place in a web site selected links to subjects or interest-oriented resources located on the WWW.

SUBJECT PORTALS

Web Search Engines had been developed initially by computer scientists, by borrowing techniques from information retrieval search such as best match searching and relevance ranking. Information professional are increasing bringing their skills to help organise the growing wealth of Internet resources.

A good example of their influence is the development of subject-specific web search engines known as subject portals, where evaluation of material covered is a major concern. Two prime UK subject portals are SOSIG Social Science Information Gateway, covering social science resources and OMNI Organising medical networked information covering medical resources. Subject portal sites can be very helpful, but they should be used with care. Users should bear the following points in their mind:

- The aim of the subject portal is to list and review the most important sites on the web relevant to that subject. The sites are usually constantly peer-reviewed to ensure that the site is relevant and up to date.
- New sites are appearing all the time. Relying on a subject portal site to find everything users require may mean that they miss an important site that has recently appeared and has not yet been reviewed by the producers of the particular subject portal.
- A subject portal is a one stop shop for information on the topic it covers. Users don't have to carry out extensive Internet searches in order to find the information require. They can simply go to the required subject portal site.
- Subject portals save users having to have long lists of bookmarks (saved addresses of web pages), which are often, cumbersome and time consuming to arrange and keep up to date. However, if users do prefer to use bookmarks they can arrange them in an order to suit the way they work and not have an order forced on them by the subject portal.
- A subject portal site is only as good as the reviewers who peer-review the site listed. The reviewers need to have a policy of keeping the portal sites up to date and of constantly reviewing the sites they list, to make sure that they are still relevant and still contain good, timely information.
- A subject portal may be available to everyone who needs to use it to only certain groups of users. A good portal should be publicly available to anyone who needs it.

ELECTRONIC JOURNALS

Electronic journals form a large part of the collection of a library for providing web based services. Today many journals are available electronically - some are full text and some contain only bibliographic information with abstract. Major advantage of electronic journals is that they are constantly updated and easy to access but disadvantage is that breaching of copyright law is very easy.

They are available as bitmaps, PostScript, PDF, ASCII, SGML and HTML. Library services may be delivering to users on CDRom, through e-mail or through web. Some international societies and associations have developed their own digital libraries through which users can get access to all their publications. Services are available to the members of society or associations through subscription.

ONLINE DATABASES

These are large collections of machine-readable data that are maintained by commercial agencies and are accessed through communication lines. Many libraries subscribe to them for easy access and use of current information. The disadvantage is that only bibliographic data is presented and not full text. The information cannot be accessed when the system is down for any reason. Examples Ei Compendex, SciFinder Scholar, Web of Science, Current Contents,etc.

SEARCH ENGINES

Search Engines are huge databases of web page files that have been assembled automatically by machines where as the subject directories are human-compiled and maintained. Search engine indexes every page of a Web site and subject directories linked only homepages.

Search Engine is the popular term for an information retrieval (IR) system. A search engine is computer software that searches a collection of electronic materials to retrieve citations, documents, or information that matches or answers a user's query. The retrieved materials may be text documents, facts that have been extracted from text, images, or sounds. A query is a question phrased so that it can be interpreted properly by search engine. Depending on the type of software, it may be a collection of commands, a statement in either full or partial sentences, one or more keywords, or in the case of Non-text searching, an image or sequence of sounds to be matched.

SUBJECT DIRECTORIES

Subject directories differ from search engines in that search engines are populated by robots that finds and index sites whereas humans making editorial decisions that populate subject directories. Subject directories are basically index home pages of sites and can be classified as general, academic, commercial or portal. Among the well known subject directories are the Argus Clearinghouse and Yahoo. Strengths include relevance, effectiveness and relative high quality of content. Weaknesses are that they lack depth in their coverage of the subjects.

FUTURE OF WEB BASED SERVICES

Library Web services will continue to spread out, offering more full-text electronic journals and indexes that do not now include full text will begin to do so, or link to external resources. Bibliographic access to full-text periodicals either through cataloging, databases, or vendors will be in improved form. There will be more Web forms for user feedback, and perhaps a virtual librarian who interacts in real time chat or video conferencing. More Document delivery services to distance education or users and Savings on Interlibrary Loan and user convenience are incentives. Information resources through creative consortia purchasing will be popular. A well-developed user education modules or tutorials, especially to support independent exploration of library and Web resources. Somebody will have to figure out how to keep Word users from saving print documents as XML, without thinking in terms of Web, not print, space. XML will be embraced as a way to control page appearance and Behaviour, but it will take a while for people to figure out how to use it well and there will be trends we haven't thought of yet.

The standards for organising web-based resources are still in the early stages of development, and librarians are forced to utilise standards for print resources that were not designed for electronic resources. Additionally web-based information resources are volatile in the sense that may be moved from one site to another or may be removed altogether from web. Web-based library services will become more widespread and sophisticated as the web becomes common place throughout the world, and to be successful players in the E-world. Libraries must continue to address the web design and implementation issues. As we actively transfer library services, our central purpose remain the same, to serve and teach users to find, evaluate, and use information effectively. The librarians should be expert to hold the hands of the users who are moving towards new communication paradigm a shift from face to face human contact to human machine interaction, from paper to electronic delivery, from text centered mode to multimedia and from physical presence to virtual presence. Despite these changes in communication technology, the reference interview will remain at the heart of the reference transaction. To meet these challenges the librarians may play a leadership role in providing better Web Based library Services facilities to their current techno savvy users.

8

Current Research Techniques in Digital Library

INTRODUCTION

Researchers have recently reviewed the status of some digital libraries from around the globe. These reviews reveal that while the digital libraries have very good information access and retrieval mechanisms in place, there is almost no provision for quality reference and information services.

However, these studies show that there is a trend towards the personalisation of digital library service, as in case of HEADLINE and GEMS (presently called iGEMS, a digital library developed at Nanyang Technological University in Singapore). Some recent research efforts have been directed at building personalised digital library environments. These studies can be grouped into three categories: user needs assessment, personalised user interface and personalised digital library, researchers reviewed literature on user interfaces, particularly in a digital library environment, and suggested the need for a task-based digital library.

Researcher discussed the personal digital library (PDL) that acts as a front-end to other electronic library systems and manages the user's information needs. Barry and Barbara discussed the creation of personal digital libraries. The North Carolina University Library developed MyLibrary @NCState as a portal application to the NCSU Library's information resources. This portal allows user profiling to build a dynamic, customised gateway to both general and discipline specific resources. MyLibrary is a Cornell University Library initiative to provide personalised library services to their students, faculty and staff on the basis of a focus group study to gauge library users.

The MyLibrary project has two components, MyLink and MyUpdate. MyLink allows patrons to save useful information resource links that they found themselves or those suggested by the librarians via a targeted notification in their personal space. Users can access this personal space from any place. MyUpdate periodically queries the online catalogue and notifies users, utilising a pre-defined user profile.

Headline is one of the eLib Programme's Phase 3 projects, developing a hybrid library system called the HeadLine Personal Information Environment (PIE), This PIE uses portal-type technology to present an information environment that is personalised to the user's needs and allows user customisation.

This project presents users with pages of resources relevant to their courses/ department. PIE users are also provided with an "all resources" page that contains all the library resources.

Users can create their own lists of resources on their own pages. Meyyappan reported on ongoing research at Nanyang Technological University in Singapore on the design and development of task-based digital library organisation and a digital work environment (DWE).

The major objective of these research projects is to allow users to personalise digital library access so that they can view their preferred resources, and hence, information is automatically filtered. These projects aim to select automatically a subset of the DL collection based on the nature and characteristics of a user.

The user then can add new resources, or delete recommended resources, to his or her page. The DWE project is somewhat different from others in the sense that the main objective of the DWE is to provide filtered access to the local digital library collections, to remote digital libraries, as well as to traditional libraries, and,most importantly, to the vast information resources on the university intranet. The system also allows users to create their own personal workspace to store selected information resources for future use.

SEMANTIC RESEARCH FOR DIGITAL LIBRARIES

During the DLI, which ran from 1994 to 1998, significant research was conducted at all six projects in the area of semantic retrieval and analysis for digital libraries. Among the semantic indexing and analysis techniques that are considered scalable and domain independent, the following classes of algorithms and methods have been examined and subjected to experimentation in various digital library, multimedia database, and information science applications:

Object Recognition, Segmentation, and Indexing

The most fundamental techniques in Information Retrieval involve identifying key features in objects. For example, automatic indexing and natural language processing (*e.g.*, noun phrase extraction or object type tagging) are frequently used to extract meaningful keywords or phrases from texts automatically. Texture, colour, or shape-based indexing and segmentation techniques are often used to identify images. For audio and video applications, voice recognition, speech recognition, and scene segmentation, techniques can be used to identify meaningful descriptors in audio or video streams.

Semantic Analysis

Several classes of techniques have been used for semantic analysis of texts or multimedia objects.

Symbolic machine learning (*e.g.*, ID3 decision tree algorithm, version space), graph-based clustering and classification (*e.g.*, Ward's hierarchical clustering), statistics-based multivariate analyses (*e.g.*, latent semantic indexing, multi-dimensional scaling, regressions), artificial neural network-based computing (*e.g.*, backpropagation networks, Kohonen self-organizing maps), and evolution-based programming (*e.g.*, genetic algorithms) are among the popular techniques.

In this information age, we believe such techniques will serve as good alternatives for processing, analyzing, and summarizing large amounts of diverse and rapidly changing multimedia information.

Knowledge Representations

The results from a semantic analysis process could be represented in the form of semantic networks, decision rules, or predicate logic. Many researchers have attempted to integrate such results with existing human-created knowledge structures such as ontologies, subject headings, or thesauri. Spreading activation based inferencing methods often are used to traverse various large-scale knowledge structures.

Human-computer Interactions (HCI) and Information Visualization:

One of the major trends in almost all emerging information systems applications is the focus on user-friendly, graphical, and seamless Human Computer Interactions. The Web-based browsers for texts, images, and videos have raised user expectations of rendering and manipulation of information.

Recent advances in development languages and platforms such as Java, OpenGL, and VRML and the availability of advanced graphical workstations at affordable prices have also made information visualization a promising area for research.

Several digital library research teams including Arizona/Illinois, Xerox PARC, Berkeley, and Stanford, are pushing the boundary of visualization techniques for dynamic displays of large-scale information collections.

The Illinois DLI Project: Federating Repositories of Scientific Literature

The Artificial Intelligence Lab at the University of Arizona was a major partner in the University of Illinois DLI Project, one of six projects funded by the NSF/DARPA/NASA DLI (Phase 1). The project consisted of two major components:

- A production testbed based in a real library
- Fundamental technology research for semantic interoperability (semantic indexes across subjects and media developed at the University of Arizona).

The Testbed

The Illinois DLI production testbed was developed in the Grainger Engineering Library at the University of Illinois at Urbana-Champaign (UIUC). It supports full federated searching on the structure of journal articles, as specified by SGML markup, using an experimental Web-based interface.

The initial rollout was available at the UIUC campus in October 1997 and has been integrated with the library information services. The testbed consists of materials from 5 publishers, 55 engineering journals, and 40,000 full-text articles. The primary partners of the project include: American Institute of Physics, American Physical Society, American Astronomical Society, American Society of Civil Engineers, American Society of Mechanical Engineers, American Society of Agricultural Engineers, American Institute of Aeronautics and Astronautics, Institute of Electrical and Electronic Engineers, Institute of Electrical Engineers, and IEEE Computer Society.

The testbed was implemented using Soft Quad (SGML rendering) and Open Text (full-text search), both commercial software.

The Illinois DLI project developers and evaluators have worked together very closely on needs assessment and usability studies. The production testbed has been evaluated since October 1997.

Six hundred UIUC user subjects enrolled in introductory computer science classes have used the system; and their feedback has been collected and analyzed. We expect to have collected usage data for about 1500 subjects at the end of the study. Usage data consists of session observations and transaction logs.

After four years of research effort, the testbed successes include:

- Willingness to build custom encoding procedures for SGML. This enabled the testbed to succeed in federating journals from different publishers with differing use of SGML, where Elsevier and OCLC failed.
- Canonical encoding for structure tags. The testbed can federate across publishers and journals.
- Willingness to build custom software for searching. The Illinois DLI system is able to show multiple views on the Web and has advanced structure search capabilities.
- Production repositories for real publishers. The project became the R&D arm of several scientific publishers and generated valuable contributions to the scientific publishing industry.

- Changing the nature of libraries with research. The project enables a research prototype to become a standard service capability for engineering libraries.

However, in the nature of research, we also have experienced many testbed difficulties: For the user interface, the project originally planned to modify the Mosaic Web browser (which was developed at UIUC). When the Web became commercial, Mosaic was quickly taken out of the control of the developers. Custom software is hard to deploy widely: the Web browser interface has widespread support, but the functionality was too primitive for professional full-text search and display.

Several practical difficulties were found in using SGML for this project. Plans to use standard BRS as full-text backend had to be abandoned. It proved essential to use an SGML-specific search engine. Good-quality SGML simply was not available. We had to work with every publisher, since nothing was ready for SGML publishing. SGML interactive display proved not to be of journal quality. Physics requires good-quality display of mathematics, which is very difficult to achieve. As the project comes to its end, several future directions are being explored:

- Technology transfer to publisher partners: Several partners have expressed interest in receiving the testbed technologies. A contract has been developed with the American Institute of Physics to clone the testbed software and processing. A similar contract is under development with American Society of Civil Engineers.
- Testbed continuance by university library: An industrial partnership programme has been established between the UIUC Library and publishers. A UIUC spin-off company has been formed to provide software and future services.

Semantic Research in Illinois DLI Project

The University of Illinois DLI project, through the partnership with the Artificial Intelligence Lab at the University of Arizona, has conducted research in semantic retrieval and analysis.

In particular, natural language processing, statistical analysis, neural network clustering, and information visualization techniques have been developed for different subject domains and media types.

Scalable Semantics become Feasible

Statistical and neural network clustering proves useful and feasible interactively and for large-scale collections. Specifically, the AI lab has developed a noun phrasing technique for concept extraction, a concept space technique for building automatic thesauri, and a self-organizing map (SOM) algorithm for building category maps. More details are provided below.

Semantic indexes for large collections

Two large-scale semantic indexing simulations were performed in 1996 and 1997, respectively. We analyzed 400,000 Inspec abstracts and 4,000,000 Compendex abstracts to generate about 1,000 engineering-specific concept spaces (automatic thesauri) using the NCSA supercomputers (Convex Exemplar and SGI Origin 2000). Results of such computations could be used for semantic retrieval and vocabulary switching across domains.

DIGITAL LIBRARIES OF THE FUTURE AND THE ROLE OF LIBRARIES

Research on digital library (DL) systems started in Europe in the mid-nineties. At that time DLs were seen essentially as repositories of digital texts accessible through a search service which was operating by indexing information stored in a centralised metadata catalogue. The construction of a DL was very resourceconsuming since, for each new DL, both the content and the software providing the DL functionality were built from scratch. As a result of this development approach, only powerful user communities or user communities with in-house computer science technical skills could afford the building up of DLs. These DLs were created to serve end-users only as consumers of information. They did not provide any functionality for submitting the documents.

The submission was usually performed either by the author or by a librarian operator by means of specific procedures residing outside the DL. Today, the requirements imposed on DLs are very different from that early time. A novel notion of DLs, also referred to as "knowledge commons" has recently emerged, whose fulfilment requires new technologies and new organisational models. This paper focuses on such new DLs by first discussing the motivations for their introduction, then presenting an innovative DL technology, called DILIGENT, and, finally, illustrating the role that libraries can play in this new scenario.

DIGITAL LIBRARIES OF THE FUTURE

According to the most recent understanding, the DLs of the future will be able to operate over a large variety of information object types - far wider than those maintained today in physical libraries and archives. These information objects will be composed of several multi-type and multimedia components aggregated in an unlimited number of formats. These, for example, can mix text, tables of scientific data and images obtained by processing earth observation data, or they can integrate 3D images, annotations and videos. These new information objects will offer innovative and more powerful means to researchers for sharing and discussing the results of their work. In order to be able to support these objects, the DL functionality has to be appropriately extended far beyond that required to manipulate the simple digital surrogates of the physical objects. In order to support these objects the DL may need considerable resources.

For example, the creation and handling of the new documents may require access to many different, large, heterogeneous information sources, the use of specialised services that process the objects stored in these sources for producing new information, and the exploitation of large processing capabilities for performing this tasks. New DLs are also required to offer a much richer set of services to their users than in the past. In particular, they must support the activities of their users by providing functionalities that may range from general utilities, like annotation, summarisation or co-operative work support, to very audience-specific functions, like map processing, semantic analysis of images, or simulation. The availability of this new DL functionality can, in principle, change the way in which research is conducted.

By exploiting such types of DL, for example, a scientist can annotate the article of a colleague with a programme that extracts useful information from a large amount of data collected by a specific scientific observatory. This programme, executed on demand when the annotation is accessed, can complement the content of the paper with continuously refreshed information. In the new DLs users are not only consumers but also producers of information. By elaborating information gathered through the DL they can create new information objects that are published in the DL, thus enriching its content. The new DLs are thus required to offer services that support the authoring of these new objects and the workflows that lead to their publication. In parallel with the evolution of the role of DL systems, we are now observing a large expansion in the demand for DLs.

Research today is often a collaborative effort carried out by groups belonging to different organisations spread worldwide. Motivated by a common goal and funding opportunities, these groups dynamically aggregate into virtual research organisations that share their resources, *e.g.* knowledge, experimentation results, or instruments, for the duration of their collaboration, creating new and more powerful virtual research environments. These virtual research organisations, set up by individuals that do not necessarily have great economic power or technical expertise, more and more frequently require DLs as tools for accelerating the achievement of their research results. This new potential audience demands less expensive and more dynamic DL development models.

They want to be able to set up new DLs that serve their needs for the duration of their collaborations in an acceptable timeframe and with an acceptable cost. The current DL development model cannot satisfy this large demand; a radical change is needed if we want to be able to address these new emerging requirements. A great contribution towards the satisfaction of all the requirements can certainly come from the introduction of mechanisms that support a controlled sharing of resources among different organisations. Sharing in this context is not only applied to repositories of content, as is usually meant today, but can be extended to any type of resource needed to build a DL, *i.e.* language and ontology resources, applications, computers and even staff with the necessary skills for supporting the DL development, deployment and maintenance.

Supporting this type of sharing requires the introduction of appropriate solutions at both the technological and organisational levels. These two levels are not independent; instead they strongly influence each other. In fact, the availability of a good technological solution favours the creation of an appropriate organisation, and vice-versa, a successful organisation stimulates the development of new supporting technologies. We present the DILIGENT infrastructure as an example of a technological solution for these new DLs. The organisational aspects stimulated by the introduction of this technology are briefly discussed afterwards.

DILIGENT

DILIGENT (DIgital Library Infrastructure on Grid ENabled Technology) is a three-year Integrated Project funded by the European Commission under the 6th Framework Programme for Research and Technological a Digital Library Infrastructure that will enable members of dynamic virtual research organisations to create on-demand transient digital libraries that exploit shared resources. Resources in this context are multimedia and multi-type content repositories, applications, and computing and storage elements. Following the understanding of DLs expressed in Borgman *et al.*, this project focuses on the development of DLs that "are not ends in themselves; rather they are enabling technologies for digital asset management, electronic commerce, electronic publishing, teaching and learning, and other activities".

From an abstract point of view, the DILIGENT infrastructure can be understood as a broker serving DL resource providers and consumers. The providers are the individuals and the organisations that decide to publish their resources under the supervision of the broker, according to certain access and use policies. The consumers are the user communities that want to build their own DLs. The resources managed by this broker are content sources (*i.e.* repositories of information searchable and accessible through a single "entrance"), services (*i.e.* software tools that implement a specific functionality and whose descriptions, interfaces and bindings are defined and publicly available) and hosting nodes (*i.e.* networked entities that offer computing and storage capabilities and supply an environment for hosting content sources and services). Providers register their resources and give a description of them by exploiting appropriate mechanisms provided by the infrastructure. The infrastructure also automatically derives other properties of the resources that are used to enrich the explicit description. The infrastructure manages the registered resources by supporting their discovery, monitoring and usage, and by implementing a number of other functionalities that aim at realising the required controlled sharing and quality of service. A user community can create one or more DLs by specifying a set of requirements. These requirements specify conditions for the information space (*e.g.* publishing institutions, subject of the content, document types), for the operations that manipulate the information space (*e.g.* type of search, tool for data analysis), for the services for supporting the work of the users (*e.g.* type of personalised dissemination, type of collaboration), for the quality of service (*e.g.* configuration, availability, response time) and for many other aspects, like the maximum cost, or lifetime.

The broker satisfies the community's requirements by selecting, and in many cases also deploying, a number of resources among those accessible to the community, gluing them appropriately and, finally, making the new DL application accessible through a portal. The composition of a DL is dynamic since the DL broker continuously monitors the status of the DL resources and, if necessary, changes them in order to offer the best quality of service. By relying on the shared resources many DLs, serving different communities, can be created and modified on-the-fly, without big investments and changes in the organisations that set them up.

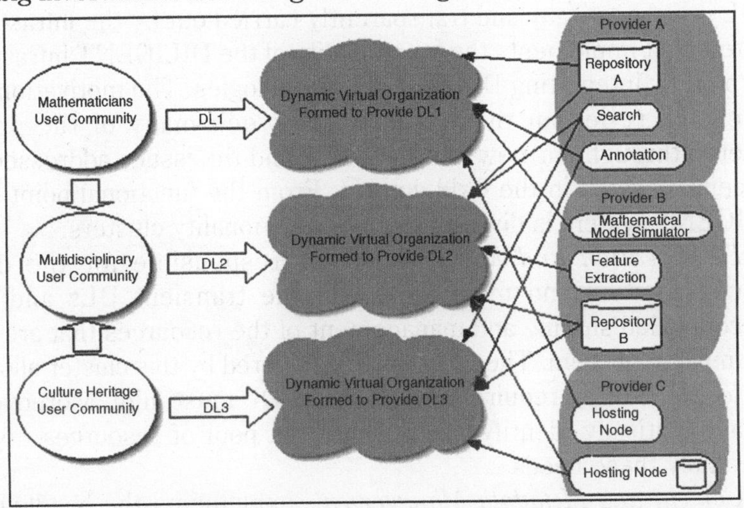

Fig. The Role of Virtual Organisations in DILIGENT.

In order to support the transactions between the providers and the consumers, the DILIGENT infrastructure exploits the virtual organisations (VOs) mechanism that has been introduced in the Grid research area. This mechanism models sets of users and resources aggregated together by highly controlled sharing rules, usually based on an authentication framework. VOs have a limited lifetime, are dynamically created and satisfy specific needs by allocating and providing resources on demand. Through the VOs mechanism the DILIGENT infrastructure glues together the users and the resources of a DL.

Figure graphically illustrates the role of VOs in supporting the brokerage model. The consumers, *i.e.* the user communities that require DLs to support their needs. The providers, each of which makes a number of resources available, are on the right. The infrastructure acts as a mediator by maintaining a framework where multiple virtual organisations, active on the same shared resources, can co-exist. The DL development model proposed by DILIGENT is radically new. Within the described framework each DL consumes the required resources only for the time it needs them.

This opens a lot of new opportunities for the creation of the functionalities required by the new "knowledge commons" environments. In particular, the exploitation of more effective, but also very computationally expensive algorithms becomes viable at an acceptable cost for many communities. For example, thanks to sharing, the use of the high processconsuming algorithms that automatically extract features from multi-media objects can be exploited in a large number of DLs. Moreover, in the framework established by the new development model, the user communities can easily, and in a timely manner, create and maintain their own DLs with limited resources since the management of the DL is automatically and transparently carried out by the infrastructure. The system that implements the functionality of the DILIGENT infrastructure is being built by integrating DL and Grid technologies. The motivation for this design choice relies on the similarity between many of the problems encountered through our new notion of DLs and the issues addressed by the most recent research in the Grid domain. From the functional point of view, the DILIGENT system is divided into five functionality clusters:

- *DL Creation and Management:* is responsible for the dynamic construction and maintenance of the transient DLs and for the controlled sharing and management of the resources that are used to implement them. The functionalities offered by this cluster allow users to express the requirements that the DL must fulfil. Moreover, they automatically identify and arrange the pool of resources needed to satisfy these needs.
- *Content and Metadata Management:* implements the handling of DL content and related metadata, the consistent and distributed management of annotations, and the integration of external content and metadata sources.
- *Process Management:* manages the creation of user processes composed of existing services, the validation of their correctness, the automatic optimisation of their definition according to the resources available and the service characteristics, and their reliable

execution. Thanks to this feature, the DILIGENT system can easily be enriched with additional operational workflows to meet new user requirements.

- *Index and Search Management:* is responsible for enabling cost-efficient search and retrieval of information in DLs, while satisfying the level of quality required for the overall data retrieval and delivery operations.
- *Application Specific Functionality:* provides the functionality needed to support user-specific scenarios, like portals, document visualisation, or features extraction.

From the architectural point of view, the DILIGENT system is designed as a Web Services Resource Framework (WSRF) application built on top of the gLite Grid middleware released by the Enabling Grids for Escience in Europe (EGEE) project. gLite hides the heterogeneous nature of the computing elements (*i.e.* services representing a computing resource) on the one hand and storage elements (*i.e.* services representing a storage resource) on the other hand by providing an environment that facilitates and controls their sharing. The DILIGENT services are being initially deployed on a project-proprietary gLite infrastructure. Architecturally, this infrastructure is completely interoperable with the EGEE infrastructure. EGEE is currently the largest European Grid infrastructure ever built.

A number of other recently funded projects will extend this infrastructure to other geographic regions, like Mediterranean countries, Latin America, or China. The interoperability with the EGEE infrastructure will allow any authorised virtual community that wishes to create DLs to also exploit the resources made available by this vast Grid infrastructure. During the project timeframe, the DILIGENT infrastructure will be populated with a number of important archives and software applications provided by the two communities that are participating in the experimentation with the results of the project, one from the environmental e-science domain and one from the cultural heritage domain.

The first community is ImpECt (Implementation of Environmental Conventions) and includes leading players in the environmental sector. This community will use DILIGENT to support the organisation of conferences and the preparation of projects and periodical reports.

Through DILIGENT this community expects to improve accessibility, interoperability and usability of environmental data, models, tools, algorithms and instruments, integrating the distributed data sources with specialised data handling services. The second community, ARTE, is a community of scholars located in different parts of the world, working together to establish a new discipline that merges experiences from research in medicine, humanities, social sciences and communication. In order to achieve their objectives, these researchers require instruments to ease the construction of multimedia artefacts and to improve support for education. At the time of the writing of this paper initial experimentation with the features of a DILIGENT DL has already been conducted by implementing simplified services for preparing environmental reports, as required by the ImpECt environmental agencies. Through the exploiting of rich information sources, ranging from raw data sets to maps and graphs archives, these agencies periodically prepare reports on the status of the environment. Currently, this task is performed by first selecting the relevant information from each of the multiple and heterogeneous sources available, then launching complex processing on large amounts of data to obtain "products", like graphs, tables and other summarised information and, finally, producing the required report by assembling all the different parts together.

This process, which is repeated periodically, requires a lot of work due to the complexity of interfacing the different sources and tools. Despite the effort expended, the resulting reports do not completely fulfil the requirements of their readers, who would like to have a picture of the environmental status which is updated at the time the report is accessed. A DILIGENT DL offers a more effective framework for the creation and maintenance of these reports. In our experimentation, for example, we have built a DL which exploits content maintained in both repositories including textual documents and archives of Earth observation raw data provided by the European Space Agency. In this DL, which is accessible through a single user interface, all the different kinds of information necessary for creating the reports can be found.

By combining this information and by defining how to derive the associated "products" (images, tables, or graphs) from raw data, the users can create their reports much more easily. Moreover, a specialised user interface allows authorised users to access these composite reports by choosing static or dynamic generation. The selection of dynamic generation triggers associated process workflows which, by combining appropriate applications, generate the required products on demand by processing both the raw data and other intermediate products stored in the DL repositories. The dynamically generated products are obtained by running those applications that are computationally intensive on the Grid. In this way the complex processes required to generate the products are executed in few minutes at a limited cost to the community that is exploiting them. In order to obtain the same performance without the Grid, an institution would have to equip its digital library with a great number of computers, while in the case of DILIGENT the institution can also exploit computer capabilities made available by third party organisations. The same is true for storage capacity. Maintaining raw data, intermediate products and high resolution images requires a large amount of storage capacity. By exploiting the Grid technology, part of this information, especially the temporary part, can be maintained in third-party storage systems.

THE ROLE OF LIBRARIES IN FUTURE DLs

In the framework envisaged by DILIGENT, libraries play an important role at the organisational level. In particular:

- As providers of resources, they can help to enhance the amount of available resources by making stakeholders aware of the importance of sharing. In particular, as far as the sharing of content is concerned, they can operate by promoting digitisation campaigns and the Open Access approach. These actions may result in a vast amount of new digital information accessible online which can be exploited by advanced services.
- Also within a digital framework, libraries are certainly the best candidates for carrying out content description, maintenance and preservation of resources. By exploiting their large experience acquired in the past, they can contribute to the long-term availability and to the quality of the resources disseminated by the DLs.
- Long-term availability also requires the implementation of models able to support the sustainability of the resources provided. Libraries, either alone or as members of library consortia, can also act as the organisations deputed to define and put in place these models.
- As main resource providers, libraries can work jointly on the definition of common policies and standards. An agreement on these aspects would strongly contribute towards facilitating the design and development of the new complex services required to fulfil the emerging user needs.
- In the future envisaged by DILIGENT, libraries can also play an important role as mediators between the infrastructure and the user communities. In particular, they can proactively promote and facilitate the creation of DLs that respond to the needs of the user communities. They can also assist users by providing, if necessary, the skills required to select, update and exploit the DL content and services.

DEVELOPMENTS IN COMPUTER AND MICROPROCESSOR TECHNOLOGY

Dramatic reductions in the size and cost of computer components and equally impressive gains in the speed, storage capacity and reliability of hardware components have expanded their use rapidly in all activities and functions of a library and information centre. Notable reductions in the size of microprocessors combined with dramatically enhanced capacity have added new dimensions to the computer new hardware technology.

Initially, small silicon chips contained only few components and circuits, but the average number of components has doubled each year Since, 1965. Early small-scale integration efforts first gave way to large-scale integration (LSI) chips that contained thousands of components, very large-scale integration (VLSI) chips that contained hundreds of thousands of components and circuits, and now ultra large-scale integration (ULSI) chips come with millions of components and circuits.

A microprocessor, also known as Central Processing Unit (CPU) of a computer, is a complete computation engine that is fabricated on a single chip. Microprocessors are manufactured by different companies like Intel, Advanced Micro Divices (AMD), Motorola,,etc. However, most widely-used microprocessors are manufactured by Intel. The first microprocessor used in a PC was Intel 8080. Introduced in 1974, it was a complete 8-bit microprocessor on a single chip. Intel 8088 used in the IBM PC in 1979, was the first microprocessor that made its presence felt in the market.

The PC market moved from the 8088, 80286, 80386, 80486, Pentium, Pentium-II, III, IV and now to Intel Dual Core and Quad Core. The new Intel Dual Core can execute any piece of code that ran on the original 8088, but the Dual Core runs about 3,000 times faster. The capacity of a microprocessor is measured in terms of the number of bits it can send or receive and the number of bits it can process internally.

The 8088 was an 8/16 bit processor, indicating that it can send or receive 8 bits of data and internally process 16 bits of data at a time. The 80286 was a 16/16 bit processor and 80386 chip had a 32-bit processor with a 32-bit data path and, as a result, was much faster than either the 8088 or the 80286 chip. The 80486 chip, introduced by Intel in late 1989, had a 32- bit processor.

It has architectural enhancements, Hence, it performed better than the 80386 chip. The Pentium is a 32-bit processor with a 32-bit data path. It is three times faster than the 80486. The Pentium II and III had a 32-bit processor with a 64-bit data path. It was three times faster than the Pentium. The Pentium IV is a 32-bit processor with a 64-bit data path, and was introduced in 2000.

It is four times faster than the Pentium. Currently, PCs and laptops are equipped with Dual Core which is a 64-bit processor with 64-bit data path and processing speed of 3.0 Ghz. Like microprocessor technology, digital storage devices have also witnessed notable reductions in its size and cost with dramatically enhancement in capacity of storage.

There are two types of data storage devices, *i.e.,* removable data storage devices and Non-removable data storage devices. The data storage devices come in many sizes and shapes. The storage devices can also be categorised based on media used for storage, for example magnetic storage media, optical storage media, metal-oxide semiconductors or flash memory devices (popularly known as Pen drives or USB drives). Magnetic storage media are commonly used for large volumes of data (*e.g.,* video, image, or remote sensing data). Large amounts of data are stored through tape drives because the capacity on the drives is huge - three billion (or three gigabits) of data per square inch can fit on a single magnetic disk.

Hard discs, floppies, tapes, cartridges,,etc., are example of magnetic media. CD-ROMs and DVD ROMs are example of optical storage media which can again be of two types,, *i.e.*, i) write-once, read-many: data once written cannot be erased; and ii) Rewritable: the data that is once written can be erased completely and the same storage device can be used again for storing different data. A typical disc used in a computer-based CD drive stores 650 MB.

Digital Versatile Disk or DVD, initially stood for Digital Video Disc. Like a CD, DVD is an optical storage system for read-only, recordable and rewritable applications. The DVD format provides several configurations of data layers, moving from 2D storage to 3D storage. Each configuration is designed to provide additional storage capacity. The similarity between the DVD and the CD gets smaller with each upgraded configuration, however, DVDs in contrast to CDs has storage capacity of 4.7 GB. Metal-oxide semiconductors-based storage devices, popularly known as pen drives or USB drives or flash memory devices, is Non-volatile computer memory that can be electrically erased and reprogrammed. It is a technology that is primarily used in memory cards and USB flash drives for general storage and transfer of data between computers and other digital products. Flash memory stores information in an array of memory cells made from floating-gate transistors.

In traditional single-level cell (SLC) devices, each cell stores only one bit of information. Some newer flash memory, known as multi-level cell (MLC) devices, can store more than one bit per cell by choosing between multiple levels of electrical charge to apply to the floating gates of its cells. Flash drives are now available with 8 GB storage capacity. Digital collections that are too large to store entirely on a disk use hierarchical storage mechanisms (HSM). In an HSM, the most frequently used data is kept on fast disks while less frequently used data is kept in nearline such as an automated (robotic) tape library.

An HSM can automatically migrate data from tape to disk and vice-versa as required. Intelligent storage networks and snap-servers are now available in which the physical storage devices are intelligently controlled and made available to a number of servers. A number of RAID (Redundant Array of Inexpensive Disks) models are also available for greater security and performance. The RAID technology distributes the data across a number of disks in a way that even if one or more disks fail, the system would still function while the failed component is replaced.

DEVELOPMENTS IN COMMUNICATION AND NETWORK TECHNOLOGY

Communication technology, with its ability to transmit data and information from one location to another, serve as a tool to exploit potentials and ability of computer to store and process vast amount of information. A computer communica-tion network is an interconnection of a collection of several computers from which the user can select the service required and communicate with any computer as a local user.

A computer communication networks can be viewed as a collection of nodes with computing resources and nodal-switching computers that facilitate communication through a set of transmission links.

Developments in communication technology have made it possible to interconnect geographically dispersed computing resources of different kinds and makes.

Users can access the network through PCs and terminals attached to a node and messages traverse these networks through the switching nodes. Since, computer communicates using digitised signals instead of electric signals, it requires different transmission facilities than those used for transmitting analogue electrical signals.

It is, however, a common practice to use conventional telecommunication links for data transmission by converting digital signals into analogue signals using a process called 'Modulation' and the device that performs the conversion is called the MODEM (MOdulator - DEModulator).

Currently, terrestrial, satellite-based data networks, Integrated Service Digital Network (ISDN) and wireless networks are available that can handle all kinds of communication requirements (, *i.e.,* voice, data, telemetry, facsimile and video) without discrimination.

The computer networks can be grouped into four categories based on geographical locations of its computer terminals,, *i.e.*,

- *Local Area Network (LAN)*: interconnection of many computers within a given local area, more often premises of a single organisation building. A very high speed of data transmission can be attained within a limited geographic area. LANs are typically configured in a star, bus or ring. Low speed LANs use telephone wires or copper cables, optical fibre cables are used to achieve high-speed transmission of data.
- *Wide Area Network (WAN)*: WAN is used to interconnect a number of widely dispersed computers in various cities of a country or different countries. WANs use communication media maintained by telegraph or telephone companies. These networks usually have land telephone lines, underground coaxial cables, microwave communication and satellite communications.
- *Metropolitan Area Network (MAN)*: MAN refers to inter- connection within geographical limits of a city or town.
- *Gateways*: Gateways consist of software and hardware that are required to interconnect networks amongst themselves. Gateways

contend with any differences in packet sizes, protocols and addressing methods between the two networks it connect. Gateways are also used to connect LANs to WANs and WANs, in turn, can be linked through gateways to create national and international data communication networks.

The communications networks can be grouped into the following three categories based on the technology and communication media used by them:

- *Public Switched Telephone Network*: PSTN are managed by common carriers usually telephone companies/departments the world over. The PSTN generally provide two basic services, the normal dial-up connections to the subscribers and permanent leased connection between two subscriber's points. The permanent leased connections provide single traceable line between two subscriber points. The leased lines are generally less prone to noise than dial-up lines.
- *Public Data Network*: Analogous to the public telephone network, many domestic common carriers provide data communications services via a specialised network called a Public Data Network (PDN). Most Internet Service Providers (ISPs) use combination of PDN and PSTN for providing Internet connectivity.
- *Integrated Services Digital Networks* (ISDN): An ISDN is a network that provides end-to-end digital connectivity to support a wide range of services, including voice and Non-voice services.

Computer networks use physical channels through which information is transmitted between computers in a network. Media may be classified as bounded, *i.e.,* wires (twisted pair telephone wires or UTP CAT 5), cables (co-axial) and optical fibres; or unbounded, *i.e.,* radio waves or microwaves.

Data communication is an integral part of the modern information storage and retrieval systems in terms of their online access.

Today, network technology works on client server architecture with middleware used for connecting software components or applications on clients and servers.

Technique of packet switching, evolved in 1960s, is used for transferring data between computer systems with an objective to facilitate networked computers to communicate seamlessly across multiple, geographically dispersed locations. The Transmission Control Protocol (TCP) and Internet Protocol (IP), called TCP/ IP suite, is the backbone of Internet and other TCP/ IP based networks.

With developments in communication technology, institutions have options to set-up fibre optic-based gigabit LAN or wireless LAN. Depending on the geographical location, institutions have options to buy terrestrial or satellite-based Internet bandwidth its combinations from a number of Internet Service Providers (ISPs).

DISTINGUISH COMPUTER TECHNOLOGY AND COMMUNICATIONS TECHNOLOGY

Computer Technology

You have certainly seen and, we would guess, used a computer. Nevertheless, let's define what it is. A *computer* is a programmable, multiuse machine that accepts data—raw facts and figures—and processes, or manipulates, it into information we can use, such as summaries, totals, or reports. Its purpose is to speed up problem solving and increase productivity.

Communications Technology

Unquestionably you've been using communications technology for years. *Communications technology*, also called *telecommunications technology*, consists of electromagnetic devices and systems for communicating over long distances. The principal examples are telephone, radio, broadcast television, and cable TV.

In more recent times, there has been the addition of communication among computers—which is what happens when people 'go online' on the internet. In this context, *online* means using a computer or some other information device, connected through a network, to access information and services from another computer or information device. A *network* is a communications system connecting two or more computers; the internet is the largest such network. Information technology is already affecting your life in exciting ways and will do so even more in the future. Let's consider how.

Information Technology and its Used in Education

In her sociology classes at Indiana University, professor Melissa Wilde uses a small wireless keypad linked to a computer to enable students to answer questions not by raising their hands but by pressing buttons, with the results appearing on a screen in the front of the room. Wilde has her students answer multiple-choice questions to see whether they understand her lecture points and to make necessary adjustments.

"I can instantly see that three-quarters of the class doesn't get it," she says. She also uses the technology to get students to answer questions about themselves—race, income, political affiliation—skewed, for example, Towards wealthier or poorer students, an event that fired up a half hour of excited class discussion. Maybe the classrooms at your school haven't reached this level of interactivity yet, but there's no question that information technology is universal on college campuses, and at lower levels the internet has penetrated 99 per cent of schools. Most college students have been exposed to computers Since, the lower grades; indeed, one-fifth of college students report they were using computers between ages 5 and 8, and all had begun using computers by the time they were 16–18 years old. At the college level, the great majority (85 per cent) of students have their own computers, and two-thirds use at least two e-mail addresses.

As you no doubt know, *e-mail* is 'electronic mail,' messages transmitted over a computer network, most often the internet. Three-quarters of college students use the internet 4 or more hours a week, and about onefifth use it 12 or more hours a week. About half are required to use e-mail in their classes. For academic purposes, most students use e-mail to set up appointments (62 per cent) with professors, discuss grades (58 per cent), or get clarification of an assignment (75 per cent). Besides using the internet to help in teaching, today's college instructors also use *presentation graphics software* such as PowerPoint to show their lecture outlines and other materials on classroom screens.

In addition, they use Blackboard, WebCT, and other *coursemanagement software* for administering online assignments, schedules, examinations, and grades. One of the most intriguing developments in education at all levels, however, is the rise of *distance learning,* or *e-learning,* the name given to online education Programmes, which has more than 3.2 million online students enrolled nationwide and grows more than 20 per cent a year. E-learning has had some interesting effects: for example, the home-schooling movement, whereby children are taught at home, usually by parents, has come of age thanks to internet resources. e-Learning has also propelled the rise of for-profit institutions, such as Devry and the University of Phoenix, which 8 per cent of full-time college students now attend.

More than a third of institutions of higher education—and 97 per cent of public universities—offer online courses, and many have attracted on-campus students, who say they like the flexibility of not having to attend their classes at a set time. e-learning has been put to such varied uses as bringing career and technical courses to high school students in remote prairie towns, pairing gifted science students with master teachers in other parts of the country, and helping busy professionals obtain further credentials outside business hours. But the reach of information technology into education has only begun.

In the future, as suggested, see software called 'intelligent tutoring systems' that gives students individualised instruction when personal attention is scarce—such as the software Cognitive Tutor, which not only helps high school students to improve their performance in math but also sparks them to enjoy a subject they might have once hated.

In colleges, more students may use interactive simulation games, such as McGraw- Hill's Business Strategy Game, to apply their knowledge to real-world kinds of problems. And employees in company training Programmes may find themselves engaged in mock conversations with *avatars*—computer depictions of humans, as are often found in online videogames—that represent imaginary customers and coworkers, combining the best parts of computer-based learning with face-to-face interaction.

HEALTH: HIGH TECH FOR WELLNESS

Computers Used in Health and Medicine

Viktor Yazykov, competing in the perilous Around Alone solo sailing competition, found himself in the stormy South Atlantic with a seriously infected arm that needed emergency surgery. So, with the help of step-bystep instructions sent by e-mail from Boston-based Dr. Daniel Carlin to his solar-powered laptop computer, Yazykov operated on his own arm. Yazykov's story is a dramatic example of *telemedicine*—medical care delivered via telecommunications. For some time, physicians in rural areas lacking local access to radiologists have used 'teleradiology' to exchange computerised images such as X-rays via telephone-linked networks with expert physicians in metropolitan areas.

Now telemedicine is moving to an exciting new level, as the use of digital cameras and sound, in effect, moves patients to doctors rather than the reverse. Already telemedicine is being embraced by administrators in the American prison system, where by law inmates are guaranteed medical treatment—and where the increase in prisoners every year has led to the need to control health costs.

Computer technology is also radically changing the tools of medicine. All medical information, including that generated by X-ray, lab test, and pulse monitor, can now be transmitted to a doctor in digital format. And image transfer technology allows radiologic images such as CT scans and MRIs to be immediately transmitted to electronic charts and physicians' offices. Patients in intensive care, who are usually monitored by nurses during offtimes, can also be watched over by doctors in remote 'control towers' miles away. Electronic medical records and other computerised tools enable heart attack patients to get follow-up drug treatment and diabetics to have their blood sugar measured. Software can compute a woman's breast cancer risk. Patients can use e-mail to query their doctors about their records.

Various *robots*—automatic devices that perform functions ordinarily performed by human beings, with names such as robo doc, RoboCart, TUG, and HelpMate—help free medical workers for more critical tasks; the four-armed da Vinci surgical robot, for instance, can do cuts and stitches deep inside the body, so that surgery is less traumatic and recovery time faster. Hydraulics and computers are being used to help artificial limbs get 'smarter.' And a patient paralysed by a stroke has received an implant that allows communication between his brain and a computer; as a result, he can move a cursor across a screen by brainpower and convey simple messages—as in *Star Trek*.

Want to calculate how long you will live? Want to go about gathering your family health history to see if you're at risk for particular inherited diseases? These are only two examples of health Web sites available to patients and health consumers. Although online health information can be misleading and even dangerous, many people now tap into health care databases, e-mail health professionals, or communicate with people who have similar conditions. For instance, hours after 10-year-old Robert Lord of San Diego fractured his spine in a fall from a tree, his father found an experimental drug on the internet, saving the boy from lifetime paralysis.

Often patients are already steeped in information about their conditions when they arrive in the offices of health care professionals. This represents a fundamental shift of knowledge, and therefore power, from physicians to patients. In addition, health care consumers are able to share experiences and information with one another. Young parents, for example, can find an online gathering spot at pediatrician Alan Greene's Web site.

MONEY: TOWARDS THE CASHLESS SOCIETY

Computers Affect and Financial Matters

"The future of money is increasingly digital, likely virtual, and possibly universal," says one writer. *Virtual* means that something is created, simulated, or carried on by means of a computer or a computer network, and we certainly have come a long way Towards becoming a cashless society. Indeed, the percentage of all financial transactions done electronically, both phone-initiated and computer-initiated, was projected to rise to 18.4 per cent in 2013, up from 0.9 per cent in 1993.

Besides currency, paper checks, and credit and debit cards, the things that serve as 'money' include cashvalue cards, automatic transfers, and digital money. Many readers of this book will probably already have engaged in online buying and selling, purchasing CDs and DVDs, books, airline tickets, or computers.

But what about groceries? After all, you can't exactly squeeze the cantaloupes through your keyboard. Even so, online groceries are expected to reach $7.5 billion in U.S., sales by 2012. To change decades of shopping habits, e-grocers keep their delivery charges low and delivery times convenient, and they take great pains in filling orders, knowing that a single bad piece of fruit will produce a devastating word-of-mouth backlash. Only about 46 per cent of U.S.,

workers have their paychecks electronically deposited into their bank accounts, but this is sure to change as Americans discover that direct deposit is actually safer and faster. Online bill paying is also picking up steam. For more than two decades, it has been possible to pay bills online, such as those from phone and utility companies, with special software and online connections to your bank. About 19 million American households do some bill paying online, and the number was expected to reach 61 million households in 2008.

Some banks and other businesses are backing an electronic-payment system that allows internet users to buy goods and services with *micropayments,* electronic payments of as little as 25 cents in transactions for which it is uneconomical to use a credit card. Micropayment, suggests futurist Paul Saffo, 'allows you to buy things by the sip rather than the gulp.' The success of Apple Computer's iTunes online music service, which sells songs for 99 cents each, suggests that micro sales are now feasible.

All kinds of businesses and organisations, from independent songwriters to comic book writers to the Legal Aid Society of Cleveland, now accept micropayments, using intermediaries such as BitPass and Peppercoin. Thus, you could set up your own small business simply by constructing a Web site and accepting micropay-ments.

LEISURE: INFOTECH IN ENTERTAINMENT AND THE ARTS

Leisure Activities be Affected by Information Technology

Information technology is being used for all kinds of entertainment, ranging from videogames to telegambling. It is also being used in the arts, from painting to photography. Let's consider just two examples, music and film. Computers, the internet, and the World Wide Web are standing the system of music recording and distribution on its head—and in the process are changing the financial underpinnings of the music industry. Because of their high overhead, major record labels typically need a band to sell half a million CDs in order to be profitable, but independent bands, using online marketing, can be reasonably successful selling 20,000 or 30,000 albums. Team Love, a small music label established in 2003, found it could promote its first two bands, Tilly and the Wall and Willy Mason, by offering songs online fREE for *downloading*—transferring data from a remote computer to one's own computer—so that people could listen to them before paying $12 for a CD. It also puts videos online for sharing and uses quirky Web sites to reach fans.

"There's something exponential going on," says one of Team Love's founders. "The more music that's downloaded, the more it sells." Many independent musicians are also using the internet to get their music heard, hoping that giving away songs will help them build audiences. The web also offers sources for instantly downloadable sheet music. One research engineer has devised a computerised scoring system for judging musical competitions that overcomes the traditional human-jury approach, which can be swayed by personalities and politics. And a Spanish company, PolyphonicHMI, has created Hit Song Science software, which they say can analyse the hit potential of new songs by "reference to a finely parsed universe of attributes derived from millions of past songs." As for movies, now that blockbuster movies routinely meld live action and animation, computer artists are in big demand. The 1999 film *Star Wars: Episode I*, for instance, had fully 1,965 digital shots out of about 2,200 shots.

Even when film was used, it was scanned into computers to be tweaked with animated effects, lighting, and the like. Entire beings were created on computers by artists working on designs developed by producer George Lucas and his chief artist. What is driving the demand for computer artists? One factor is that animation, though not cheap, looks more and more like a bargain, because hiring movie actors costs so much—some make $20 million a film. Moreover, special effects are readily understood by audiences in other countries, and major studios increasingly count on revenues from foreign markets to make a film profitable.

Digital manipulation also allows a crowd of extras to be multiplied into an army of thousands. It can also be used to create settings: in the film *Sky Captain and the World of Tomorrow,* the actors—Gwyneth Paltrow, Angelina Jolie, and Jude Law—shot all their scenes in front of a blue screen, and computer-generated imagery was then used to transport them into an imaginary world of 1939. Computer techniques have even been used to develop digitally created actors—called 'synthespians.' Actors ranging from the late James Dean to the late John Wayne, for instance, have been recruited for television commercials. And computerised animation is now so popular that Hollywood studios and movie directors are finding they can make as much money from creating videogames as from making movies. But animation is not the only area in which computers are revolutionising movies. Digital editing has radically transformed the way films are assembled.

Whereas traditional film editing involved reeling and unreeling spools of film and cutting and gluing pieces of highly scratchable celluloid together, nearly burying the editor in film, today an editor can access 150 miles of film stored on a computer and instantly find any visual or audio moment, allowing hundreds of variations of a scene to be called up for review. Even Non-professionals can get into movie making as new computerrelated products come to market. Now that digital video capture-and-edit systems are available for under $1,000, amateurs can turn home videos into digital data and edit them. Also, digital camcorders, which offer outstanding picture and sound quality, have steadily dropped in price.

IT'S ROLE IN MANAGING ORGANISATIONAL CHANGE

IT and Environment - Goals-Structure

Researcher defined environment as those factors which not only are outside the system's control but which determine in part how the system performs.

Uncertainty is the difference between the amount of information required to perform the task and the amount of information already possessed by the organisation:

- *Proposition* 1: Turbulent environment drives organisations to use IT for monitoring the preferences of the environment. System theorists have recognised the importance of 'feedback' for the survival of the system and for maintaining a 'steady state' or 'homeostasis'. Organisations are purposive systems that learn of the impending threats by scanning. Scanning is the process by which the organisation acquires information for decision making. The modes of scanning are primarily determined by the external environmental stimuli and are determined by the magnitude and by the direction of the discrepancy between the goal and its realisation. While surveillance is useful for information-gathering process, search is oriented towards finding a satisfactory solution to a specific problem. Complex systems require complex controllers. IT will provide the 'complex controller" to the increasingly complex organisation. The information systems of an organisation need to evolve to remain consistent with the changing organisational structure. Referring to the obscurity of causal laws of turbulence, Aldrich argued that scanning could provide the firm with the desired 'competitive edge.'
- *Proposition* 2: Turbulent environment drives organisations to use IT for translating the information on environmental preferences into goals. Continuously changing environment requires organisations to continuously reassess their goals. Effective structuring requires a consistency among the design parameters and contingency factors have demonstrated that organisations' goals can be generated by external forces, such as other groups seeking to use the organisation to further their own ends.
- *Proposition* 3: Turbulent environment drives organisations to use IT to align their structure with environmental preferences. The very efforts of the organisation to maintain a constant external environment produce changes in organisational structure. Scott argued that organisational structure and goals are driven by the preferences in the environment. The structure is determined by the information-processing capacity requirements of the organisation which in turn are governed by the IT being used. Aldrich, Perrow, Walker and Woodward have attributed structural differences to the organisation's technology. Mintzberg had suggested that the organisation's environment and technology are the independent variables that determine the structural variables of the organisation. Fowles, in his narrative on the history of organisational communications technologies

contends that the phenomenal expansion of organisations can be largely attributed to advances in the technologies of organisational communication. Yates argued that in absence of technological communication organisations could have evolved differently. Preliminary econometric analyses of the overall U.S., economy for the period 1975-1985 further confirms that the increased use of IT is correlated with decreases in firm size and vertical integration.

IT and Organic Structure

- *Proposition* 4: Turbulent environment drives organisations to make more use of IT for increasing their 'organic' characteristics. 'Organic' firms are better equipped to sustain themselves in turbulent environment. A dynamic environment will drive the structure to an organic state despite other forces; the more complex the environment, the more decentralised the structure. Introduction of IT at the 'operating core' level transforms a bureaucratic administrative structure into an organic one. Effectively, automation of routine tasks eliminates the source of many of the social conflicts throughout the organisation. Law of requisite variety implies that the rate of change of organisational systems must correspond to the rate of change of environmental systems, *i.e.*, organisations with complex environmental interactions would develop complex structures like adhocracies or networks. Adhocracy is suitable for a dynamic and complex environment, when the firm has sophisticated technical systems and the focus is upon consistently offering differentiated products for retaining the customers. Future organisations would be 'networks' characterised by adhocracies with flexible systems of projects and teams brought together quickly to accomplish specific tasks. Some existing organisations have already 'farmed out' their operations by establishing them as separate organisations or contracting them out to other organisations.
- *Proposition 4a:* Turbulent environment drives organisations to use IT for empowering workers at all levels. Growing availability of telecommunications has offered technologies like distributed systems and client-server architecture that facilitate the process of empowerment of the lower levels. In the 'informated' organisation, workers would be 'empowered' by virtue of access to necessary information to perform higher-level tasks. Ramstrom has argued that tactical decisions relating to 'soft' information would be delegated to the 'grass-roots' where there is easy access to relevant information concerning the immediate environment, at the same time providing these levels with the information generated within the system by means of 'cheap' internal information systems.

- *Proposition 4b:* Turbulent environment drives organisations to use IT for increasing the spans of control. Information technologies, by facilitating the standardisation of coordination would facilitate larger spans of control or work units which would be characterised by extensive lateral communication and self- contained authority structures.
- *Proposition 4c:* Turbulent environment drives organisations to use IT for increasing lateral communications. Selective use of lateral decision processes for situations involving task uncertainty increase the information processing capacity of the organisation. Bringing the points of decision down to the points of action reduces the information overload on the managers. Since specification of 'procedures' in complex situations creates inefficiencies, organisations in turbulent environments would use more IT resource for delegating the decision-making to workers. Increased use of groupware for lateral coordination will spell the demise of middle management.

IT and Differentiation - Integration

- *Proposition* 5: Turbulent environment drives organisations to reduce their 'dimensions' by focusing on core competencies by leveraging their use of IT.
- *Proposition 5a:* Turbulent environment drives organisations to use IT to reduce differentiation and integration to focus on increased specialisation. Organisations structure themselves to minimize coordination costs and group together similar activities to achieve the benefits of process specialisation. Environmental uncertainty or 'task predictability' is the basic independent variable influencing the design of the organisation. Faced with increased uncertainty, organisations can reduce the need for information processing by decreasing the 'diversity of outputs'. Reduced differentiation and integration of activities would decrease the coordination effort involved thus reducing the information processing requirements. Reduced coordination costs with IT would result in the substitution of IT for human coordination. Greater specialisation would be achieved by focusing on few core competencies.

IT's Role in Managing Organisational Interdependencies

- *Proposition* 6: Turbulent environment drives organisations to actively seek Inter-organisational relations to leverage their core competencies. Cooperation, especially in the international context, will be necessary to gain a competitive advantage in the future. To survive in an increasingly competitive environment, firms would form alliances that would bring together their core competencies to create the 'best of all" products.
- *Proposition 6a:* Turbulent environment drives organisations to reduce

environmental complexity and uncertainty by seeking interdependencies with other organisations in the environment.

- *Proposition 6b:* Turbulent environment drives organisations to use more IT - effort to establish coordinating mechanisms with other firms.

To survive in the fast-changing environment the 'adaptive organisation" would be more like a shifting 'constellation' that has 'linkages' with independent and semi- autonomous organisations. Use of inter organisational linkages such as EDI would enable new forms of organisations and reduce the coordination costs of increasingly market-driven organisations. Increasingly, electronic linkages are becoming the necessary condition of doing businesses with larger firms. Using an analogy to the study of community chests conducted by Litwak and Hylton, we observe that in the increasingly global competition, the firms are competing for the common customers' 'fund' and the increase in one firm's revenue would come at the expense of other firm's loss. Coordination, being a function of interdependency, should grow in periods of increased competition for 'funds.'

The IT Paradox

- *Proposition* 7: Increasingly turbulent environment would feed the need for further advancements in IT which would further increase turbulence.

Business needs are incessantly driving the demands for increased capabilities of IT. In turn, increasingly advanced IT is being utilised in more and more sophisticated ways by the businesses to outdo competition. IT, which is being deployed as a solution to the increased complexity and uncertainty of the environment, has paradoxically contributed to the situation by 'compressing time and distance.' In absence of the present day advances in IT, would we be talking of globalisation or time based competition? Perhaps, not.

The pace of complexity is increasing fast. Hopefully, the advances in technology would be able to keep up with the environmental changes. Turbulence refers not to chaos in the environment, but to an increasing causal interconnection that renders environments obscure to local observers. Thus how can IT help organisations in responding to the challenges of an increasingly complex and uncertain environment? How can IT help the organisations achieve the 'flexible' organisation structure? We provide academic libraries as a living educational example that has been impacted by the strong trend of convergence of the technological advancements.

SORTING SEARCH RESULTS OF ONLINE LITERATURE DIGITAL LIBRARY

An OLDL (Online Literature Digital Library) is a library in which collections, *i.e.*, publications from one or more domains of study, are stored in digital formats and accessible by users through the Internet.

Examples of well-known OLDLs are:

- IEEE Xplore
- CiteSeer
- Google Scholar
- PubMed

Digital libraries are rapidly growing in popularity. For instance, ScienceDirect, the world's leading scientific, technical and medical information resource celebrated its billionth article download in November'06 since, launched in 1999. Besides usage, digital libraries are also rapidly growing in terms of size and diversity of topics. For instance:

- In Computer Science, ACM Digital Library has close to one million full-text publications collected over 50 years, to search and download.
- In Electrical Engineering and Computer Science, IEEE Xplore, another OLDL, provides users with on-line access to more than 1,700 selected conferences proceedings.

These high growth rates introduced several challenges facing the information access capability of OLDLs. Next we list few challenges that probably guides future research related to LDLs.

LARGE SIZES AND TOPIC DIVERSITY OF SEARCH OUTPUT RESULTS

Search outputs of OLDLs tend to suffer from the 'topic diffusion' problem, where commonly, keyword-based searches produce a large number of publications over a large number of topics, where not all topics are of interest to the user. One way to solve this problem is to assign scores to search results. Assigning scores to publications helps OLDLs to present the most important relevant publications to the user first, Citation-based publication score measures are commonly used for ranking publications. At the present time, OLDLs lack effective and accurate publication ranking.

LACK OF EFFECTIVE SCORING FUNCTIONS FOR PUBLICATIONS

At the present time, OLDLs lack effective and accurate publication rankings. Providing accurate publication scores can help users in reducing the time spent in searching OLDLs, and thus enhances the scalability of OLDL usage as users can quickly identify important relevant publications to their topic of interest.

LACK OF EFFECTIVE SCORING FUNCTIONS FOR SEARCH OUTPUTS

In the field of literature digital libraries, citation analysis is employed to order digital library search outputs. Examples of citation-based measures are citation-count and PageRank. However, as noticed by, citation-based measures compute popularity of publications based on the 'current' state of a citation graph that continuously changes and evolves.

Thus PageRank is effective in capturing the popularity of publications based on the current citation-graph inhand. We show that PageRank may assign inaccurate popularity scores for both old and recent publications.

And thus PageRank cannot be used to rank OLDL search outputs. We therefore need effective techniques to order search results based on their importance and relevance to users' interests.

INFORMATION ACCESS IN DIGITAL LIBRARIES

A digital library (DL) system comprises a large, distributed information space, where the objects carrying the knowledge required by the users, live. Setting up and maintaining a DL would be entirely useless if users were not provided with the adequate tools to access the DL information contents.

In defining the information access service of a DL, there are at least 3 areas of the information system field which can give significant contributions:

- *Information retrieval* (IR) can contribute content-based methods, that is methods that exploit the signal level of an information object. For textual objects, these include all classical methods based on the statistical properties of language, such as the vector-space method and the probabilistic method. For non-textual objects, in the last decade there has been a fluorishing of methods for similarity-based retrieval of images, video and audio objects.
- The *database* area can contribute all methods for attribute-based information querying, ranging from traditional databases, to semi-structured databases; the methods falling under the last category are especially useful when ad- dressing the *structure* of objects.
- *Knowledge representation* can contribute methods for accessing objects by querying descriptions of their contents; these descriptions are typically couched in terms of representations of the underlying domain of discourse, or *ontologies* as these have come to be termed lately.

Putting the techniques found in the fields all together at work, requires a conceptual schema which integrates in a unique framework the different aspects of DL objects addressed by each of them. In what follows as suggested, try to sketch such a schema.

A CONCEPTUAL SCHEMA OF INFORMATION ACCESS

We characterise the space of information access by the following, orthogonal dimensions:

- The information access model, which establishes the basic terms of the system/user interaction;

- The information access mode, which establishes the role of the user and that of the system during their interaction.

Information access Models

Similarly to an information retrieval model, an information access model specifies:

- A representation of the objects to be accessed;
- A representation of the user information needs; and
- A function associating a set of objects to each user information need.

Information access models can be categorised according to the options available on each one of their dimensions. For object representation, following we distinguish between simple objects and composite objects. Simple objects cannot be further decomposed, and can be represented along the following dimensions:

- *Content abstractions*: these are representations used to access objects via IR techniques. They are created by IR indexers in an automatic way, by extracting low-level features from objects, such as the number of word occurrences in a text, or the energy level in a certain region of an image); content abstractions retain that part of the information originally present in the object content that is considered sufficient to characterise the object for access purposes;
- *Content representations*: these are symbolic representations of the meaning of documents, that is descriptions formulated in some suitable knowledge representation language, spelling out the truth conditions of the object. Content representations can be constructed manually, sometimes with the assistance of some knowledge extraction tool, or automatically, for instance via object classification methods. They can be precise or uncertain, depending on whether or not the content representation formulas are expressed in an un- certain logic, such as fuzzy or probabilistic logic.

Composite objects are structured set of simple objects, thus they are typically represented as mathematical *structures*, reflecting their internal organisation. Finally, objects, whether simple or composite, can have a *profile*, that is an attribute-based description of their external properties, such as the author and the publisher of a book, or the data and time at which an image has been taken, and the like. In the context of digital libraries, the 4 dimensions of object representation reduce to 3 only, since content representations and profiles are typically grouped together under the label of discovery metadata. The metadata associated to a DL object can therefore vary from simple records typically adhering to some standardised schema to very complex representations expressed in some knowledge representation language which must be coupled with a representation of the underlying domain of discourse, in order to be properly used for, *e.g.* information access. In summary, as suggested, therefore consider object representation as being categorised as:

- Content,
- Metadata, and
- Structure.

For information need representation, we have 2 options: formal language queries or natural language queries. For the retrieval function, we have 2 options: exact match or best match. Not all combinations of these options give rise to meaningful information access models. Considering the object representation options we have the following:

- Content is typically addressed via IR techniques, based on natural language queries and best-match retrieval function. For instance, users access the con- tent of an image base by providing as a query an image itself In so doing, users are implicitly asking the system to retrieve images which 'looks' similar to the image query, at least as far as the system can tell. For this reason, methods providing access by content are often called '*similarity-based*' access methods. An analogous pattern is found in access models for textual or for audio content. Notice that in some models of this kind, the query may not be expressed in the same medium as the sought objects. For instance, when accessing by content a video database, users may provide an image as a query, and the system is expected to retrieve the scenes sharing visual similarity with the provided image. Similarity-based access models are medium-dependent, in that different media require different techniques, and the possibility of using the same or a similar technique across different media is very limited. In addition, experience has shown that even within the same medium, the effectiveness of techniques is application-dependent: for example, retrieving by similarity sport images requires different techniques from those necessary to establish the similarity of X-ray images.
- Metadata is typically addressed via formal language queries, thus we are in the realm of databases or knowledge representation, depending from the degree of sophisticatedness of the involved representations. For instance, to query a Dublin Core scheme, one needs a very simple language allowing to state basic relational conditions on simple numeric- or string-based attribute values; instead, to query an OWL representation the ability to state conditions involving taxonomies and navigation of graph structures is required. In general, a query to metadata takes the form of a logical formula, and an exact match retrieval function is employed for query evaluation, grounded in some logical theory. We call these models *semantic* access models. Some retrieval engines allow to exploit information retrieval techniques

when accessing objects via their metadata records. This is achieved by seeing metadata records as pieces of text whose words are the attribute values. Such a text is treated in the same way as textual content, and matched against a natural language query as in a similarity-based textual access method. This kind of access model is widely employed on bibliographic records, as it frees users from the necessity of knowing the meaning of meta- data attributes.

- Also object structure can be queried in two different ways:
- Via exact match retrieval functions, such as the one underlying the query language XPath. In this case, the structural query is mostly embedded into a larger query addressing either content or metadata. We do not have therefore separate classes of access models but sophistications of similarity-based or semantic access models allowing also the specification of structural clauses in queries.
- Via best match retrieval functions, which express in a quantitative way the degree of similarity between the structure of each object and a user provided structure class. These models have been investigated in the con- text of XML, and are a structural variation of similarity-based models. We call the models falling in this class 'similar structure-based access models'.

In summary, we have the following information access model categories:

- Similarity-based access models, possibly with structural conditions;
- Semantic access models, possibly with structural conditions; and
- Similar structure-based access models.

Information Access Modes

Independently from the access model, the information access modes establishes the role of the system and that of the user. Each of these two can be either passive or active. Excluding the case in which they are both passive, we have the following 3 types of information access systems:

- *Query-answering systems*: in this case the user is active, that is, poses a query, while the system is passive, that is it just evaluates the user query and returns the result.
- *Filtering systems*: In which the user is passive, that is, does not pose any query, and the system is active, that is it selects on a stream of incoming objects, those that are deemed as relevant for the user; the relevance assessment is performed by relying on a user profile.
- *Personalised query-answering systems*: in which the user is active, that is, poses a query, and the system is active too, in that it alters the query evaluation process by taking into account the user preferences, represented as a profile. Recommendation systems also fall into this category, since they propose recommendations along with the answer to the query.

EVALUATING PUBLICATION SCORING FUNCTIONS IN DIGITAL LIBRARIES

This section deals with the issues of defining score functions for publications in digital libraries, and evaluating how good they are.

Presently, digital libraries do not assign scores to publications, even though they are potentially useful for:

- Providing comparative assessment, or 'importance', of papers; and
- Anking papers returned in search outputs.

Using social networks or bibliometrics, one can define a number of publication score functions. Existing citation-based publication score functions are all based on the notion of prestige in social networks and bibliometry. The well-known PageRank algorithm determines the importance of a publication by the number and importances of publications with links to it. The Hyperlink Induced Topic Search (HITS) algorithm is similar to the PageRank algorithm in that HITS involves computing two scores for each publication; hub and authority scores. Authorities represent high-prestige publications, whereas hubs are publications that have links to authorities. Other citation-based score functions can be derived as follows:

- Use normalised citation count as the basis for a score function.
- Revise the score of a paper using the score of its publication venue.
- Add weights to citations, *e.g.*, citations by an 'important' author's work are more significant.
- Revise the score of a paper using temporal distributions of citations; *e.g.*, citations in the last 10 years are more significant than earlier citations.
- Revise a paper score using the score of its citation venue; that is, capture the notion of a hub or an authority, *e.g.*, survey journal represents a hub, whereas a research paper represents an authority.
- Revise a paper score by the score of its author.

Citation-based Publication Score Functions

PageRank

Importance of papers that cite a particular paper determines its importance. PageRank and HITS were designed based on this assumption. PageRank scores is computed recursively using the formula

$$P_{i+1} = (1-d)M^T P_i + E$$

Where *Pi* and *Pi+1* are the current and next iteration PageRank vectors respectively. *M* is a matrix derived from the citation matrix *C* by normalising all row-sums in *C* to *1*. *C*, in turn, is the adjacency matrix of the graph *G* formed as follows; the papers represent the graph nodes, and the citation relationships between these papers represent the edges. C is of size NxN, where N is the total number of papers in the system. Finally, d and $(1\text{-}d)$ are the future citation probability. Given that an author A who is writing a new paper and already cited paper u which in turn cites paper v, and let w be a paper in AnthP selected randomly. The parameter d represents the probability that A will cite w, and $(1\text{-}d)$ is the probability that A will cite v. To guarantee the algorithm convergence, it is assumed to have a hidden link between each pair of the graph nodes. This link is represented by the user-defined parameter E. A variation of E is simply $E1=d$. Another variation of E that is used in is,

HUBS AND AUTHORITIES

Authority score of paper P is computed by summing up the hub scores of the papers citing P. Hub score of P is computed by summing up the authority scores of the papers that P cites. Computation is recursive until results converge after a number of iterations. One difference between HITS and PageRank is that the first one works on papers in the result set of a query, while the latter considers all the papers independent of the query.

Citation Count

A paper, normally, does not cite another paper unless the cited paper is relevant. And, large number of citations to a paper gives an indication that the paper is important. Based on this fact, one can use citation count as a measure for paper importance. For a given paper P, let CitationCount (P) be the number of times paper P is cited by other papers. Using the number of citations, paper P is as important as those papers that have the same number of citations and more important than those papers that have fewer citations. As suggested, refer to this paper ranking measure as PCitation_Count.

Evaluating Publication Score Functions

Figure shows the three score functions, namely, PageRank (PPgRank), Authorities scores of HITS (PAuth) and, the Citation-count (PCitCnt). As it is clear from the figure the three functions are highly skewed, and do not separate scores well over the interval. This figure is based on the AnthP digital collection from the field of data management. In the author observed the skewness and inseparability of these functions independently in computer science and life sciences publications as well. And, it is shown that distributions of citation-based score functions are also highly skewed and decay very fast. Studies show that the cause is topic diffusion since, scores are computed with respect to the full publication set.

In the authors compared and evaluated several publication score functions, including PageRank and Authorities scores, both adopted from the www search domain, and citation-count scores from the bibliometrics domain. The authors observed the separability problem with all of these functions which is that none of these scoring functions assigns scores that distribute well over a given scale, *e.g.* Instead, distributions of existing publication score functions are highly skewed, and decay very fast resulting in a much less useful comparative publication assessment capability for users.

This lack of separability is caused by the 'rich gets richer' phenomena, *i.e.*, a very small number of publications with relatively high numbers of in-citations have even higher chances of receiving new citations. Yet, these scoring functions are still not very accurate, probably caused by topic diffusion in search outputs. In the following section, and by using the research-pyramid model proposed in, the authors in normalise scores of publications within their own research pyramids, which allows for a fair comparative assessment of publications as publications are compared to their peers in their own research pyramids.

9

Designing for Collaboration in E-Research

Collaboration has always been at the heart of the e-Science vision to the extent that it has almost been taken for granted that research is a collaborative activity and that collaboration is desirable and useful. Some recent studies have started to unpack the role that collaboration plays and have observed that research practices are not simply and unreservedly collaborative and open but that researchers are quite deliberate and careful about just when and who they share and collaborate with. Instead of treating collaborative behaviour as a given, we need to start to unpack the different ways in which researchers make choices about collaboration and just what collaboration might mean in a particular context.

The question is how environments for research can be designed so as to facilitate and support the formation and work of virtual organisations addressing complex research questions. Clearly, this process needs to be shaped in a way that allows designers and users to attend to the working practices involved and to the ways in which these change as research progresses. The increased emphasis on sharing of resources and reuse of data and artefacts such as workflows or scientific software raises issues of ensuring their provenance and quality as well as security, confidentiality and appropriate use.

As previous work on the use of electronic records in health care has shown, these issues are intimately tied in with peoples' *working practices*, located in an organisational and regulatory *context* and that therefore development of support for such work needs to be attentive to these matters. For example, the secondary use of such data brings with it additional problems of consent and confidentiality but also has to deal with the inherent problems of making sure that record keeping practices and the use of records are sufficiently aligned. This is just one example of how design of collaboration support for e-Research needs to be attentive to the specific practices involved and the organisational contexts in which e-Research takes place.

We would argue that the specific circumstances of and practices involved in research make it necessary to establish a reflexive tie between the normally separate activities of design and use. Such a tie needs to exist both at the local level where support of specific research endeavours is the key concern, at the institutional level where decisions are made about the institutional support of research IT and at the level of the formation and shaping of (multi-)disciplinary research communities. Drawing on studies from the areas of computer supported cooperative work and participatory design may help us to formulate a systems development approach that will support local research practices while at the same time being attentive to how these fit in with generic technical architectures and global infrastructures. For example, Büscher *et al.* point to the "deeply consequential relationships between use and software architectural design" and develop an approach to distilling local innovation into generic architectures and more generally applicable component parts.

We would argue that the development of virtual research environments needs to be underpinned as much by sound architectural principles as by an understanding of collaborative practices in e-Research and that much can be gained by aligning this development with wider developments in the area of collaborative work environments and the tradition of computer supported cooperative work and participatory design.

VRES AND CWES

As research is a particular kind of work, similar to other kinds in some respects but different in others, virtual research environments can be seen as special cases of collaborative work environments. However, it would seem that the development of VREs is progressing independently of the development of CWEs and that the communities involved in these projects overlap only very partially. This is not to say that there is no exchange but it is our impression that collaborations are opportunistic and contingent rather than strategically arranged. There is a real danger here not only that effort is duplicated but also that valuable lessons learned over many years in the field of computer supported cooperative work are ignored in the development of cooperation support for e-Research.

These lessons relate to general findings about work as a socially organised activity, to the design of collaboration support and to the ways in which technology development can be informed and driven by an understanding of collaborative work practices. Our aim is to sketch out and provide strategies for exploiting this overlap for the benefit of both projects. We can roughly characterise them as being related to conceptual issues, methodology and technology, each of which as suggested, discuss in turn.

CONCEPTUAL ISSUES

The way we conceive of work and the concepts we use to describe its features has an important impact on how we go about designing collaboration support for innovative work contexts. For example, we might want to look at extracting general lessons from studies of risks in scientific collaborations and use them to inform the debate about collaborative work environments and the way we might go about setting up communities of distributed knowledge workers. A taxonomy of collaboration environments, populated with examples of efforts that have been successful might help us understand what good practice is in this area as well as to disseminate this understanding.

An excellent example of such a resource is the Science of Collaboratories database of successful e-Research environments or collaboratories. Based on such common ground, we can also start exploring the differences in conceptualisations of social structures in VRE and CWE research as well as the relationship between the visions involved and real-world experiences. For example, a study of FBIRN, a large-scale multi-organisation scientific collaboration suggests that local contexts and organisational alignments are still of crucial importance to the way in which work gets done. This is despite the emphasis placed in conceptualisations of e-Research on inter-organisational work in "virtual organisations".

When we consider similar statements about work within collaborative work environments, can we assume that these individuals will be divorced from such organisational contexts? Will this be true for the majority or at least a significant minority of workers? Or do we need to treat organisational alignments as one in a number of factors? Building upon these understandings will be essential for collaborative technologies to be easily *embedded* within social arrangements and wider socio-technical contexts, be *transparent* in the sense that their use does not require a lengthy setup process and have a *reach* beyond individual projects or activities and beyond individual institutional contexts: that is, to embody infrastructural qualities. Such an arrangement would mean that use is *learned* as part of membership, *i.e.*, taken for granted within a community of practice, would involve established *conventions of practice*, build on an *installed base* and the technology would become *visible only upon breakdown, i.e.*, it would normally be seen-but-unnoticed. Building systems and use practices that acquire these properties is still a challenging task and we need to gain a better understanding of what factors further or hinder the emergence of an infrastructure.

For example, Olson have suggested the related concepts of collaboration readiness, collaboration infrastructure readiness and collaboration technology readiness as a means to guiding our understanding of the factors that further or hinder collaboration. An example of a factor relating to collaboration readiness is the issue of whether established rules for data sharing exist within a community. Collaboration infrastructure readiness relates to questions about the operational environment of collaboration environments such as the existence of high-bandwidth multicast networks for multiparty video conferencing or the availability of technical support. Finally, collaboration technology readiness relates to the question of skills and experiences that individual researchers have with collaboration support tools. Depending on where we locate the barriers to uptake, different kinds of responses will be necessary to address issues falling into one or more of these categories.

METHODOLOGY: USER-DESIGNER RELATIONS AND INNOVATION

There is a need for technological innovation and a developing understanding of the changes in modern workplaces to progress hand in hand if we want to develop technologies that will turn out to be useful, usable and socially beneficial. Technology push needs to be balanced with application pull and reflection on the changes made to the working practices of researchers. A user-centric approach is crucial here if we do not wish to disenfranchise researchers who may feel that their work is being reshaped by technologists who understand very little of it and do not share the concerns of the research communities for what constitutes good practice. As suggested, discuss various approaches to practically addressing these issues by creating particular forms of relationships between technology design and use, allowing local innovation to be distilled into more generally applicable components that fit in with a generic open architecture for collaboration support.

It is paramount to avoid the design fallacy, *i.e.*, the notion that building ever more knowledge about users and use *into* designed artefacts is going to lead to more useable and useful systems and wider uptake. Requirements are moving targets as contexts and work practices are continuously evolving. This is especially true in research where innovation is part of the game rather than an occasional exception. This does not mean that traditional methods of requirements gathering like the use of workplace studies, focus groups or user surveys do not have a role to play but they need to be complemented with at least an element of ongoing engagement that is aimed at supporting the innovative uses that occur only after the initial design of technologies is completed and artefacts get used in anger in real-world settings.

Corealisation is one approach that aims to provide a suitable orientation to design as an ongoing activity involving not only professional designers and other IT professionals but, crucially, all people playing a part in the overall socio-technical ensemble of which IT is a part. In e-Research, a related strategy that has been pursued is "embedding" researchers in the design team or designers in research teams. Another approach developed within the area of CSCW and palpable computing is the use of facilitation as a way of exploring innovative uses of technology in real-world settings, on a routine basis or in the form of scenarios played out in the field. The strength of these approaches is that they foster a long-term engagement between technologists and users to explore possible designs and their uses in real-world contexts.

While the use of facilitators in traditional work contexts is quite well explored as, *e.g.*, user-advocates in participatory design or technology-use mediators in organisational studies, further research is needed for inter-organisational or communitybased settings. The distributed nature of such contexts makes it necessary to think about new ways of supporting the collaborative appropriation of otherwise general-purpose media, *e.g.*, by using the collaboration technologies itself for the mediating processes.

TECHNOLOGY

Many VREs are built as portals that allow web-based access to various resources as well as providing collaboration support. The existence of a recognised standard makes it possible not only to select from a wide range of development tools and supporting technologies but also potentially enables the resulting VRE components to be traded and integrated in institutional portal environments using the same standards. However, JSR 168 provides for integration only at the level of the presentation layer, allowing different, independently developed *portlets* to be displayed together in a web browser, coexisting but not interoperating.

This leaves the coordination and integration between different portlets which is needed in many contexts unaddressed. One reason why the Sakai virtual learning environment is quite attractive as a development platform for VREs is that it provides APIs for a closer integration and coordinated existence of components. It is becoming increasingly apparent that what is needed is an underlying framework that can bind together independently developed collaboration tools as we move from scenarios where these merely co-exist to integrated environments. In addition, we should not forget that the Web and its standards were not originally designed to support complex applications but were rather meant to facilitate the relatively coarse-grained process of document transfer.

Mobile applications required, *e.g.*, in the context of archaeological excavations or high-bandwidth VRE environments supporting large scale synchronous collaborations make it necessary to complement browser-based tools and to provide for integration between different modes of access to a VRE. One issue this raises is the dynamic transition between synchronous and asynchronous collaboration and the interplay between and integration of scientific applications and collaborative environments. The aim of the ECOSPACE project to produce collaboration upperware and services to enable seamless and instant collaboration within communities is very consonant with approaches taken in e-Research, especially service oriented approaches adopted in the Grid community. What is important, though, is to ensure that the solutions chosen at the middleware and upperware layers are compatible or can be adapted. For example, strategies will be needed to provide federated authentication and authorisation mechanisms that integrate well with back-end identity and user profile management systems run by institutions or resource providers. The selection and use of standards as well as awareness of existing work are important elements that can be achieved through initiatives such as the e-Framework and the eReSS study of standards used in JISC VRE projects.

E-SCIENCE VERSUS E-RESEARCH

We would like to begin with a distinction between e-science and e-research. Terminology is not innocent and the differences in the integration of cyberinfrastructures and tools in scholarly dominant use of the term e-science in discussions of new information infrastructures for the humanities and social sciences carries with it an emphasis on data-oriented, computational, or quantitative analysis. We propose to use the term e-research instead. This term is more inclusive of a variety of research modes, and thereby acknowledges disciplinary practices.

e-Science, termed cyberinfrastructure in the US, is generally defined as the combination of three different developments: the sharing of computational resources, distributed access to massive datasets, and the use of digital platforms for collaboration and communication. The core idea of e-science is that knowledge production will be enhanced by the combination of pooled human expertise, data and sources, and computational and visualization tools. e-Science has become a buzzword for funding large-scale facilities in research fields driven large-scale data processing. It claims to be no less than a revolution in the way knowledge can be created. This development started in the US at the end of the 1990s in the framework of supercomputer centers. It was picked up in the UK in 2001, when an "e-science" research programme was launched, with funding of 250 million pounds for a period of 5 years.

The Grid technology developed by computer scientists working in particle physics settings played an important role for e-science. In the framework of their research, it was important to go from sharing information to sharing computation, turning "the global network of computers into one vast computational resource". The idea then took the shape of a generic computational infrastructure for scientific research. The domains that are supposed to be affected by this revolution vary according to the national variety of e-science. But, so the claim goes, almost all disciplines will be transformed in some way or other.

We have discussed elsewhere the tension this has created between e-science as a generic novel paradigm of research and its practice as a local infrastructure in a limited set of fields. This led us to a plea for forms of non-computational e-science, and for the use of e-research as the more inclusive term. e–Research acknowledges forms of research that are not reliant on high-performance computing, as well as other ways of making use of new media and digital networks. E-mail and web sites, used by hundreds of thousands of scholars may have more import than a grid application used by a few hundred.

As far as we know, the term e-research in a methodological sense was used first by Terry Anderson and Heather Kanuka in 2002. In their research manual addressed to researchers in the field of education, they define e-research basically as "Net research". It includes online surveys and interviews, log file analysis, analysis of social behaviour in virtual reality environments and online evaluation of knowledge. Their use of the term e-research is very close to Christine Hine's use of the term virtual methods or the term Internet Research by a growing group of social and humanities scholars, in particular the group organized in the Association of Internet Researchers AoIR.

Since 2004, we have used e-research differently, as a critique of the notion of e-science rather than as a generic word for internet research or virtual methods. Our critique addresses three different aspects of e-science: the underlying philosophy of science, assumptions about diffusion of e-science across academia, and expectations about the technological infrastructure needed.

First of all, in contrast to the implied philosophy of science in most e-science writing, we wish to celebrate rather than diminish the pluriformity that exists in academia. We do not expect that making clever use of ICT will in itself make the social sciences or humanities "harder" or more like experimental science. Nor should it: our use of e-research is both descriptive and performative. Our second point of critique addresses the assumption that e-science is supposed to diffuse across academia. With respect to the diffusion model, we emphasize that if more fields make use of ICT, this will not be a simple wholesale adoption. Rather, we foresee an active transformation, in which the models of research prevalent in the relevant field shape the way ICT is conceptualized and used. Rather than a *diffusion* of e-science, we propose to think along the lines of *translation* of e-research. The implication is that it is not a matter of simply setting up a proper Grid infrastructure, and then expecting that users will flock to it and become e-scientists. A translation model of e-research posits a different dynamic between tools and users, where mutual shaping and adaptation takes place, and where what 'e-science' can mean as a practice is also subject to transformation.

This leads to the third element of our critique: which technologies are actually needed by scholars in a variety of fields? Or perhaps more precisely, which technologies could support and enhance research practices in a given field? Very often, researchers will not need a Grid– nor whatever paradigm comes next in computer science. They may will be more interested in some rather 'low-level' technology like better e-mail applications – robust and portable rather than cutting edge – which may not be very exciting for computer scientists, but may be far more helpful to advance the field in question. Our critique implies a particular stance, and this too has implications for the kind of work supported. This user-oriented perspective may lead to conservatism, since it emphasizes a business-as-usual focus.

By making the user so central, we run the risk of undermining the dynamic of innovation that can be coupled to initiatives like e-science. In this respect we are on the side of some of the champions of e-science, in that we also feel that it should be possible to play more creatively with both concepts and technologies in many fields in the social sciences and humanities than is currently the case. We think this type of innovation of epistemic cultures will always need to start from the position of a group of researchers in a particular field and the creation of room and support for activities that explicitly involve exploration and experimentation, however, rather than with a technology looking for users. This forces us to play a rather complicated game in which we both promote innovation in academia and are suspicious of the innovation talk that comes with it. We expand on how we are dealing with these tensions later in this chapter.

On this issue of e-research, let us finally note that the term seems to have become far more widespread recently. This is partly due to discussions at the series of international conferences on e-social science, and partly due to the creative activities in "digital humanities". The Oxford E-research Centre has also taken up the term, and shifted from the use of e-science to e-research to designate their new research programme. This development reached a high point in 2007 at the Third International Conference of e-Social Science in Ann Arbor, where the former director of the UK e-science programme Tony Hey explicitly noted the restrictive character of the label e-science, and affirmed that in the social sciences, e-research would be a much better term instead.

E-RESEARCH AS INTERVENTION

We conceptualize the development of e-research in the humanities and social sciences as an intervention in the practice of knowledge creation. The drive to create new modes of knowledge generation that is dependent on, and mediated by, high-performance computing networks has usually not been the result of the autonomous development of the field in question, but rather of interactions. For example, cell biologists did not accidentally hit upon the idea of simulating a living cell in a three-dimensional graphical immersive environment. Rather, this resulted from interaction with computer scientists involved in the creation of virtual reality environments and of visualizations, initially mainly funded by DARPA, leading to projects such as the Virtual Cell.

Coalitions are therefore created around advanced research instrumentation. Funding schemes, tools, researchers, institutional frameworks and research agendas interact to form these coalitions. Presently, we are witnessing the emergence of this type of interaction in the social sciences and humanities. The result of these interactions can perhaps best be characterized as a parade of prototypes, applications developed within the framework of a particular project but aimed at broader area of scholarly communities.

For example, papers presented at the First International Conference of e-Social Science in 2005 in Manchester showed ways to put social science applications on the Grid, a spatial decision support system, tools for distributed data analysis, modeling and simulation environments and a prototype for networking social science resources on the Web. It is not yet clear to what extent these prototypes will survive their initial period of funding and contribute substantively to social science research. If other researchers do not use them, this may simply be because they are not sufficiently relevant to the field, or even invisible to the core group of experts in the field. It may also be that certain kinds of actors, such as large firms and professional software developers need to be involved in these coalitions, because of their ability to shape availability and usability of tools.

In all these cases, it may be fruitful to conceptualize e-research as an intervention in current practices, potentially upsetting these practices and disrupting the existing fabric of social relationships that carry knowledge creation. This conceptualization also emphasizes the recognition of theoretical and methodological pluriformity we attach to the term e-research. By seeing e-research as intervention, we not only underline that translation work is needed if e-research is to be adopted in new fields, but also that this has a cost. It is not only a matter of spreading the wealth around; it is also a matter of redirecting and thereby upsetting research agendas.

Conceptualizing e-research as intervention, we make visible the complexities of the work involved and the difficulties in prospective evaluation of its possible outcomes. It is not enough to weigh the costs and benefits of one research agenda over the other. It is also relevant to acknowledge the fact that e-research as intervention needs to be understood in sociological as well as epistemological terms. We need to step back from involvement in the culture of a particular field to be able to see these intricacies. This is why we find the expertise developed in the field of science and technology studies especially useful. Because our primary accountability as scholars is not in the particular field being investigated, this provides a relative distance from its dominant paradigms.

We thereby have a degree of freedom to engage in experiment and play with new forms of research that may be enabled in e-research, and to reflect on the consequences. This leads, of course, to an immediate new involvement in that field, opening a virtuous cycle of engagement and disengagement. This cycle can only be sustained on the basis of a theory about innovation in a particular field that is partly independent of the state of affairs in that field. For example, in one of our projects at the VKS, we work together with economic historians to create a collaboratory for their research. In order to understand the problems historians may encounter in switching to mediated and large-scale forms of collaboration, we can draw on experiences in other fields. We therefore need to draw upon knowledge such as developed in the "science of collaboratories", while maintaining an analytic standpoint that remains aware of the particularities of economic history. In other words, having a conceptual framework to understand the dynamics of knowledge production enables a different appreciation of new practices around new tools. The field of science and technology studies has not only developed well-honed theories and methodologies to understand these dynamics, but has also thought hard about the balance between engagement and distance.

DETACHMENT/RESEARCH

Approaches in this quadrant are concerned with the interrelationship between micro-level research practices, on the one hand, and macro-level policy and technology implementation, on the other. Whether from the perspective of critiquing e-research in the context of social and institutional factors, or from the perspective of potential social science users with concerns regarding the social implications. Sustainability viewed from this approach is concerned with social barriers and perceived relevance of e-research.

CRITICAL/REFLEXIVE OR PROSPECTIVE

The critical/reflexive approach is concerned with the social implications of e-research and tends to highlight the discrepancy between visions and practice. The focus is often on the analysis of high-level discourses around e-research, such as policy documents or future visions. The discussion typically revolves around the 'values' and 'expectations' embedded in technologies as well the evolving meaning of terminology, definitions, and boundaries. This perspective tends to couple its argument with the need for researcher immersion in ethnographic case studies.

Vann and Bowker, for example, explore 'prospective texts' around e-research and argue that in order to understand the impact of e-research on knowledge-producing practices, social scientists need to "consider decisions that get made about how the skill, commitment, performance, and product demand of scientists can be coordinated and stabilized". In other words, visions lock in particular trajectories of the way in which the work of the research is done. This approach thus looks to concrete instantiations of local scientific practices – such as how the 'labor' of research of different forms of research is talked about – or at new disciplinary identities and forms of accountability in scientific practice.

Hine's work is a good illustration of this approach. She explores the relationship between the visions for global online cataloguing and digitization of species and the cultural specificity of the systematics field in biology. To do this, she examines the discourse of the House of Lords Select Committee on

Science and Technology review of the state of systematics in Britain, combining this with ethnographic observation of the problems encountered in practice. In the process, she challenges the inevitability of the digital solutions perspective: 'if you build it they will come'.

Systematics is also an interesting case study for exploring what Hine describes as the 'political geography' of a discipline, whereby the geopolitical history of a discipline shapes collective notions of social justice in the present. For example, human geographers try to distance themselves from the colonial geographies of the 18th century, and anthropologists are also keen to rectify and distance themselves from the cultural imperialism of the same period. In the case of systematics, access to the world's most critical taxonomic collections has historically been held by national institutions of developed countries, often with a history of colonization.

This centralization of resources and exclusion of developing countries in the past make the rhetoric of open access and data sharing compelling to a sense of social justice within the disciplinary community. The 'political geography' of systematics also converges with the "archaic image of systematic biology" to ensure that digital technologies are perceived within systematics to hold both 'practical purchase' and 'symbolic qualities'. Indeed, Hine argues that "particular sets of expectations around digital technologies have played an important part in shaping the discipline's response to the internet, playing out both on a level of individual practices and in high level policy forums where the discipline's activities are evaluated".

Researchers who adopt the critical/reflexive perspective argue that the compelling rhetoric around the transformative nature of digital technologies will preclude appropriate discussions about the real needs for digitizing resources and for evaluating the needs of users.

SKEPTICISM/NON-USE FROM WITHIN THE DISCIPLINES/SUSTAINABILITY AS PROJECT

A skeptical approach may lead to non-use or resistance to e-research. The U.K. *National Centre for e-Social Science* (NCeSS) perceives that potential users of e-Social Science will fall into three main categories: early adopters; enthusiasts; and the unengaged. In this quadrant the perceived development and uptake will be viewed with skepticism, with resources perhaps better allocated to an agenda that is less technology-driven and that sees the extension of tools to the 'unengaged' as being of doubtful value.

THE STATUS OF INTERNET-BASED RESEARCH

Although the Internet may be portrayed as a communication technology unique to the 1990s, this depiction is somewhat misleading. The Internet's origins are in fact traceable to the 1960s development of the military-funded communication network, ARPANET, with the Internet officially making its debut as a civilian tool for communication in 1983.

However, widespread public awareness of the Internet's existence did not occur within the United States until the early 1990s when it was privatized and online services such as America Online (AOL) were developed to serve the general public. Hence, there is a tendency to think of it as a turn-of-the-twenty-first-century phenomenon.

Prior to the 1990s, early public access to the Internet was limited mostly to government agencies, universities, and computer-related organizations, such as hardware and software developers. Initially, users experienced the Internet in the form of text-based communication applications such as e-mail and navigation systems such as Telnet.

In 1992, the World Wide Web (WWW) became publicly available in the United States and began to diffuse widely in 1993 with the release of the iconbased web browser Mosaic, which made web navigation more "user friendly" and visually appealing. Subsequently, use of the Web helped to popularize the Internet in general. As use of the Internet has shifted from a small community of researchers and government employees to a worldwide community, researchers recognize the Internet as an important area in need of study. The widespread diffusion and adoption of the Internet in the United States and abroad provides scholars with numerous research opportunities.

Because the Internet functions as a channel for communication, this is especially true for the field of communication. However, as with any innovation, it can be difficult at first to know how to approach the investigation of an innovation's contribution to and effects on the society into which it is introduced. With regard to the Internet, communication researchers, as well as others, must grapple with numerous decisions, such as determining how applicable existing theories and methods of enquiry are to this newest communication technology.

While the arguments for why and how to study the Internet vary, a common theme to arise within our discipline concerns the unique opportunity that today's communication scholars have to witness and record, first hand, the introduction of a major communication technology. Scholarly journals are one forum where communication researchers record the results of their research for the benefit of current and future generations of scholars.

Published articles inform other researchers of the types of approaches being used to study a wide variety of topics, including the Internet. A number of disciplines are conducting Internet research as is evident when searching electronic databases.

For example, a simple keyword search conducted in December 1999 in the Social Sciences Abstracts database on the term "Internet" yielded a return of 969 articles published across a diversity of disciplines, most notably in the areas of business, demographics, law, and policy studies.

Each discipline, including communication, typically contains a core set of journals considered to be "leaders" among all others in terms of their coverage of subject matter, length of publication, and quality of published articles. The question asked in this study concerns how leading journals in the field represent Internet-based research conducted by communication scholars, because an important goal of scholarly journals is to document a field's evolution over time.

This study examines the content, frequency, and pattern of published Internet-based research articles-studies that focus on some aspect of the Internet-in leading communication journals for the purpose of assessing how these journals are keeping pace with the Internet's influence on the communication process. It also considers how these journals represent our response to these changes to other disciplines in the social sciences.

THE IMPORTANCE OF COMMUNICATION SCHOLARS RESEARCHING THE INTERNET

Within the discipline, a handful of articles has addressed the importance of communication scholars studying the Internet. The reasons for study as well as the ways in which the Internet should be studied are varied. For example, in 1996, the Journal of Communication devoted the majority of its winter issue to "The Net." Within this issue, in a dialogue between Newhagen and Rafaeli, Rafeali pointed out that the development of the Internet, in part, is rooted in academe and, as such, "this alone behooves our involvement" in its study.

Beyond this statement Rafeali suggested that researchers focus on what he called the "five defining qualities of communication" on the Internet which, although somewhat abstract, included "multimedia, hypertextuality, packet switching, synchronicity, and interactivity." Newhagen argued that communication researchers must take a more active role in understanding the Internet by first understanding computer architecture, an area often left to engineers.

A bridge must be constructed between the worlds of communication and engineering so that communication researchers no longer find themselves in the position "where the engineers roll out a new technology, and we hold up numbers from 1 to 10, rating it."

Concerning the benefits of studying virtual reality, Biocca stated, "Communication researchers rarely have had the chance to observe the introduction, diffusion, and sociocultural presence of what may become the next dominant communication medium." However, he cautioned against viewing new communication technologies as a revolutionary by stating that many "new" technologies build upon, and borrow from, existing ones.

As such, researchers are likely to start out using existing theories and methods to study a new technology. He suggested focusing on questions such as the shape the medium is taking, and how the medium shapes and is shaped by the user-areas well suited to communication research. In a 1993 article, writing more broadly about humancomputer interface design, Biocca, as Newhagen was to do later in 1996, called for communication scholars to be more proactive in researching computer-mediated communication (CMC) by taking part in the design and development of new communication technologies.

Although, both of Biocca's articles were written just prior to the Internet's widespread public diffusion, his ideas, as if in anticipation of its introduction, are very applicable to the Internet and have been echoed in the later writing of Newhagen and Rafaeli.

Other communication scholars assuming the importance of studying the Internet have suggested additional approaches to its study. December argued for the need to define specific units of analysis for Internet research that would act as guideposts for researchers, helping to facilitate cross study comparisons.

These four units were defined as media space, media class, media object, and media instance. He also proposed a definition of Internet-based computer-mediated communication as that which involves information exchange that takes place on the global, cooperative collection of networks using the TCP/IP protocol suite and the client-server model for data communication.

Messages may undergo a range of time and distribution manipulations and encode a variety of media types. The resulting information content exchanged can involve a wide range of symbols people use for communication.

As such, he argued that the Internet is not a single medium but is instead made up of several media. Additionally, he cautioned that researchers studying on-line services such as Prodigy or America OnLine (AOL) should be aware that they were not actually conducting Internet-based research because these access providers offer proprietary services not available on the Internet. While this caveat is technically correct, it is perhaps overly restrictive. In addition to offering proprietary services to its users, on-line vendors such as AOL also function as Internet Service Providers (ISPs), allowing for communications to be exchanged via the global network.

In contrast to December, Morris and Ogan viewed the Internet as a single flexible mass medium capable of the synchronous and asynchronous transmission of text, audio, and video communication. They argued that the Internet provides the opportunity for communication researchers to rethink rather than abandon traditional views on mass media and to adopt a more flexible perspective on communication models. Additionally, they suggested that researchers study the Internet using a variety of existing frameworks, such as network analysis, and theories, such as social presence.

In summary, these scholars essentially argue that communication in relation to other disciplines should be a leader, if not the leader, in researching the Internet because it is a communication phenomenon. Communication scholars need to be proactive and creative in their research designs in order to reach this goal. To do this, they must possess a thorough understanding of how the technology works by taking an active role in the design and evaluation of future Internet applications.

RATIONALE

Knowledge of the extent to which Internet-related topics have been addressed and what methods of enquiry have been applied can assist communication researchers in placing their work within a broader range of studies. This information also identifies over- and under-emphasized topics and methods. Lastly, knowledge of the degree to which the Internet is represented within a discipline can provide researchers with a sense of the area's development and relative importance to the field as a whole.

It is not uncommon for communication researchers to analyse articles within an individual journal or a range of journals in order to assess the status of the discipline as a whole with respect to a particular issue. Examples of these studies include analyzing the frequency with which qualitative research is published, investigating the content and quality of published content analyses, and assessing the status of published mass communication articles by women across eight journals. Continuing this type of enquiry, this study examines the publication history of Internet research among five leading journals in the field.

JOURNAL SELECTION CRITERIA

While acknowledging the presence of newer electronic Internet and new technology-specific publications such as Internet Research and Journal of Computer-Mediated Communication, this study purposely focuses on mainstream, established communication journals. The reasons for this emphasis are threefold. First, and most obvious, the Internet is a channel for communication and as such it falls within the realm for study by communication researchers and, in turn, publication in our leading, established communication journals.

Second, established journals-those in existence for a period of decades-have the distinct advantage of having built both a reputation and a following over time. These journals are widely read within the discipline, contributing to scholars' perceptions of and currency with changes in the field. A third reason, closely related to the second, is that established journals can be viewed as historical records that document the field's evolution. Ideally, these journals reflect trends in the development of a discipline and the segments of society with which it deals as accurately as possible for the benefit of current and future scholars.

Selection of the five journals examined in this study employed two criteria: previous research identifying leading journals in the field and the reputation of Social Sciences Abstracts as a valid resource for communication research. In a content analysis of women's published research in mass communication, Dupagne, Potter, and Cooper identified eight leading communication journals, defined according to high circulation counts and low acceptance rates.

The journals identified in their study included: Communication Monographs, Communication Research, Critical Studies in Mass Communication, Human Communication Research, Journal of Broadcasting and Electronic Media, Journal of Communication, Journalism Quarterly, and Quarterly Journal of Speech. These journals functioned as a starting point for this study; however, application of the second criterion, communication research indexed in Social Sciences Abstracts, resulted in the omission of four titles from the original list.

The decision to further limit the journals examined was based on a twofold rationale. First, electronic databases are increasingly used by scholars to conduct literature searches because of their ease of use and convenience in comparison to print indexes. Within the vast realm of electronic indexes available for searching, Social Sciences Abstracts is a widely used leading index published by the highly reputable indexing service, H. W. Wilson Company. Second, subject-specific indexes, such as Social Sciences Abstracts, are typically more useful to and more likely to be used by scholars than general indexes, such as Expanded Academic Index, because they cover indexed journals in more detail, are more likely to index all articles in a journal rather than a chosen few, and they provide longer, more detailed abstracts.

By restricting the focus to leading communication journals indexed in Social Sciences Abstracts, this study attempts to take into consideration a broader view concerning how scholars in other disciplines might perceive the role of our discipline in the area of Internet research based on the presence of communication journal articles contained in the index. With the application of this second criterion, the final list of journals examined in this study include: Communication Research, Human Communication Research, Journal of Broadcasting and Electronic Media, Journal of Communication, and Journalism and Mass Communication Quarterly.

MEASURES

This study uses December's definition of Internet-based communication but with a slightly more liberal view on what constituted Internet-based communication. An article was considered Internetbased if it focused on computer-mediated communication technologies requiring access to an ISP, including services such as AOL or Prodigy, or closely simulated an Internet-based communication environment (*e.g.*, intranets, e-mail exchange between AOL members). This definition broadly included the Internet in general, intranets, World Wide Web (WWW), e-mail, mailing lists, bulletin boards, newsgroups, chat, virtual reality games such as multi-user domains (MUDs), and video/audio/ text computer conferencing. From the interfaces specified above, it can be seen that in most instances Internet access was necessary for communication to occur.

As with any area of research, certain information is useful in providing scholars with an overall sense of an area's progress or current status. For the purpose of this study, the concept of current status is operationalized into nine measures-author name, authorship, author rank, affiliation, topic, interface, method, total number of Internet-based articles per issue, and total number of research articles per issue.

Identification of an area's primary researchers provides scholars with a sense of which perspectives may be dominant in an area of study. While quantity of publication by an author does not necessarily equate with quality of research, it can provide scholars, especially those new to an area, with a starting point in the literature. The same can be said for the order of authorship on an article.

Distinguishing between primary and secondary authors can indicate, but not necessarily guarantee, which researchers are initiating studies, taking primary responsibility for the studies, and acting as primary contacts or "experts" in an area. Knowledge of which universities or organizations are conducting research in a particular area is beneficial for those interested in matters such as networking, educational, and employment opportunities.

The rank (*e.g.*, faculty, staff, student) of an author provides information on the diversity or homogeneity of the contributors to an area of research.

RESEARCH QUESTIONS

This study attempts to answer two basic questions. First, what is the frequency and pattern, if any, of published Internet-based research articles in five of the leading communication journals? Second, what do the contents of these articles reveal about the status of Internet research within and outside of the communication discipline?

UNIT OF ANALYSIS

The unit of analysis for this study was the scholarly communication research article that focused on Internet-based communication. This included "research in brief" articles but excluded editorials, rejoinders, and book reviews. Coders primarily read titles and abstracts to determine if an article fit this study's definition of Internetbased research. In instances where article titles and abstracts did not provide sufficient information, coders skimmed the articles for details.

POPULATION DATA

All research articles were examined in four major communication journals between the years 1994-1999. Because frequency of publication over time was one question asked by this study, population data were used instead of sample data in an effort to obtain a more accurate depiction of publishing trends across time by these journals.

The four journals selected for the main study included Communication Research, Human Communication Research, Journal of Broadcasting and Electronic Media, and Journal of Communication.

A fifth journal, Journalism fa Mass Communication Quarterly, was selected for a pilot study to test the codebook. To identify leading communication journals publishing Internet-related articles, a basic keyword search was conducted using the term "Internet" in the Social Sciences Abstracts electronic database; four journals were consistently referenced in the search results and thus selected for closer examination. One limitation of this selection process concerns the exclusion of some communication journal titles from the Social Sciences Abstracts index.

However, this limitation was considered acceptable given the broader focus of the study discussed earlier. Despite this limitation, the five journals selected for this study are examples of the mainstream publication outlets available through most of the field's major associations: the Association for Education in Journalism and Mass Communication, Broadcast Education Association, and International Communication Association.

The starting year for the study, 1994, was selected because, based on the Social Sciences Abstracts search results, in general, Internet publications did not begin to increase until that point in time. The first recorded Internet article in the database occurred in 1992; one article was referenced in 1993. However, in each year thereafter, the number of articles increased steadily. This pattern is consistent with the growing popularity of the Internet with the general public in the United States. The communication journals selected for study during this time frame contained a total of 961 research articles (323 from the pilot study and 638 from the main study). Each article was examined to determine if it met the definition of Internet-based research. Those articles that qualified were then coded.

OPERATIONAL DEFINITIONS

To answer the questions proposed in this study, nine measures were recorded for each Internet-based research article: author name, authorship, author rank, affiliation, topic, interface, method, total number of Internet-based articles per issue, and total number of research articles per issue. For each article the last name and initials of all authors were recorded. Authorship was coded as primary (first author) or secondary (all additional authors). The rank of each author was coded as faculty, student, staff (university affiliated, non-faculty/non-student employees), government employee, business employee, or other. Author affiliation was recorded as the name of the university or organization with which the author was identified at the time of publication.

Rather than attempt to anticipate the range in subject matter, article topic was recorded as open text by each coder and then later grouped into six broad categories: access, adoption/diffusion, policy, research/theory, social interaction, and other. Interface, the application used to communicate via a computer, was divided into eight categories: World Wide Web, e-mail, mailing lists/newsgroups/ bulletin boards, chat rooms, virtual reality game sites (*e.g.*, MUDs, MOOs), video/audio/text-based conferencing, Internet in general (no specific interface identified), and other (coders recorded the specific interface).

Method of enquiry was coded as policy study, critique/essay (non-policy studies), interview/case study, content analysis (qualitative and quantitative), experiment, survey, other (coders recorded the specific method) and combination for multiple methods used within a single study (each method was recorded and then weighted). Lastly, for each journal issue, coders recorded the total number of Internet-based articles and overall total number of research articles.

CODING PROCEDURES

The author and another communication researcher acted as coders. The codebook was created by the author and reviewed for clarity by the second coder. A pilot test to check for intercoder reliability was conducted on all issues of Journalism and Mass Communication Quarterly, 1994-1999, resulting in a 100 per cent overlap of 323 articles.

Discrepancies in coding were discussed, and slight modifications for the purpose of clarification were made to the codebook before proceeding to the four journals selected for the main study. Reliabilities for the number of Internet-based research articles and total number of articles for the pilot test were at the acceptable levels allowing for the inclusion of these articles in the study, under separate reporting.

Intercoder reliability for the main study was calculated using a 20 per cent overlap. Issues for the reliability check were selected using a stratified random sample. The total overlap between the coders contained 128 articles.

INTERCODER RELIABILITY

For the main study, the level of agreement concerning which articles qualified as Internet-based research was 98.4 per cent. Percentages of agreement and Scott's pi corrections for chance (where applicable) were as follows for the measures: author name, 97.9 per cent; authorship, 97.9 per cent.96; author rank, 97.9 per cent.97; affiliation, 97.9 per cent; topic, 94.3 per cent; interface, 96.9 per cent.96; method, 97.7 per cent.97; and total number of research articles per issue, 96.9 per cent. For the pilot study, percentage of agreement for Internet-based research articles was 84.6 per cent and 99.7 per cent for total number of articles per issue.

RESULTS

Frequency analyses are reported for each measure. With the exception of overall trends in publishing, all other measures report data collected from the four journals in the main study. This is because intercoder reliability for the pilot study was only reached on the two measures: Internet-based articles per issue and total articles per issue.

TRENDS IN PUBLISHING

Of the 961 research articles analysed, 37 (3.9 per cent) were Internet-based. Among the four journals in the main study, 4.1 per cent (26 of 638 articles) were Internet-based. Trends in the publication of Internet-based articles across the five journals revealed no distinct pattern of increase, decrease, or stabilization during the six-year time period. This finding was also the case within each of the five journals.

Overall, the Journal of Communication (32 per cent) published Internet research articles the most frequently followed by Journalism and Mass Communication Quarterly (30 per cent), Journal of Broadcasting and Electronic Media (24 per cent), Human Communication Research (8 per cent), and Communication Research (6 per cent). The percentage of published Internet-based research articles varied widely by year; however, a trend line reflecting a moving average suggests that the number of articles has increased over time.

TOPIC, INTERFACE, AND METHOD

Social interaction (31 per cent) was the topic most often researched. This was followed by research/theory (23 per cent); other (15 per cent), which included the topics of competition among local news web sites, digital art on the WWW, TV audience feedback via e-mail, and portrayals of the Internet in magazines; access (12 per cent) and adoption/diffusion (12 per cent); and policy issues (7 per cent). The interface studied most often was the Internet in general (42 per cent) followed by mailing lists/ newsgroups/bulletin boards (19 per cent), WWW (15 per cent), e-mail (12 per cent), and chat rooms (4 per cent), video/ audio/text conferencing (4 per cent), and other (4 per cent) which included an Internet-based interactive health programme.

The two most frequently used methods of enquiry were content analysis (27 per cent) and critique/essay (27 per cent). These were followed by experiment (11 per cent) and survey (11 per cent), and, lastly, policy study (8 per cent), interview/case study (8 per cent), and combination (8 per cent), which included groupings such as network analysis and content analysis, and surveys and content analysis.

DISCUSSION

The results of this study present a somewhat vague picture as to where this newest area of study is positioned within the selected journals. In part, this is due to the low number of Internet articles available for examination and thus discussion.

The results also indicate that scholars searching the Social Sciences Abstracts would find a scarcity of Internet-related research in our leading journals. It may be that the infrequent and uneven publication of Internet research in the journals examined is simply a typical reflection of any field's initial attempts to come to terms with a new area of study.

This finding suggests that Internet research is an area within the field that is clearly open for study. Within the four journals analysed, only two authors stood out in total number of publications potentially providing greater opportunity for other scholars to become better known through their research in comparison to more established areas in communication. Not surprisingly, faculty are the dominant group publishing Internet research articles, but, again, because of the newness of the area student authors may have more opportunities to publish than in more established areas. While certain universities are represented more than others, it remains to be seen which programmes will eventually come to the fore regarding Internet-based communication research.

In the areas of topic, interface, and methods, similar opportunities for growth exist. However, as speculated by Biocca and Morris and Ogan, thus far, communication researchers primarily are using traditional methods to study the Internet (*e.g.*, content analysis, essays/ critiques) with a few studies employing network analysis, as suggested by Morris and Ogan.

Additionally, research has tended to focus largely on the Internet in general, leaving specific interfaces such as mailing lists and e-mail in need of attention. Topics also seem to follow widely used categories (*e.g.*, adoption/diffusion, social interaction) in communication research. This trend may be useful for making comparisons across different types of media; however, it also risks overlooking effects that may be unique to the Internet.

The low number of Internet-based research articles (3.9 per cent) and the sporadic publication of the articles within the five communication journals examined may be attributed to several factors. To begin with, the Internet, despite nearly a three-decade history, is still a relatively new area of study. Although the World Wide Web, which helped make the Internet popular, became publicly available in 1992, it was not until 1995 that awareness of the Internet by the media and the general public began to increase. With this increased awareness among the populace, researchers are realizing the importance of researching the Internet, but this can be a slow process. In 1995, Dennis Davis, the editor of Journal of Broadcasting and Electronic Media, wrote in his annual summary, "One of my editorial priorities is to increase the number of articles dealing with new technologies. To do this, the number of submissions will need to be increased. This past year 10 submissions (4.9 per cent) dealt with new industries or new technologies. Three times as many manuscripts dealt with existing industries (30 papers, 14.8 per cent). I would like to see a more even balance between submissions dealing with old and new industries."

To its credit, the Journal of Communication published a symposium on "The Net" in its 1996 winter issue. Factoring in the timeframe necessary for the review, decision, and printing process, the calls to action contained within this issue may partially explain the noticeable increase in the publication of articles during 1998. The drop off in 1999 may be a reflection of this cycle as well, or possibly a reflection of changes in editors' interests. Still, it seems clear that some of these journals are demonstrating a desire to publish Internet-based research articles; however, as Davis indicates, perhaps few studies are being submitted.

Alternatively, it may be that a number of studies are being submitted; however, because of the relative newness of Internet-based research some of these studies may lack the theoretical grounding often desired in published works by our leading journals. A review of the literature reveals that communication researchers are attempting to unveil the parallels and distinctions between new and traditional technology theories and methodologies, but the research waters are still murky in this area. Additionally, the emergence of new technology journals such as Internet Research and New Media and Society, may serve as alternative outlets for these studies, thus siphoning off submissions to the mainstream, established communication journals. As well, given the crossdisciplinary nature of the Internet (*e.g.*, computing, communication, human factors), depending on the topic, communication researchers may be submitting their works to journals in other fields. If this is the case, then the communication journals examined might more actively solicit Internet research submissions in an attempt to better represent the amount and type of research being conducted in this area.

While this author does not advocate the lowering of acceptance standards for research articles, communication journals could potentially foster increased publication of Internet research, following the lead of the Journal of Communication, by dedicating issues to symposia on the topic. These symposia could be viewed as debuts of Internet research that, while possibly less theoretically rigorous, would be considered valuable contributors to the development of future, more theoretically based studies.

The main point to be emphasized is that the communication research community is widely dispersed across numerous universities and organizations worldwide. Scholarly journals function, in part, as a communication link between researchers. Communication scholars interested in studying the Internet benefit most by knowing who else is researching in the area and what results have been found. Leading journals play an important role in conveying this information, but only if that information is being published. If it is the case, which remains to be seen, that Internet research is not being published because of a lack of strong theoretical foundations, then an important question needs to be addressed. Namely, how are scholars to build theory if they do not have access, which these journals can provide, to studies on which to build a foundation? The answer may lie in the emergence of topic-specific journals such as New Media and Society.

In 1996, Morris and Ogan, commenting on the Internet's growth (25 million at the time), asked, "Why, then, have communication researchers, historically concerned with exploring the effects of mass media, nearly ignored the Internet?" This is a question still in need of an answer, or possibly reformulation. We might also ask why our leading journals appear to be slow on the uptake. Notably, Wartella and Reeves, in a 1985 study that examined historical trends in publishing about children and the media, observed "that the relationship between research activity and media popularity is not simultaneous." Their findings illustrated that research related to a communication technology (*e.g.*, film, radio, television) often lags behind the diffusion rate of the technology, a pattern confirmed in this study.

Nevertheless, Internet research appears to be an area of study with which communication researchers must become more comfortable and skilled at conducting. Unlike television, radio, or print media, the computer requires certain knowledge and skills to operate-and ultimately to study. As Biocca and Newhagen and Rafaeli argue, communication scholars are being called upon to take a more active role in the understanding and design of new communication technologies. These challenges, as well as knowledge and skills requirements, may act as barriers for some researchers who are less technically oriented. This particular barrier may be offset over time as communication programmes develop tracks of study in new technologies on both the graduate and undergraduate levels that emphasize familiarity with and understanding of computer communication technologies.

Additionally, the Internet can simultaneously function as an interpersonal and mass channel for communication. This hybrid nature tends to blur the traditional lines used to distinguish different types of communication from one another. Is the Internet really a form of mass communication? Questions such as this one make it difficult for communication scholars to identify perspectives from which to study the Internet.

Finally, because Internet research is more or less in its infancy and as such lacks a strong history of research on which to build, communication researchers must be especially thoughtful about and creative in their approach to its study. They must also make the effort to network, outside of journal publications, with other Internet researchers to share research strategies and results. Certainly, not every communication researcher is interested in studying the Internet nor, given the numerous areas available for study within the field, should it be the focus of every communication scholar or the sole topic of our leading publications. However, in general, to overlook the Internet as an area for study is to be remiss as a discipline.

Before concluding, two limitations must be addressed regarding the narrow focus of the research. First, the conclusions drawn from this study are primarily limited to the five journals examined. It should be noted, though, that these journals have historically attempted to keep pace with changes in the discipline so that cautious speculations of a more general nature about the discipline's response to the Internet might be made. However, additional research examining a broader range of communication journals is necessary to confirm these speculations. Second, the definition used to identify Internet-based research excluded articles examining computer-mediated communication more generally. Future studies may wish to examine this broader category of research as well.

This study makes two primary contributions to the field. First, it informs communication scholars of the content and amount of published Internet research in leading journals that represent our research efforts both within and outside of the discipline. Second, it generates discussion concerning why the numbers are relatively low in light of earlier calls to action regarding the importance of studying the Internet. Both communication journals and communication scholars play important roles in determining where Internet research will be positioned within the discipline, as well as where the discipline will be placed relative to other fields investigating the technology. Despite the small number of Internetbased articles published by five of our leading journals during the sixyear time period examined, communication scholars studying the Internet should be encouraged in that, overall, the number of articles published appears to be increasing.

However, to more accurately reflect the Internet's importance as a research topic within the discipline, it is hoped that the findings in this study will encourage communication scholars to submit more of their Internet-based research to our leading journals while current and future editors of these journals will be encouraged to include more of these articles in their publications. As a discipline we possess the potential be a leader in Internet research, and our core journals can, and should, reflect this potential not only to scholars within the field but also to the larger academic community.

THE CHALLENGE OF APPLYING CONTENT ANALYSIS TO THE WWW

Content analysis has been used for decades as a microscope that brings communication messages into focus. The World Wide Web has grown rapidly since the technology that made it possible was introduced in 1991 and the first Web browsers became available in 1993.

The Commerce Department estimates that one billion users may be online by 2005, and the growth in users has mirrored growth in content. More than 320 million home pages can be accessed on the Web and some Web sites are updated almost constantly. This growth and change makes the Web a moving target for communication research. Can the microscope of content analysis be applied to this moving target?

The purpose of this chapter is to examine ways that researchers have begun to apply content analysis to the World Wide Web. How are they adapting the principles of content analysis to this evolving form of computermediated communication? What are the unique challenges of content analysis in this environment? This review of pioneering work in Web-based content analysis may provide researchers with insights into ways to adapt a stable research technique to a dynamic communication environment.

Krippendorff found empirical enquiry into communication content dates at least to the late 1600s when newspapers were examined by the Church because of its concern of the spread of non-religious matters. The first well-documented case of quantitative analysis of content occurred in eighteenth-century Sweden. That study also involved conflict between the church and scholars. With the advent of popular newspaper publishing at the turn of the twentieth century, content analysis came to be more widely used. It was with the work of Berelson and Lazarsfeld in the 1940s and Berelson in the 1950s that content analysis came to be a widely recognized research tool that was used in a variety of research disciplines.

Berelson's definition of content analysis as "a research technique for the objective, systematic and quantitative description of the manifest content of communication"8 underlies much content analysis work. Budd, Thorp, and Donohew built on Berelson's definition defining content analysis as "a systematic technique for analyzing message content and message handling." Krippendorff defined content analysis as "a research technique for making replicable and valid inferences from data to their context."

Krippendorff identified four primary advantages of content analysis: it is unobtrusive, it accepts unstructured material, it is context sensitive and thereby able to process symbolic forms, and it can cope with large volumes of data. All of these advantages seem to apply equally to the Web as to media such as newspapers and television. The capability of coping with large volumes of data is a distinct advantage in terms of Web analysis.

Holsti identified three primary purposes for content analysis: to describe the characteristics of communication, to make inferences as to the antecedents of communication, and to make inferences as to the effects of communication. Both descriptive and inferential research focused on Web-based content could add value to our understanding of this evolving communication environment.

How-to guides for conducting content analysis suggest five primary steps that are involved in the process of conducting content analysis research. Those steps are briefly enumerated below with consideration for application to the Web. First, the investigator formulates a research question and/or hypotheses. The advent of the Web has opened the door for many new research questions. The challenge for researchers who apply content analysis to the Web is not to identify questions, but rather to narrow those questions and seek to find a context for them either in existing or emerging communication theory. The temptation for researchers who are examining a "new" form of communication is to simply describe the content rather than to place it in the context of theory and/or to test hypotheses.

Second, the researcher selects a sample. The size of the sample depends on factors such as the goals of the study. Multiple methods can be used for drawing the sample. But Krippendorff noted that a sampling plan must "assure that, within the constraints imposed by available knowledge about the phenomena, each unit has the same chance of being represented in the collection of sampling units." This requirement for rigour in drawing a sample may be one of the most difficult aspects of content analysis on the Web. Bates and Lu pointed out that "with the number of available

Web sites growing explosively, and available directories always incomplete and overlapping, selecting a true random sample may be next to impossible." Not only do new Web sites come online frequently, but old ones are also removed or changed. McMillan found that in one year 15.4 per cent of a sample of health-related Web sites had ceased to exist.16 Koehler found that 25.3 per cent of a randomly selected group of Web sites had gone off-line in one year. However, he also found that among those sites that remained functioning after one year, the average size of the Web site (in bytes) more than doubled.

The third step in the content analysis process is defining categories. Budd, Thorp, and Donohew identified two primary units of measurements: coding units and context units. Coding units are the smallest segment of content counted and scored in the content analysis. The context unit is the body of material surrounding the coding unit. For example, if the coding unit is a word, the context unit might be the sentence in which the word appears or the paragraph or the entire article. Many researchers use the term "unit of analysis" to refer to the context from which coding units are drawn. Defining the context unit/unit of analysis is a unique challenge on the World Wide Web. Ha and James argued that the home page is an ideal unit of analysis because many visitors to a Web site decide whether they will continue to browse the site on the basis of their first impression of the home page. They also argued that coding an entire site could be extremely timeconsuming and introduce biases based on Web-site size. Web Techniques estimated that Web sites range from one page to 50,000 pages. Other researchers have attempted to take a more comprehensive approach to defining the unit of analysis. For example, in a study of library Web sites Clyde coded all pages mounted by a library on its server.

Fourth, coders are trained, they code the content, and reliability of their coding is checked. Each step of this coding process is impacted by Web technology. The Web can facilitate training and coding. For example, McMillan trained two coders who were living in different parts of the country to assist in coding Web sites. Instructions and coding sheets were delivered by e-mail and coders were given URLs for sites to be coded.

The coding process was carried out remotely and without paper. Wassmuth and Thompson noted potential problems in checking intercoder reliability for changing content. They controlled for possible changes in content by having sites that were being coded by multiple coders viewed at the same day and time by all coders. Massey and Levy addressed the problem of changing content by having all sites evaluated twice with the second visit made twentyfour hours after the initial visit to the site.

Fifth, the data collected during the coding process is analysed and interpreted. The statistical tools used to analyse the data will depend on the type of data collected and on the questions that are addressed by the research. Similarly, the interpretation will grow out of the data analysis as well as the researcher's perspective. The fact that the content that has been analysed is Web-based is not expected to change the basic procedures of analysis and interpretation used in content analysis.

METHODOLOGY

The author took several steps to identify both published and unpublished studies that have applied content analysis to the Web. First, a search of the electronic Social Sciences Citation Index was conducted searching for key words "Web" and "content analysis."

The SSCI was also searched for "Internet" and "content analysis."

Selected communication journals were also reviewed for any articles that applied content analysis to the Web. The author also sought out papers from communication conferences that applied content analysis to the Web. Finally, bibliographies were checked for all studies that were identified using the above techniques. Any cited study that seemed to apply content analysis to the Web was examined.

Eleven studies were identified that applied content analysis to computer-mediated communication technologies other than the Web.

Three studies analysed content of listservs designed for academicians and practiboners of public relations and advertising. Two studies analysed newsgroups that served as online support/information groups on the topics of abortion and eating disorders.

Two studies analysed pornographic materials found on Usenet. Two studies focused on e-mail and electronic bulletin board postings related to public affairs: Newhagen, Cordes, and Levy examined e-mail sent to NBC Nightly News and Ogan examined content of an electronic bulletin board during the Gulf War. The final two studies focused on organizational communication issues with analysis of e-mail messages related to an online training programme and an Internet discussion group established in conjunction with a conference.'

In addition to the studies that examined computer-mediated communication forms such as e-mail and listservs, nineteen studies were found that focused specifically on content analysis of the World Wide Web. The five steps in content analysis identified in the literature are the basis for examination of how these nineteen studies applied the microscope of content analysis to the moving target of the World Wide Web.

FINDINGS

The first step in content analysis is to formulate research questions and/or hypotheses. The majority of these studies were descriptive in nature. However, a few of these studies do seem to be moving more towards hypothesis testing and theory development. For example, McMillan proposed four models of funding for Web content based in part on level of interactivity that was determined by analysis of Web site features. Wassmuth and Thompson suggested that their study might be a first step in developing a theory that explains relationships between specificity of banner ad messages and the goal of information tasks.

The second step in conducting a content analysis is to select a sample. The sampling frame from which sites were drawn varied widely. One common way of defining a sampling frame was to use an online list of sites in a given category. A second popular technique was to use search engines) to identify sites that met criteria related to the purpose of the study. Two studies used off-line sources to identify Web sites and two studies combined online and off-line listings of Web sites. Finally, one site analysed three newspaper Web sites with no discussion of the sampling frame.

After defining the sampling frame, researchers typically draw a sample for analysis. Nine of the nineteen studies did not sample; instead they analysed all sites in the sampling frame. The goals of these studies were typically to describe and/or set a benchmark for analysis of a given type of Web sites.

Among studies that used sampling, use of a table of random numbers was the most common sampling technique. McMillan pointed out challenges of applying a table of random numbers to an online listing or search engine results.

Most lists generated in this way are not numbered leaving the researcher a tedious hand-counting task. Search engine listings may be presented in multiple hypertext sub-menus that further complicate the task of assigning random numbers. Howeverz, few of the studies cited here provided much, if any discussion, of how to address sampling difficulties that arise from using online sources to identify the sampling frame. The sample size for these nineteen studies varied dramatically from three to 2,865. The majority of the studies (fourteen) analysed between fifty and 500 sites.

The third step in content analysis is defining categories. In content analysis of traditional media, one of the first steps is to define the time period of the study (*e.g.*, a constructed week of newspaper issues). But, in analysis of Web sites, study authors placed emphasis on the time frame (*e.g.*, April 1997) of the study. As noted earlier, changes in the content of Web sites necessitates rapid collection of data. The most rapid data collection reported was two days and the longest was five months. Most studies collected data in one to two months.

After identifying the time frame of the study, researchers need to identify context units for coding. The most common context unit used for these studies was the "Web site." Many of the studies did not specify what was meant by the Web site. However some did limit analysis to the "home page" or initial screen seen upon entering the site while others specified examination of all pages that could be found at a given site and others indicated that they had searched sites in "sufficient detail" to identify key features.

Given the magnitude and changing nature of sites, some creativity would seem to be needed in defining the context unit. Wassmuth and Thompson devised one creative approach in their analysis of banner ads that were encountered when the coder performed a specific task at a newspaper Web site (find a classified ad for a BMW). Another approach was to have coders analyse all sites for a specific length of time-about ten minutes.

This helps to reduce bias that might be involved in coding sites of varying lengths. However, it might introduce "error" in that different coders may choose to examine different parts of a Web site during the ten-minute examination period.

These nineteen studies varied widely in terms of coding units used by the researchers. The most common coding unit was "content categories." However, no standard list of categories emerges from these studies. Nor do they rely on established lists such as the fifty categories identified by Bush. Instead, content categories seem to be specifically related to the goals of the given study. For example, Bar-Ilan developed content categories related to a specific historical figure, and McMillan and Campbell developed content categories related to the community-building features of city-based Web sites.

Another common coding unit is structural features of the Web site (*e.g.*, links, animation, video, sound, etc.). Two studies used Heeter's conceptual definition of interactivity as a frame for organizing analysis of Web site features.

One study conducted an in-depth analysis of e-mail links. Many of the other sites also coded e-mail links as a structural element. Tannery and Wessel developed a three-level categorization system for evaluating overall sophistication of Web sites based on both content categories and structural features, Some studies also reported on "demographic" characteristics of sites such as country of origin and type of institution that created the site while others explored the nature and/or purpose of the sponsoring organization in more detail. The Wassmuth and Thompson study is unique in its analysis of banner advertisements in Web sites. The fourth step in content analysis is training coders and checking the reliability of their coding skills. One of the primary reasons for this attention to training and checking coders is that, as Budd, Thorp, and Donohew noted, an important requirement for any social-science based research is that it be carried out in such a way that its results can be verified by other investigators who follow the same steps as the original researcher. Krippendorff wrote that at least two coders must be used in content analysis to determine reliability of the coding scheme by independently analyzing content.

Eight of the nineteen studies did not report any information about coders. Of those that did report on coders, the number of coders used ranged from two to twelve with an average of about five coders. Only seven studies reported on training of coders and most said little about how training was done.

Eleven studies reported cross-coding techniques. Most cross-coded a percentage (10 to 20 per cent) of all sampled sites. Elliott had all sites cross-checked by two coders while Li had two coders cross-check all the data collected in the first three days ofa ten-day sample. Ha and James used a pre-test/posttest design that enabled them to correct coding problems prior to the start of data collection as well as to check reliability of collected data.

Ten studies reported reliability of the coding. Formulas used for testing reliability included Holsti's reliability formula, Perreault and Leigh's reliability index, Spearman-Brown Prophesy Formula, and Scott's Pi. Bar-Ilan did not indicate what type of test was used to generate a 92 per cent reliability score for her study. Reliability scores ranged from.62 to 1.00.

The fifth stage of content analysis is to analyse and interpret data. As noted earlier, the purpose of most of these studies was descriptive in nature. Therefore, it is not surprising that key findings are also descriptive in nature. One theme that emerged from several of these studies was the diversity found at Web sites. For example, Bates and Lu found that the "personal home page" is an evolving communication form, Clyde found variety in the structure and function of library Web sites, and McMillan concluded that the Web has diversity of content, funding sources, and communication models.

A second theme found in these studies is commercialization of the Web. Some studies view commercialization as positive for marketers and/ or consumers while others express concern about impacts of commercialization on public life and/or academic expression. As a counterpoint to these concerns, Gibson and Ward found the Web offered a forum for minor political parties to have a voice.

A third major theme was the fact that many site developers are not using the Web to its full potential as a multi-media interactive environment. Researchers found many sites made limited use of interactivity, graphics and motion video, and search functions. And Elliott's study suggested that there is still significant room for development of new content in important areas such as family life education.

RECOMMENDATIONS FOR FUTURE RESEARCHERS

The studies reviewed above found that the stable research technique of content analysis can be applied in the dynamic communication environment of the Web. But using content analysis in this environment does raise potential problems for the researcher. Some of these studies exhibit creative ways of addressing these problems. Unfortunately, others seem to have failed to build rigour into their research designs in their haste to analyse a new medium. Future studies that apply content analysis techniques to the Web need to consider carefully each of the primary research steps identified in the literature: formulating research questions and/or hypotheses, sampling, data collection and coding, training coders and checking the reliability of their work, and analyzing and interpreting data.

For the first step, formulating the research questions and/or hypotheses, content analysis of the Web is both similar to and different from traditional media. Content analysis of traditional media, such as newspapers and broadcast, assume some linearity or at least commonly accepted sequencing of messages. Hypertext, a defining characteristic of the Web, defies this assumption. Each individual may interact with content of a Web site in different ways. Furthermore, the Web is both "like" and "unlike" print and broadcast as it combines text, audio, still images, animation, and video. These unique characteristics of the medium may suggest unique research questions. However, in some fundamental ways, the first step in the research process remains similar. Researchers should build on earlier theoretical and empirical work in defining their Web-based research.

Approaches taken by the authors cited above tend to be consistent with Holsti's first purpose of content analysis: describing the characteristics of communication. This is appropriate for early studies of an emerging medium. However, researchers also need to move on to the other two purposes identified by Holsti: making inferences as to antecedents of communication and making inferences as to the effects of communication.

The second step in content analysis research, sampling, presents some unique challenges for Web-based content analysis. As noted earlier, a key concern in sampling is that each unit must have the same chance as all other units of being represented.

The first challenge for the researcher is to identify the units to be sampled. This will be driven by the research question. For example, if the researcher wants to examine a sample of Web sites for Fortune 500 companies, it may be fairly simple to obtain a list of these sites and apply a traditional sampling method (*e.g.*, a table of random numbers, every nth item on the list, etc.) But, if one seeks a different kind of sample (*e.g.*, all business Web sites) the task may become more difficult. Essentially, the researcher has two primary sources from which to develop a sampling frame: offline sources and online sources.

If the researcher draws a sample from offline sources (*e.g.*, directories, lists maintained by industry groups, etc.), then drawing a random sample is fairly non-problematic. Because the sample universe exists in a "set" medium, traditional methods of sampling can be used. However, a major problem with offline sources is that they are almost certainly out of date. Given the rapid growth and change of the Web, new sites have probably been added since the printed list was created while others have moved or been removed. Online sources can be updated more frequently, and thus help to eliminate some of the problems associated with offline sources. And, in many cases (*e.g.*, directories, lists maintained by industry groups, etc.), the list can appear in the same kind of format that is found in an offline source making sampling fairly straightforward.

But, human list-compilers are less efficient than search engines for identifying all potential Web sites that meet specific criteria. And in some cases no compiled list may exist that directly reflects the criteria of a study. In these cases, search engines may be the best way of generating a sample frame.

However, care must be taken in using search engine results. First, authors must make sure that they have defined appropriate key words and that they understand search techniques for the search engine that they are using.

If they do not, they run the risk of either over registration or under registration. Human intervention may be needed to insure that the computer-generated list does not include any spurious and/ or duplicate items.

Once a list has been generated, the researcher needs to determine the best way to draw a random sample. One way to ease the problem of random assignment may be to generate a hardcopy of the list, Then the researcher can assign random numbers to the list and/or more easily select every nth item. However, if a hierarchical search engine (such as Yahoo!) is used, special care must be taken to ensure that all items in subcategories have equal chance of being represented in the sample. In some cases, stratified sampling may be required.

Research needs to be done to test the validity of multiple sampling methods. For example, does the use of different search engines result in empirically different findings? What sample size is adequate? How can sample techniques from traditional media (*e.g.*, selection of "representative" newspapers or broadcast stations be applied to the Web? A key concern is that sampling methods for the Web not be held to either higher or lower standards than have been accepted for traditional media. The rapid growth and change of the Web also leads to potential problems in the third stage of content analysis: data collection and coding. The fast-paced Web almost demands that data be collected in a short time frame so that all coders are analyzing the same content.

Koehler has suggested some tools that researchers can use to download Web sites to capture a "snapshot" of content. However, as Clyde noted, copyright laws of some countries prohibit, among other things, the storage of copyrighted text in a database system.

Whether or not the site was downloaded prior to analysis, researchers must specify when they examined a site. Just as newspaper-based research must indicate the date of publication, and broadcast-based research must indicate which newscast is analysed, so Web-based content analysis must specify the timeframe of the analysis. For sites that change rapidly, exact timing may become important.

Researchers must also take care in defining units of analysis. The coding unit can be expected to vary depending on the theory upon which the study is based, the research questions explored, and the hypotheses tested. However, some standardization is needed for context units. For example, analyses of traditional media have developed traditional context units (*e.g.*, the column-inch and/or a word count for newspapers, time measured in seconds for broadcast), but no such standard seems to have yet emerged for the Web. The fact that multiple media forms are combined on the Web may be one of the reasons for this lack of a clear unit of measurement.

The majority of the studies reviewed above simply defined the context unit as the "Web site." Future studies should specify how much of the Web site was reviewed (*e.g.*, "home page" only, first three levels in the site hierarchy, etc.). But as analysis of the Web matures, entirely new context units may need to be developed to address phenomena that are completely non-existent in traditional media.

For example, Wassmuth and Thompson measured the ways in which the content of the Web was "adapted" in real-time to become more responsive to site visitors' needs. The fourth step in content analysis, training coders and checking the reliability of their work, involves both old and new challenges on the Web. Given the evolving nature of data coding described above, training may involve "learning together" with coders how to develop appropriate context and coding units.

But the rapid change that characterizes the Web may introduce some new problems in checking intercoder reliability. This does not mean that well-developed tools for checking reliability should be abandoned. Rather, the primary challenge is to make sure that coders are actually cross-coding identical data. If Web sites are checked at different times by different coders and/or if the context unit is not clearly defined, false error could be introduced.

The coders might not look at the same segment of the site, or data coded by the first coder might be changed or removed before the second coder examines the site. Only one of the studies reviewed above directly addressed this issue. Wassmuth and Thompson carefully defined a task to be preformed at a site and had two coders perform that identical task at exactly the same date and time.

This is one viable alternative. However, if the content of the site is changing rapidly, this control may not be sufficient. Another alternative is to have coders evaluate sites that have been downloaded. These downloaded sites are "frozen in time" and will not change between the coding times. However, as noted earlier, there may be some legal problems with such downloaded sites. Furthermore, depending on the number of sites being examined, the time and disk-space requirements for downloading all of the studied sites may be prohibitive.

The Web does not seem to pose any truly new challenges in the final step in content analysis: analyzing and interpreting the data. Rather, researchers must simply remember that rigour in analyzing and interpreting the findings are needed as much in this environment as in others. For example, some of the studies reported above used statistics that assume a random sample to analyse data sets that were not randomly generated. Findings and conclusions of such studies must be viewed with caution. Such inappropriate use of analytical tools would probably not be tolerated by reviewers had not the Web-based subject mater of the studies been perceived as "new" and "innovative."

But new communication tools are not an excuse for ignoring established communication research techniques. In conclusion, the microscope of content analysis can be applied to the moving target of the Web. But researchers must use rigour and creativity to make sure that they don't lose focus before they take aim.

Bibliography

Ajay Kumar Srivastav and Rajesh Kumar Singh: *Glossary of Library Information Communication and Technological Terms and Acronyms*, Shree Pub, 2007.

Ajit Singh Siwatch: *Encyclopedic Dictionary of Library and Information Science, Vols. I to III*, Shree Publishers, 2010.

Amjad Ali: *Ane's Encyclopedic Dictionary of Library and Information Science*, Ane Books India, 2006.

Ann Peterson Bishop, Nancy A Van House and Barbara P Buttenfield: *Digital Library Use : Social Practice in Design and Evaluation*, Ane Books Pvt. Ltd., Delhi, 2005.

B. Rajasree and P. Aravinda: *Glossary of Library and Information Science*, Anmol Publication, 2003.

B.S. Aggarwal: *Issues in Library Information Science*, Oxford Book Company, 2007 .

C.D. harma: *Advances in Library and Information Science Vol. 1: Computer Applications*, Scientific, 1995.

C.K. Sharma: *Encyclopaedic Dictionary of Library Information Science and Network*, JBD, 2002.

C.R. Karisiddappa: *Current Studies in Library and Information Science,* Manak, 1994.

J. Sridevi and Vijay Laxshmi: *Model of Digital Library*, Shree Publication, Delhi, 2004.

K. Nazeer Badhusha: *Digital Library Architecture*, Ane Books Pvt. Ltd., Delhi, 2008.

K.A. Isaac: *Glimpses of Library and Information Science*, Ess Ess, 2001.

K.L.M. Swaminathan: *Encyclopaedia of Library and Information Science (3 Vols-Set)*, Sarup and Sons, 2001.

Khalid K. Faruqi and Mehtab Alam: *Library Information Systems and E-Journal Archiving*, Authorspress, 2005.

Mahendra Nath: *Handbook of Library Services*, Pointer Publication, New Delhi, 2001.

Mange Ram and Ram Chander: *Recent Trends in Library Services*, Vayu Education of India, Delhi, 2011.

P. Kaushik: *Library Information Services and Systems*, Anmol, 2006.

P.P. Rawat, O.P. Gupta and V. Venkatappaiah: *Current Developments in Library and Information Science : Papers presented in honour of Prof. P.N. Kaula on his 71st Birthday*, Reliance, 1998.

R.C. Chakravarthy and P.R.S. Murthy: *Information Technology and Rural Development*, Pacific Books International, Delhi, 2012.

R.C. Mishra: *Information Technology and Poverty Reduction in South Asia*, Authors Press, Delhi, 2003.

R.K. Singh: *Basic Facts of Digital Library*, Shree Publication, Delhi, 2004.

S.P. Agrawal: *Directory of LIS Education in India : All in one Compendium on Library and Information Science Study*, Reliance, 1996.

Sandhya Aggarwal and R.D. Mehla: *Library Services : Challenges and Solutions in Digital Era*, Ess Ess Publications, Delhi, 2012.

Santosh Patel: *Library Information : Preservation and Access*, Authors Press, 2003.

Savita Mittal: *Digital Library Resources*, Ess Ess Publication, Delhi, 2005.

V.K. Jain: *Information Technology for Digital Library Management and Automation*, Atlantic Publication, Delhi, 2009.

V.M. Mohanraj: *Library Services for Children*, Ess Ess Publication, Delhi, 2004.

Y.L. Chopra and Mamta Chopra: *Challenges Before Library and Information Science in New Millennium*, Ess Ess, 2001.

Index